POLITICAL SCIENCE BASICS

An Introduction to American Government

R. L. Cohen

Humanities
ACADEMIC PUBLISHERS

ISBN: 9781988557908 (Hardcover)
ISBN: 9781988557915 (Softcover)

Published in New Zealand and the United States

Humanities Academic Publishers

A catalogue record for this book is available from the National Library of New Zealand.

CONTENTS

CHAPTER 1

KEY DEFINITION
IN POLITICAL SCIENCE

1.1 Governments and regimes

Political Science is defined as the social science that examines politics by means of the empirical method. **Politics**, from Greek *politiká* (affairs of the cities), is the activity through which people make, preserve and amend the general rules under which they live. Being a social science and concerning the management of our communities, politics is unavoidably connected to both conflict – a competition against opposing forces -- and cooperation – the act of achieving goals through collective action. That is, human beings are social animals, but they have different wants, needs, and opinions, so they differ in the decisions about the **rules** by which they live. These latter are thus essential for any social system, since rules help to determine who will win or lose future power struggles without having to resort to violence.[1]

Politics is a **process** and not an outcome: due to the inescapable presence of diversity and scarcity, not all conflicts in society can be resolved, so the process of setting rules can create disputes among the population. These disputes are at the basis of two essential concepts to understand politics: **authority** and **power**. The latter can be defined as the ability to influence others, so it may not necessarily be political, while the former is a form of **legitimate** power, which means that authority is itself the right to exercise power. That is, individuals acknowledge that society requires a form of common agreement to ensure that rules are upheld, so politics is connected to exercise of

---

[1] Roller, E. (2005), *The Performance of Democracies: Political Institutions and Public Policy*. Oxford University Press, Oxford.

authority, such that Easton defines it as the "authoritative allocation of values."[2] Yet, to reach this agreement, it is essential that human beings cooperate one with another up to the point that political power can also be defined as "acting in concert" as done by Hannah Arendt[3].

The concept of legitimacy is essential to understand what **the State** – the current prevalent form of political organization of our societies -- is, since Max Weber defines it as a "human community that (successfully) claims the monopoly of the legitimate use of physical force within a given territory."[4] This means that other actors may use violence, but the state is the only actor legitimized to do so. To exercise its power, the State power must be organized, and in order to decide who is in charge of allocating citizens' different values, societies need a form of **government,** namely a system or an organization for exercising authority over a body of people.

Politics produce different kinds of governments according to the level of control and authority exercised by the government over its population. At one end of the spectrum, the government makes all decisions about how individuals live their lives, and citizens are powerless to push back. At the other end, there is an anarchic system where individuals make the decisions for themselves, and government does not exist. Hence, governments can exercise this authority in different ways, and the form of government, or the set of rules that regulate the operation of a government, are defined as the political **regime.** This latter defines only a form of government and must not be misunderstood with its negative connotation, namely regime as an authoritarian political system that restricts the people's liberties.[5]

The difference between 'government' and 'regime' is important. For example, the United States federal government is composed of the three main branches (**legislative**, **executive** and **judiciary**) and draws its powers from the Constitution, the President and federal courts. With the elections, citizens decide which party (**Democratic Party** or **Republican Party**) they want to direct these branches and who should be the President. Instead, regime defines the political institutional framework of the country. Examples of regimes can thus be "**democracy**," "**authoritarian**," or "**totalitarian**." The United States system of governance, namely its regime, is a **democratic republic**

[2] Easton, D. (1976). "Theoretical approaches to political support.", Canadian Journal of Political Science, 9 (3), pp. 431-448.

[3] Phillips, J. (2013), "Between the Tyranny of Opinion and the Despotism of Rational Truth: Arendt on Facts and Acting in Concert.", New German Critique, 40 (2), 97-112.

[4] Weber M. (2004 [1919]), The Vocation Lectures. "Science as a Vocation". "Politics as a Vocation", Ed by David Owen D. and Strong T.B., Hackett Publishing Company, Cambridge.

[5] Dietrich, S. and Bernhard M. (2009). "State or regime? The impact of institutions on welfare outcomes." The European Journal of Development Research, 28 (2), 252-269.

style, and this does not change with the elections. Elections are made to select – and to replace – governments while they cannot change regime type. Hence, regardless whether Republicans or Democrats win the elections, the United States regime will remain a democratic republic.

Overall, we can find four main types of regime: democracy, theocracy, autocracy, and totalitarianism. A regime is **democratic** if it guarantees the people's basic liberties and rights. Democracy's etymology comes from the Greek word *demos* ("the people") and *kratos* (power), and this implies that any democratic system must be based on a **popular sovereignty**, namely the principle for which the authority of the state and its government are created and sustained by the consent of its people, who are the source of political power.[6] This sovereignty can be exercised in two main forms.

First, in a democracy as self-government, citizens can be directly involved in politics and make the rules that govern themselves, as it was in the case in Athens, Greece. Today, direct democracy can be recreated in several ways, from deliberative assemblies, to direct decisional means such as referendum, or the initiative process. The method by which citizens can become directly involved on a single issue by voting directly on an issue and proposing new laws or amendments to a state constitution is referred to as a **referendum**.

Second, modern democracy does not necessarily require a direct involvement in politics by the whole populace. A democracy can also assume the form of a **republic**, namely a form of government in which the people hold the power, but they rule indirectly by means of their representatives. This form of representative **democracy**, supported by Madison in his *Federalist Papers*,[7] is adopted in the United States and defines a regime where politicians rule society according to the constitutional law on behalf of the citizenry, but where the people still retain power due to democratic procedures such as **elections**, **party system**, and the **division of powers**. However, this form of government is not necessarily democratic, since there could be republics where citizens do not hold sufficient institutional means to control the elites ruling the country.

On the contrary, a regime is defined as **authoritarian** if the government restricts some of the basic liberties enjoyed by the citizenry. In this regard, it is important to underline the difference between an authoritarian and a **totalitarian** regime. The former restricts only certain liberties of the population; it may also accept certain independent organizations and it does not necessarily rely on a strong ideology to influence the people's values. On the contrary, **totalitarianism** aims at controlling every aspect

---

[6] Held, D. (2006), *Models of Democracy*, Stanford University Press, California.
[7] Madison J. (1982 [1788]), *The Federalist Paper by Alexander Hamilton*, James Madison and John Jay, Bantam Books, New York.

of citizens' life and does not accept any independent organization.[8] As mentioned by Benito Mussolini, father of Italian **fascism**, in a totalitarian state there is "all within the state, none outside the state and none against the state."[9] While there are still several authoritarian regimes in the world, North Korea is the last totalitarian regime left.

Finally, a regime can also be a "**theocracy**," namely a political system where the government is controlled by religious officials who are regarded as divinely guided. Such government leaders are members of the clergy, and laws are not based on political constitutions but rather on religious law. This form of government was typical of early civilizations, and while the **Enlightenment** has rendered this regime obsolete in Western societies, some theocracies still exist in the Middle-East, such as in Saudi Arabia and Iran.[10]

1.2 Theories of power

While 'government' and 'regime' are terms that define the way political power is organized within a certain state, different theories exist concerning the way scholars believe power should be framed, of which we can find four main paradigms. First, there is the **pluralist theory**, for which, if elected, representatives manage to represent equally the different interests present in our societies. Their rule could be both democratic and respecting the people's liberty. **Pluralism** developed after the end of the Second World War and reached its height during the 1950s and 1960s, periods of economic and political development for the Western societies characterized by low social conflict.[11]

During this time, scholars stressed the beneficial consequences of social diversity for politics, advocating for constitutional ways of accommodating this diversity on public policy issues. In this framework, group interest is the building block of politics, since this helps citizens develop their political skills and understand how democracy necessitates bargaining and compromise. For this framework to work properly, no group must be blocked from competing on equal terms with another one, and any category of people who share an interest must have the chance to form a group. Therefore, **pluralists** believed that electoral competition creates a ***polyarchy***, namely a government of minorities where elections are competitive. In this system, diverse groups have the opportunity to make themselves heard effectively in the political system with politicians relying on the electorate's support for their re-election.

---

[8] Curtis, M. (1979), *Totalitarianism*, Transaction Publishers, New Jersey.
[9] Ibid.
[10] Cosgel M.M. & Miceli T.J, (2013), "Theocracy", *Working papers 2013-29*, University of Connecticut, Department of Economics.
[11] Dryzek J.S., Dunleavy P. (2009), *Theories of the Democratic State*, Palgrave Macmillan, Basingstoke.

Considering politics as the result of the mediation between the requests of competing groups, pluralists hold that representative procedures ensure the representation of a large number of influential groups, thus avoiding the concentration of power in the hands of few individuals, which was the theoretical pillar of the second paradigm, namely the **elitist scholars**. This literature developed with Italian sociologists such as Gaetano Mosca[12], Roberto Michels[13] and Vilfredo Pareto[14], but later developed also in the United States thanks to scholars such as Charles Wright Mills.[15] This philosopher maintained that the common man cannot control politics, since power is centralized in the hands of a political **elite** that makes the fundamental decisions for everyone. Therefore, Mills defined elites as: "those political, economic and military circles which, arranged in a complex and stratified order, make decisions of at least national importance."[16]

Mills noticed that in the American society of his time, the greatest power existed in the economic, political, and military spheres.[17] These elites determined the direction of the state and reduced all minor institutions to below these top powers. Moreover, each sector extended and thickened its relations with the others, so there was a strong interdependence between them. The members of these elites could also be considered as a single whole, since they behaved in a benevolent way among themselves and had common interests with similar social origins. Therefore, despite the theory that democracies should spread political power equally, these elites ruled centralized power in their hands.

The power of the elites is connected to the third paradigm, namely the **bureaucratic theory**. This view relies on Weber's famous theory for which bureaucratization was intertwined with the development of the **territorial state** and the **capitalist economy**.[18] That is, the development of a mass citizenship increases both the quantitative demands on the state administration, and the qualitative demand for uniformity of treatment, which can only be met by a **supra-local** administrative system, operating on the basis of impartiality between persons. Hence, bureaucracy is a distinctive feature of the modern world because it constitutes an efficient structure of power and of administration over a large territory.

---

[12] Renzo S. (1952). "Note on Gaetano Mosca.", *The American Political Science Review*, 46.2 (1952), 603-605.

[13] Michels R. (1915), *Political Parties: A Sociological Study of The Oligarchical Tendencies of Modern Democracy*, Hearst's International Library Company, New York.

[14] Pareto V. (1935), *A Treatise on General Sociology*, General Publishing Company, Memphis.

[15] Mills C.W. (1956), *The Power Elite*, Oxford University Press, Oxford.

[16] Ibid.

[17] Ibid.

[18] Lutzker, M. A. (1982), "Max Weber and the analysis of modern bureaucratic organization: Notes toward a theory of appraisal.", *The American Archivist*, 45 (2), 119-130.

This process influences also the structure of democratic systems, since bureaucratization reduces the importance of the parliament in favour of the party, its leaders, and of specialized agencies. For example, the bureaucratic theory suggests that in the United States, those within agencies like the EPA, CIA, and the FBI, are the ones who have the real power within the nation. That is, '**democratization**' did not lead to a great dispersal of power to the masses, even though this does not mean that parliament has become obsolete. Rather the opposite: certain democratic processes have become essential in politics, such as the selection of leaders by electoral competition, the provision through Parliament of a forum for public debate and review of policy, and a mechanism for removing leaders in the event of a serious loss of confidence.[19]

Finally, the last paradigm connected to political distribution of power is the **social movement theory**. This theory explains how social mobilization occurs, under which forms it manifests, and which political consequences it may have. This paradigm became particularly influential in the 1960s, when many in both the United States and Europe began to see civic protests as a means to improve politics. At first, these protests puzzled scholars because studies relied on a **deprivation theory** which taught that protests were a result of social sufferance, while social movements in the 1960s were the result of an increase in social welfare. Furthermore, answers to this puzzle created differences between American and European sociology.[20]

On the one side, American theories relied more on structural approaches that examined which social and political contexts enabled or restricted protests. Among the factors that increased political movements, scholars underlined features such as an increased access to political decision making power, an instability in the ruling elites, and a lower ability of the state to repress these actions. Moreover, resource mobilization was of particular importance, since the more organized a community, and the more material, moral, cultural and human resources it possessed, the more likely a protest was to begin.

On the other side, the European strand focused more on social-constructivist approaches that focused less on social-class and material explanations, to argue instead that current protests are different from past labor movements based on social-class, since social movements are now based on post-material features as collective identity, gender, and sexuality. On top of that, recent scholars such as Goodwin and Polletta

---

[19] Waters T, Waters D (2015), *Weber's Rationalism and Modern Society: New Translations on Politics, Bureaucracy, and Social Stratification*, Palgrave Macmillan, London.
[20] Morris, A. (2000), "Reflections on social movement theory: Criticisms and proposals.", *Contemporary Sociology* 29 (3), 445-454.

argued that emotions, construction of meaning and agency, play a significant part as well in leading to the formation of social movements.[21]

As described by these paradigms, power is not organized in the same way in each country and this has significant consequences, not only for the people's political power, but also for one of the pillars of any political system, namely the people's liberty.

1.3 Types of liberty

Overall, two main conceptions of liberty have dominated the political debate, namely Isaiah Berlin's division between a "**negative liberty**" and a "**positive** (or **organic**) **liberty.**"[22] Negative liberty, which is freedom from external restraint on one's actions, include such examples such as civil and political rights such as freedom of speech, life, private property, freedom from violent crime, freedom of religion, habeas corpus, a fair trial, and freedom from slavery. Positive liberty requires the agent to take an active part in gaining control of themselves, since it claims "I am free to the extent that I achieve self-mastery." Positive liberty mainly focuses on answering the question: "By whom am I ruled?" Therefore, the positive desire to govern myself is connected to the belief that it is essential to determine who is making the political decisions to assess if citizens are free or not. Hence, the main question on which this conception of liberty is framed is: "What does it mean to be free to govern myself?"

First, self-mastery entails that individuals must be a *subject* and not an *object*, namely a self-directed doer able to make decisions by herself and not something moved by external forces. Being a subject is important because only insofar as I am able to conceive policies and goals of my own (and I am afterwards able to realize them), can I consider myself a self-mastered human being. Otherwise, I will just be an object, a mere 'thing' directed by others according to their needs. In this framework, I am free to the degree that I can realize my own will, while I am enslaved to the extent that I cannot do so.[23]

On the contrary, **negative liberty** is the concept describing individuals having a personal sphere that must not be constrained by any external interference – a space within which they can act unobstructed by others. Conceiving freedom in terms of non-interference, it becomes essential to understand which hindrances damage personal liberty and which could instead be accepted. The negative liberty scholars' answer to this dilemma has a pivotal social component, since they maintain that citizens are

---

[21] Buechler, S. M. (1995). "New Social Movement Theories", *The Sociological Quarterly*, 36(3): 441-464.
[22] Berlin I. (1958), *Two Concepts of Liberty*, Oxford University Press, Oxford.
[23] Berlin I. (2002), *Liberty*, Oxford University Press, Oxford.

unfree if others prevent them from doing what they could otherwise do. Individuals are then politically unfree when – and only when – they are prevented from attaining a goal by another human being: the wider the area where they are not hindered by other human beings in exercising their choices, the freer they are[24].

At first glance, it may seem simple to guarantee this liberty in a framework where all coercion is conceived as bad because it represses human desires. Total freedom lacking coercion. However, the fact that we live in social systems, where personal liberties are inevitably connected, creates disputes among scholars regarding how many "bads" we ought to impose to avoid larger evils. The problem is then how wide each individual's personal sphere should be, since if everyone was given unlimited freedom, we would live in a chaos where the will of the stronger would prevail over that of the weaker. In a negative liberty framework, the argument is thus: the line between the area of private life and that of public authority should be drawn to have the maximum degree of non-interference compatible with the minimum demands of social life.

Thus, the negative liberty solution differs from the one given by positive liberty. Whereas the latter aims to put authority directly in the hands of the citizenry, the former focuses on finding a minimum area of personal freedom that cannot be violated by anyone, and by this means, they aim to block authority. Hence, these two views focus on two different aspects of power: whereas positive liberty scholars focus on the *source* of the power in the hands of those ruling the social system, negative liberty scholars address the problem of the *intensity and amount* of power that rulers ought to have.

Berlin's division has yet been criticized by the republican conception of liberty as non-domination, whose origins can be found in Rome and later in the commonwealthman tradition, with books such as *Cato's Letters* by Trenchard and Gordon[25] or Madison's essays in the *Federalist Papers*. This ideal centres around the threat of having to live at the mercy of another, since it maintains that liberty involves **emancipation** from any **subordination** under **domination**. That is, it is important to determine when a party 'A' is actually dominating party 'B.' According to Philipp Pettit, the answer is that 'A' is dominating 'B' if – and only if – the former practises interference at will and with impunity, thus posing an arbitrary imposition on the latter's life.[26]

Republican liberty as non-domination has two main features. First, liberty is the opposite of slavery, and even if the master were to be benign, 'living at the mercy of another' is considered a great evil to avoid. Second, if the interference is not arbitrary, but controlled by the interests and opinions of those affected, it is not a form of

---

[24] Berlin 2002; 171-177.
[25] Trenchard J., Gordon T. (1971), *Cato's Letters*, Da Capo, New York.
[26] Pettit P. (1997), *Republicanism: A Theory of Freedom and Government*, Clarendon Press, Oxford.

domination. This view cannot be represented by Berlin's dichotomy. On the one hand, the fact that I am free from the mastery of another individual has no direct connection with the achievement of my self-mastery. On the other hand, republicanism focuses on a different X from which we should be free than the one chosen by negative liberty scholars, since the latter think that X should be "interference," whereas the former maintain that it ought to be "mastery."[27]

For this reason, there are two main differences between non-domination and non-interference. First, if one individual is subjected to a master, even though she does whatever she likes, thus enjoying non-interference, she is still a slave, since it is the opportunity to interfere at will that gives the dominating power to the master, despite whether or not the master will eventually use it. The problem of non-interference is even though the master may let the slave decide freely under some conditions, the slave will never be free. Conversely, non-domination grants greater security to personal freedom, since the master cannot interfere with the individual in any case.[28]

Second, interference may occur without people being rendered thereby unfree, since no domination exists if one interferes with my liberty but does so according to my will. Conversely, non-interference entails that every interference limits people's set of choices of some degree, and as such it constrains their freedom. Some interferences in people's lives are thus acceptable, especially if a third party interferes in a relationship where A dominates B to defend and free the latter. This aspect is central in relation to the rule of law, since it entails that a proper law is a non-mastering interferer if it does not compromise the people's liberty. On the contrary, in a non-interference framework, the fact that each law is an interference creates a difficult puzzle for the state, since its actions are seen as an inevitable constraint on an individual's set of choices.

---

[27] Pettit 1997; 52-61.
[28] Pettit P. (2012), *On the People's Terms: A Republican Theory and Model of Democracy*, Cambridge University Press, Cambridge.

Chapter 1: Key definition in Political Science

1) In a republic, who is in charge?

   a. the people

   b. the president

   c. the Supreme Court

   d. the bureaucracy

2) What does the theory of pluralism mean?

   a. Pluralism is the ideal of multicultural coexistence.

   b. Pluralism suggests that people can influence government through the many interest groups that spring up to champion everything from fighting for energy independence to banning abortions.

   c. Pluralism suggests that people can influence politicians by advocating their views on a large scale.

   d. Pluralism is the idea that one can believe in both Christian and Muslim religious tenets.

3) According to the pluralist theory, where is influence displayed in government?

   a. religious groups

   b. interest groups

   c. political groups

   d. union

4) Where does the elite theory place the source of political influence?

   a. "power elite" in government, the judicial branch, and the military

   b. "power elite" in college institutions, business, and the Central Intelligence Agency

   c. "power elite" in unions, corporations, and banks

   d. "power elite" in government, corporations, and the military

5) Where does the elite theory place political power?

   a. status based on economic influence and religious background

   b. status based on economic influence and leadership position

   c. status based on economic influence and academic background

   d. status based on economic influence and party affiliation

6) What does the social movement theory identify as the source of influence?

    a. controversial uprisings/movements

    b. religious uprisings/movements

    c. popular uprisings/movements

    d. economic uprisings/movements

7) Where does the social movement theory locate political power?

    a. strength of mass demands

    b. strength of student demands

    c. strength of union demands

    d. strength of private demands

8) What is a republic?

    a. A government system that rests ultimate governing power in its people, who may rule directly or via representatives.

    b. A government system that rests most governing power in the elite selected for authority based on obtaining superior education.

    c. A government system that rests none of the governing power in its people but instead allows a single individual to exercise sole political control to ensure the well-being of all people.

    d. All of the above.

9) The principle of checks and balances ensures that which branch of government has the authority to block the other branches?

    a. the executive branch

    b. the judicial branch

    c. the legislative branch

    d. all three branches

10) The Declaration of Independence explained the role of government—securing each individual's three rights. Which of the following is one of those rights?

    a. life

    b. freedom

    c. success

    d. none of the above

11) The Declaration of Independence explained the role of government—securing each individual's three rights. Which of the following is one of those rights?

a. wealth

b. land

c. liberty

d. none of the above

12) Which of the following is not one of the seven big ideas espoused in the Declaration of Independence?

a. liberty

b. individualism

c. freedom of religion

d. freedom to bear arms

13) What is the definition of freedom?

a. It means that the government will protect one's life, one's liberty, and one's property from the coercion of others (excluding government) in order to permit you to pursue the goals you define for yourself.

b. It means that the government will protect one's life, one's liberty, and one's property from the coercion of others (including the government) in order to permit you to pursue the goals you define for yourself.

c. It means that the government will protect one's life, one's liberty, and one's guns from the coercion of others (including the government) in order to permit you to pursue the goals you define for yourself.

d. none of the above

14) What is the view of negative liberty?

a. Freedom is granted with limited restrictions.

b. Freedom is the absence of constraints.

c. Freedom is the inclusion of constraints.

d. None of the above.

15) What is the definition of positive liberty?

a. The freedom to pursue one's goals with government restrictions.

b. The freedom to pursue one's goals with some exceptions.

c. The freedom to pursue one's goals.

d. The freedom to pursue one's goals without government control.

16) What is the concept of individualism?

a. The idea that individuals, with some government assistance, are responsible for their own well-being.

b. The notion that individuals, with some assistance from the greater society, are responsible for their own well-being.

c. The idea that individuals, not the society or the community, or the government, are responsible for their own well-being.

d. None of the above.

17) What do social democrats believe?

a. Members of a society are responsible for one another except for some assistance from the government.

b. Members of a society are responsible for one another and should support other developing countries.

c. Members of a society are responsible for one another.

d. None of the above

18) Social democracies are based on _____, the idea that people have a tight bond and are responsible for one another.

a. solidarity

b. social cohesiveness

c. interdependence

d. social collaboration

19) Which economist famously wrote, "The world runs on individuals pursuing their separate interests"?

a. Susan Richards

b. Michael Samuels

c. Milton Friedman

d. Roger Hernandez

20) Which sociologist defined the State as a "human community that (successfully) claims the monopoly of the legitimate use of physical force within a given territory"?

   a. Milton Friedman

   b. Max Weber

   c. Karl Marx

   d. Juan Domingo Perón

21) True or False: democracy's etymology comes from the Greek word demos ("the people") and kratos (power).

22) Which politician said that, in a totalitarian state, there is "all within the state, none outside the state and none against the state"?

   a. Benito Musolini

   b. Donald Trump

   c. Adolf Hitler

   d. Iosif Stalin

23) Which is the last totalitarian regime left in the world?

   a. China

   b. Russia

   c. Cuba

   d. North Korea

24) True or False: Pluralism developed after the end of the First World War and reached its height during the 1950s and 1960s.

25) True or False: Positive liberty is based on the claim that "I am free to the extent that I achieve self-mastery."

Discussion questions

   1. Define contemporary American culture.

   2. Identify current theocratic, authoritarian, and totalitarian regimes throughout the world. What are the threats these regimes pose to American democratic leadership?

   3. What does the Manifest Destiny represent in American political culture?

   4. Define fascism. What are the contemporary forms of fascism?

5. True or False. America is a democracy. Why? Why not?

6. True or False: Russia is a democracy. Why? Why not?

7. What do social democrats believe in?

Video Resources

USA.gov Channel https://www.youtube.com/usagov1

Icount https://icount.com/

PBS Frontline http://www.pbs.org/wgbh/pages/frontline/watch/

Firing Line Debates https://www.hoover.org/library-archives/collections/firing-line

Bill Moyers http://billmoyers.com/

President Benjamin Harrison (1889-1893) https://youtu.be/pU4gGEL5c8g

Oldest Footage of a President https://youtu.be/gAesU_GOe_4

Introduction to Political Science https://www.youtube.com/watch?v=Xhjl-MvnqAc

Website Resources

Data and Statistics about the United States https://www.usa.gov/statistics

A Chronology of US Historical Documents www.ushistory.org/documents/

The Founders' Constitution http://press-pubs.uchicago.edu/founders/

Follow the Money http://www.followthemoney.org/

Political Resource Directory http://politicalresources.com/

The Internet Classics Archive classics.mit.edu

The Online Library of Liberty http://oll.libertyfund.org/

CHAPTER 2

AMERICAN POLITICAL CULTURE

2.1 American Political Culture

American political culture is unique and different from all other countries in the world. American political culture is built upon values that limit the power of government. Political culture is a set of *shared* ideas, values, and beliefs that define the role and limitations of government and people's relationship to that government. The American political culture is woven together from political narratives that are vastly different across the nation. Every state has unique stories and a history defining the political narrative. We also see many instances when states do not get along or cooperate, and in these instances, cultures clash. Take, for example, the American Civil War, arguably the darkest and bloodiest hour in the country's history. That conflict represented an enormous fracturing in the political culture. The Union states maintained one set of beliefs on slavery, tariffs, suffrage, and government power, whereas the Confederates held diametrically opposite views. For years, the United States was divided on the most fundamental aspects of political culture, and it culminated in war. It was a loss of social cohesion that led to widespread suffering. This is one of the most critical reasons for studying the topic of American political culture and developing a better understanding of its dynamic input and output functions.

It is impossible to provide a tangible understanding of the American political culture. The political culture is unembodied and unspoken. Disparate views abound, especially with things based on personal experiences and exposure to other cultures. Those who have not traveled or met many people from other countries are more likely to think that the beliefs they share are objective reality, not just one set of many optional sets of narratives. In the political science subfield of comparative politics, scholars research other countries and discover widely different values on everything from group identification to suspicion of government, to tolerance of outside cultures. Examining these differences is one the primary methods researchers use to analyze societies objectively, avoid ethnocentrism, and disseminate information for learning purposes.

Political culture is easiest to recognize when one steps outside of it. Being inside of a political ideology or system can keep a person from seeing the 'big picture' of the political system. Political culture gives people a common set of assumptions about the world and a common political language within which they can agree.

2.2 Fundamentals of American political culture

American political culture is defined by the concept of limited government. Limited government is the political philosophy of a government limited in power. This is a key concept in the history of liberalism. Liberalism is a school of thought derived from the Enlightenment, found particularly in thinkers such as John Locke. Locke's beliefs in limited government were the inspiration for the Declaration of Independence and the primacy of "life, liberty, and the pursuit of happiness." One might notice the similar sounding of the words "liberty" (from the Latin *"libertas"*, meaning freedom from despotic control) and "liberal" (meaning free from restraint in speech or action). Each of these terms, in their most classical sense, refer to freedom and an aversion to external coercion. Locke and his adherents, like Thomas Jefferson, wrote in a time when many began to bring into question the legitimacy of the old, sometimes despotic, European monarchies.

American political culture focuses on individualism more than collectivism. Individualism has an emphasis on individual rights rather than on the collective whole. Individualism is the idea that individuals, not society, the community, or the government, are responsible for one's own well-being.

In American society, we hold the expectation that people will provide for their own forms of retirement and social welfare. Other countries, such as Great Britain, embrace community and communitarianism, insisting that people be protected by the government. For those people who prefer to have a social democracy, or community-focused democracy, the public interest is best served when all of society uses the government as a mechanism to take care of its citizens through things such as universal healthcare and a social welfare system. In the United States, with individualism, it is not the government's responsibility to provide for full coverage of one's retirement, well being, or employment.

American political culture provides a belief in core values of freedom, equality, and representative democracy, in a context of minimal government coercion so that the political culture ensures that the people have true 'freedom.' Freedom is understood by Americans as freedom *from* government. Equality in America is equality under the law. All forms of equality that require minimal governmental intervention. What is the origin for the concern for equality in modern political culture? In 19ᵗʰ century France, the motto of "liberte, egalite, and fraternite" (liberty, equality, and fraternity) became a chief concern after the violent French Revolution. Philosophers like Jean-Jacques Rousseau and Maximilien Robespierre emphasized equality as an important ingredient in forming a social contract between members of society. Equality paves the way for the possibility of thriving democratic republics.

Equality, defined, expresses that all citizens enjoy the same privileges, statuses, and rights in the eyes of the law. Social equality means that all individuals enjoy the same lawful status in society. Social equality is where the political/social hierarchy is free from institutional nobility. This would bar the existence of titled privileges such as those of barons or archdukes who inherit special benefits when they are born. Civil servants in the government are elected or appointed based on the law rather than heredity. Political equality is the means that every citizen has the same political rights and opportunities. This includes suffrage (voting) but it also includes the right to due process (trial by jury, right to an attorney). Although America has a dark history of universal suffrage being denied to anyone other than white landowning property owners, the United States has made great strides to create political and social equality for all people. Equality also is considered to be economic equality. Economic equality focuses on the differences in wealth. Social critics scrutinize wealth/income inequality out of concerns for justice and the loss of quality of life for those with less wealth. Others counter this by claiming that some inequality is unavoidable and that equality under the law is the only thing worth safeguarding. At any rate, the issue of equality, social, political or economic, retains an important point of divergence in today's political culture.

2.3 Democracy in American Political Culture

Democracy is a decision-making process by which individuals register their preferences for their rulers (and the policies they promise). A democracy is a government which citizens rule directly and make government decisions themselves. In a democracy, the citizens have power over their government's decision making.

Is the United States considered a democracy? Yes, in some sense, but it is important to maintain precision of terms. With some exceptions (see the next section), the United States is not what you would call a "direct democracy," but rather a constitutional republic or representative democracy. Aristotle was one of the first to use the term "republic," which accounts for the United States and most countries in western civilization today. Under this model, citizens participate in politics by voting on representatives (members of Congress, the Senate, the President) who are expected to carry out the general will of those they govern. Elected officials, even your local mayor or councilmember, have a fiduciary responsibility to govern with the best interests of the people in mind. They are held accountable electorally. If they fail to satisfy their constituents, or are found guilty of a scandal, they run the risk of getting voted out of office.

In a democracy, the use of referendum can allow citizens to have direct access to creating a democratic state. A referendum is an election in which citizens vote directly on an issue. This is a way to employ "direct democracy." California passes laws and removes people from office with this method. An example of this, in 2020, was Proposition 17. This gave citizens the opportunity to vote on a referendum regarding voting rights for convicted felons released on parole. In that instance, it passed with 58% of Californians voting in favor.

In a democracy, we would assume a social, political, and economic equality amongst the people. Equal opportunity is the idea that every American has the same chance to influence politics and achieve economic success regardless of their race, gender, or class. It is the American dream that anyone can pull themselves up by their bootstraps, rich or poor, and have the same opportunities as anyone else. In the American political culture, the attitudes, beliefs, and assumptions that we create give order and meaning to public life. In a democracy, the American political culture gives Americans the ability to disagree but remain united ultimately.

2.4 American Political Ideologies

America has several different political ideologies. In modern times, it may feel like the competing political ideologies are polarized and in constant disagreement. **Ideologies** are the competing narratives we create to explain those disagreements. Typically, ideological division in the United States has been along economic terms, disputes between conservatives and liberals. Sometimes the disputes involve social dimensions as well though.

In the American political spectrum, **conservatives** on the right call for less regulation of the economy (lower taxes, freer trade, unrestricted competition). Conservatives are Americans who believe in reduced government spending, personal responsibility, traditional moral values, and a strong national defense. It is common to see conservatives known as "right wingers." **Liberals** are the second political group in the American political spectrum. Liberals on the left call for more government regulation (like social welfare programs, universal health care, and free preschool programs).

Liberals value cultural diversity, government programs for the needy, public intervention in the economy, and individual's right to a lifestyle based on their own social and moral positions. Modern liberals may differ from the Locke's classical emphasis on abundant liberty, but they still emphasize social liberty, couched within a need to safeguard society with economic safety nets. For example, a modern liberal would be socially-libertarian on something like drug possession, preferring not to criminalize it, but would seek state intervention on economic measures such as Social Security, a regulatory safety net.

Starting in the 1960s and 1970s, however, other non-economic issues started to motivate voters—issues like racial desegregation, civil rights, women's rights, including reproductive rights, prayer in school, and reducing crime. These issues split Americans along a political dimension much like a vertical line. When you combine the horizontal, economic ideological dimension with the vertical, social ideological dimension, you get four ideological categories that are important for understanding American politics today.

2.5 A closer look at American ideologies

American ideologies are distinct along economic lines. American **economic conservatives** are those that believe in the narrative that the government that governs best, governs least. Proponents of this ideology want to see the government provide less oversight on fiscal policy. An example of a political ideology that believes in less oversight is libertarianism. **Libertarians** believe in minimal government. They tend to favor policies like gun rights, reproductive rights, civil rights, assisted suicide, and legalized marijuana. Most want only as much regulation of the economy as it would take to keep competition fair and the market from tanking. Robert Nozick, author of *Anarchy, State, and Utopia*, gives the model of a "night-watchman" state, where the government exists only for the most basic functions. It would go no further than minimal governance such as police, courts of law, and a small military. This model omits most state intervention into economic and social matters.

The economic liberal, on the other hand, seeks to utilize the government to empower people who may be disadvantaged. **Economic liberals** are distinguished from economic conservatives by two beliefs. They see citizens not just as individuals but as members of groups, some of whom are often not treated equitably by society. The second ideology is they believe government action may be necessary for all people to reach their full potential. Economic liberals favor economic policies that would provide a basic standard of living to all individuals.

The progressives are those who are on the most extreme left end of political ideology. **Progressives** are those who are the farthest to the left on the political continuum. Economic liberals are those who believe in an even stronger role for the state in creating equality. Progressives made a substantial impact in America around the turn of the 20th century under the leadership of presidents like Theodore Roosevelt and Woodrow Wilson. This was during a time when the United States saw an expansion in population, industrialization, and urbanization. Progressive critics, like Upton Sinclair, believed that this coincided with an increase in corruption, business monopoly, and worker exploitation. The response to this was the creation of several new government bureaucracies such as the Food & Drug Administration (FDA), the United States Department of Agriculture (USDA), the Federal Trade Commission (FTC), and the passage of the 16th Amendment, which enabled the income tax. This would eventually go on to include the Prohibition of alcohol with the 18th Amendment. The biggest takeaway from this era was the bipartisan (Republicans and Democrats) embracing of a more hands-on and active approach to governance.

Social issues are a source of division between conservatives and liberals as well. **Social conservatives** put a priority on the government preserving a traditional social order. Social conservatives include several groups who believe that their vision of the social order (that is, how people should live their lives) is absolute and want to put it into law. Social conservatives receive some of the intellectual foundation for their views in the works of the Irish philosopher/statesman, Edmund Burke. Burke, as opposed to Rousseau, was more suspicious of the concept of social contract because he thought it would lead to the disintegration of tradition and customs. Social conservatives seek to enact protective laws for maintaining social norms but are wary of what they consider to be the "social engineering" of social liberals.

Social liberals have concrete ideas about what they think is right and don't mind stepping on civil liberties if necessary to realize them. The social liberal doesn't always gain many adherents because it pushes the limits of Americans' limited government, individualistic culture. There are some occasions, however, when social liberals can make an impact. Whenever a perceived crisis gains public visibility (i.e., the Vietnam War or the Civil Rights Era), social liberals may have a chance to persuade the public to vote to enact legislative changes that contradict the prevailing social milieu. Exceptional circumstances notwithstanding, since we tend towards limited government, Americans distrust the government and place limits on the authority the government can exercise over people.

As you can see, political culture is manifest in many shapes and forms. You have probably encountered friends, family, and opponents who represent some or all of these viewpoints. It is not difficult to see how the competing sub-cultures might clash as they did during the American Revolution, the American Civil War, the Civil Rights Era, and perhaps today as federal, state, and local elections continue to be contentious. With this framework for comprehending political culture, we can learn about the current political context. What are the major points of contention between social conservatives and social liberals? How do they fuel the debate over the hot-button political issues (war, abortion, drug restrictions, education costs, etc.)? Can we reconcile these cultural differences without incurring violence and civil wars? How do individualists and communitarians get along under the umbrella of the same government? Understanding political culture is a useful way to make sense of the various political forces at play in American civic life.

Chapter 2: American Political Culture

1) True or False: The American founders based their ideas for a new form of government on the philosophies of John Locke.

2) Americans largely accepted the political ideas of which philosopher, whose ideas of political change challenged British ideology?

    a. Thomas Hobbes

    b. Patrick Henry

    c. John Calvin

    d. John Locke

3) Why did the colonists find the philosophical work of John Locke the most appealing?

    a. It laid the groundwork for a completely anarchical society, which is what the founding fathers ultimately wanted.

    b. It introduced the idea that a social contract was conditional on the protection of rights and could be revoked if the government failed to protect those rights.

    c. It upheld the morality of slavery as a necessary evil to successful economics in a country that would struggle otherwise.

    d. Another country had previously based their structure of government on his ideas and it worked out well for them.

4) Under a _____ government, a small group of elites exercise unlimited power over individuals in all aspects of life.

    a. totalitarian

    b. theocratic --- Consider This: A theocracy refers to government rule by a religious order.

    c. authoritarian

    d. republican

5) Why do many Americans believe that they have limited power to change the course of government?

    a. Government is viewed as distant and remote.

    b. Their votes are counted the same as everyone else's.

    c. Government exists to oppose the elite.

    d. Few people try to contact their representatives. --- Consider This: Federal elected officials receive messages from hundreds of constituents daily.

6) Which of the following statements expresses the central idea of democracy?

    a. Every person in the country should be allowed to vote. --- Consider This: Voting is not the defining feature of democracy; elections take place in dictatorships, but they are not considered free.

    b. Ordinary people want to rule themselves and are capable of doing so.

    c. Security, along with religious laws and values, is the most important function of government.

    d. Governing should be carried out by a single, enlightened leader.

7) An important aspect of representative democracy is _____.

    a. a class structure that lets the elite rise to the top

    b. periodic elections so citizens can replace those whose views no longer reflect the views of the majority

    c. elections that limit competition so that citizens aren't confused by too many choices --- Consider This: This form of election for this purpose is not consistent with the free and fair elections characteristic of representative democracy.

    d. control over a candidate's message so that he or she doesn't mislead the people

8) True or False: American Civil War is arguably the darkest and bloodiest hour in America's history.

9) True or False: British political culture embraces community and communitarianism, insisting that people be protected by the government.

10) True or False:American political culture provides a belief in core values of equality, socialism, and popular democracy.

11) How do Americans understand freedom?

    a. Freedom from the government

    b. Freedom to do whatever they want to do

    c. Freedom to make political choices

    d. Economic freedom

12) True or False: Individualism has an emphasis on the collective whole rather than individual rights

13) What does equality mean in the American political system?

    a. All people within a specific society have the equal rights, liberties, and status

    b. Equality of opportunity.

    c. Equality under the law.

    d. None of the above.

14) Democracy is a decision-making process by which:

    a. Autocrats decide what policies are the best for the country.

    b. groups register their preferences for their officials and the policies they promise.

    c. individuals register their preferences for their officials and the policies they promise.

    d. None of the above.

15) Is the United States considered a democracy?

    a. Yes. Absolutely.

    b. America is both a democracy and a republic. A representative democracy, to be more precise.

    c. No.

    d. None of the above.

16) Which is the initiative that allows the citizens citizens to have direct access to creating a democratic state

    a. A referendum

    b. A plebiscite

    c. Advertising campaigns

    d. Rioting

17) What is a good example of the referendum as a way of direct democracy?

    a. Proposition 18, 2018.

    b. Proposition 5, 2001.

    c. Proposition 13, 2012.

    d. Proposition 17, 2020.

18) What do Americans understand by equal opportunity?

    a. the idea that first class citizens are the ones that should influence politics and achieve economic success.

b. the idea that every American has the same chance to influence politics and achieve economic success regardless of their race, gender, or class.

c. the idea that every white American has the same chance to influence politics and achieve economic success regardless of their race, gender, or class.

d. the idea that Americans have the chance to influence politics and achieve economic success according to each one's contribution.

19) True or False: Ideologies are the competing narratives we create to explain disagreements

20) True or False: In the American political spectrum, conservatives on the right call for more regulation of the economy.

21) American conservatives do not believe in:

a. reduced government spending

b. liberal and unorthodox moral values

c. personal responsibility

d. robust national defense

22) True or False: In the American political spectrum, liberals on the left call for more government regulation, in broad and diverse areas such as social welfare programs, universal health care, and free preschool programs.

23) Which of the following is incorrect?

a. Modern liberals in America value cultural diversity.

b. Modern liberals in America call for public intervention in the economy.

c. Modern liberals in America value individual's rights to a lifestyle based on their own social and moral positions.

d. Modern liberals in America demand mandatory religious education.

24) True or False: Modern liberals strictly adhere to Locke's classical emphasis on abundant liberty.

25) Why are social issues a source of division between conservatives and liberals?

a. Conservatives and liberals cannot understand each other

b. There is no middle point between both groups

c. Social conservatives put a priority on the government preserving a traditional social order

d. None of the above

Discussion Questions

1. According to the text, what is political culture?
2. What is the concept of limited government?
3. What is the concept of liberalism?
4. True or False: American political culture focuses on individualism more than collectivism.
5. True or False: Americans understand freedom as freedom from government. Equality in America is equality under the law.
6. What are the values and cultural beliefs that are most ingrained in American citizens?

Video resources

USA.gov Channel https://www.youtube.com/usagov1

Icount https://icount.com/

American political culture - Harvard University https://www.youtube.com/watch?v=kUXCGYCJiZE

Political Culture - Harvard University - Thomas Patterson https://edx-video.net/d1c70b49-878a-45ad-9a37-7a071b93a1a5-mp4_720p.mp4

Civics and Government https://www.pbslearningmedia.org/subjects/social-studies/civics-and-government/

Website Resources

US History - American Political Culture https://www.ushistory.org/gov/4a.asp

American political culture - University of Minnesota http://open.lib.umn.edu/americangovernment/chapter/6-1-political-culture/

The Alexis de Tocqueville Tour: Exploring Democracy in America https://www.c-span.org/series/?tocqueville

Smithsonian: History and Culture http://www.si.edu/history_and_culture

Data and Statistics about the United States https://www.usa.gov/statistics/

A Chronology of US Historical Documents www.ushistory.org/documents/

CHAPTER 3

POLITICS AND ECONOMIC MODELS

3.1 Politics and economics

Why would the discussion of economic models and politics occur intertwined? The first answer to why these two fields are connected is that human beings are a social species. That is, each individual defines her own needs and desires in cooperation with others, so we must find a way to socially organize these relations. If we lived in a world where resources are infinite, this would not be necessary, since all citizens could just fulfil any of their desires as they please. However, in our empirical world **scarcity** plays an essential role. This refers to the fact that human and non-human resources are finite and society is thus only capable of producing a limited amount of goods.[29] In short, there are not sufficient resources to produce all the wares that people desire or want to consume. For this reason, societies have to find a way to redistribute the limited amount of goods and wares at their disposal. This is the role of **economics**, which is defined as the process for deciding who gets the material resources and how they get them. Hence, economic goods are those wares that are relatively scarce and need to be allocated according to a certain criterion.

Economics is a social science not only because it concerns the way society organizes itself to provide good to its citizens, but also because it aims to explain the economic behavior - how these latter exchange scarce resources - of individuals, groups and organizations. To do so, economics relies on the **rational choice theory**, namely the conception for which economic agents take their decisions according to what they mostly

---

[29] Hahnel R. (2003), *ABCs of Political Economy. Modern Primer*, Pluto Press, London.

prefer and to the hindrances they encounter and the aggregate behavior in society reflects the sum of the choices made by individuals. At the individual level, this means that the agent evaluates the alternative options she encounters in terms of costs and benefits, choosing the one whose outcome offers the most amount of benefits and the least amount of costs[30].

At the aggregate and social level, economics assumes that each economic agent knows the economic model and that her actions are consistent with what decision-makers would do in a situation with the same nature, amount of information and social structure. This is the **rational-expectations theory**, which is not only an assumption related to present behavior of economic agents, but also an assumption regarding their future decisions and the fact that even if agents may not be perfectly correct, they will be right on average over time. In this regard, rational-expectations theory is slightly different from the rational choice theory. Whereas the latter concerns how individuals take decisions, the former is an assumption about the economic system, since it maintains that over time and on average, economic agents tend to be correct.[31]

Overall then, economics concerns the decision related to how to allocate the resources. To do so, we must create some forms of social institutions, namely a social arrangement by means of which we decide how to satisfy our needs and desires. This is where politics intervene and become intertwined with the economy: politicians influence the types of economic decisions implemented by deciding how assets are utilized in our economy. The goal for politics is then to decide which economic system better fulfils the economic needs of our communities.

Throughout history, societies have created different social institutions to organize citizens' needs and desires by assigning in different ways duties and economic rewards to individuals according to how they participate in the economy. Of all the different typologies, two economic systems in particular have framed the way economics is shaped nowadays, capitalism and socialism.

Capitalism

Capitalism is usually defined as an economic regime where enterprises and/or private citizens own the means of production and where employers pay a wage to their employees to manufacture goods with the purpose of afterwards selling them to produce profits. Even though these general traits are usually largely accepted in the literature, there is not a specific definition of capitalism that is unanimously accepted, so

---

[30] Sen, A.K. (1982), *Choice, Welfare and Measurement*, Blackwell, Cambridge.
[31] Gourieroux, C., Jacqueline Pradel J. (1986), "Direct test of the rational expectation hypothesis", *European Economic Review*, 30 (2), 265-284.

it is difficult to trace back its origins. If one argues that capitalism is simply the most natural way to allocate resources within an economic community, then it has always existed and it is an intrinsic feature of human beings. That is, human beings' nature is made of the will to enrich oneself or her community, so capitalism has always existed and will always exist. Yet, others argue that capitalism is not related to human beings' nature, but it rather developed as a result of specific economic phenomenon, such as the development of agriculture, or slavery in ancient societies. Hence, capitalism is a precise historical feature that has not always existed and it will not necessarily last forever[32].

That said, there is a widespread agreement concerning the fact that capitalism is an economic system where production is not planned by a central government, but it is dictated by laws of **demand and supply** – defined as the economic relationship between the amount of a commodity that producers want to sell at a certain prince and the quantity consumers wish to buy - in the market economy. The term **market** is thus central to capitalism and it refers to decision making of multiple individuals about what to buy or sell, which creates different levels of demand and supply.

This is also how price is determined, since **prices** represent the equilibrium point at which the quantity of goods supplied by producers equals the amount required by consumers. More in detail, prices represent the compensation – usually measured in a certain currency - given by consumers to producers in return for one unit of goods or services. Prices are thus influenced by different factors that do not remain constant over time, such as production costs, demand of the product and availability. These features rather change continuously causing another important economic process, namely **inflation**, which is the decline of purchasing power of a given currency over time. Inflation is not a completely random process, but it is possible to quantify according to changes in the increase of an average price level and a basket of selected goods and services over time. The opposite may occur as well, since a deflation period results in an increase of the purchasing power of money over time.

Inflation does not only affect consumers' purchasing power, but it also changes financial mechanisms such as **currency exchange rates**, holding costs and bank loans. For what concerns exchange rates, namely the amount of currency needed in a specific country to buy the same unit of another country's currency (how many $ you need to buy 1 euro), money supply and interest rates strongly influence the demand for a currency. This is an important aspect of the economy, so governments and their central banks use interest rates as a tool to control their domestic currency and thus their economy.

---

[32] Weingast B., Wittman D.A. (2006), *The Oxford Handbook of Political Science*, Oxford University Press, New York.

For what concerns the banking system, banks both pay an **interest rate** on the people's savings in order to attract depositors and they receive an interest rate for the money that is loaned from their deposits. When interest rates are low, businesses and individuals are more inclined to ask for loans. Banks respond to these requests by offering more loans, which increases the money supply in a fractional reserve banking system. This results in a growing money supply that increases inflation, which means that more money will be needed to buy the same unit of goods and services. These processes may be unstable if left on their own, so governments create specific economic institutions – such as the Federal Open Market Committee – to regulate interest rates as a means to keep inflation rates under control and to maintain a balanced economy.

This is an oversimplified explanation of why interest rates and inflation tend to be inversely correlated, but it well describes why even in capitalist systems there may be the need for governmental and/or private interventions. For example, one of the economic tasks implemented by governments is to use taxes to balance economic inequalities, to fund public services and also to encourage or discourage certain behaviors. That is, taxes can be seen to serve a similar function to that of prices in private transactions, namely they can determine what actions should be done by governments and who will pay for them. There are different ways to do so and one of these is the **benefit principle**, for which resources should be allocated by the public sector directly according to consumer wishes. Conversely from private transactions, this principle is difficult to implement because citizens do not want to pay for a public service if they can be excluded from its benefits, so many important aspects of welfare could be negatively affected in this way.[33]

From this brief description, it follows that capitalism is not a monolith, but it presents itself in many facets and forms in political science. As aforementioned, all scholars agree that capitalism is the economic regime where capital goods belong to private citizens, but since the way it is organized has differed significantly over time, there have been different visions related to what capitalism actually is. Due to this difficulty in defining what capitalism precisely is, there has never been an academic agreement on its 'political economy', but rather many different perspectives on some specific questions related to its ethics, equality and morality. More pertinent to the economy, there has always been a debate on how much we ought to regulate markets.

On the one hand, there are those sustaining a **Laissez-faire capitalism**, for whom capitalist markets should be completely free from any economic interventionism such as subsidies and regulations. This view is based on two pillars. First, on an integral

---

[33] Frank, R.H. (2000), "Why is cost-benefit analysis so controversial?", *The Journal of Legal Studies*, 29 (2). 913-930.

conception of freedom as non-interference for which individual economic liberty must not be curtailed by the state's intervention. Second, that markets are capable of self-regulating and that best results are thus achieved when the market is left to its spontaneous order.[34] Hence, there is no space for government intervention in the economic sector. Laissez-faire developed in the 18th century, but this view is still influential, since **neoliberalism** - one of current the dominant economic paradigms - has drawn from it most of its structural features.[35]

On the other hand, most scholars acknowledge that we should have forms of **regulated capitalism** to control markets in a certain way, even though decision-makers should mainly be individuals rather than public agents as the government. In this system, individuals may decide they want the government to step in to regulate behaviors that are not in the public interest and to fix externalities created by economic liberty. As for previous features, the spectrum of "how much" government ought to intervene is wide and can be differently connected to capitalism. Yet, another important economic theory, socialism, maintains that it is not a matter of regulating capitalism, since we can reduce capitalism's problems only insofar as governments keep total control of the economy.

Socialism

Socialism is defined as an economic system where there is a social ownership of economic means of production, together with a planned market economy. According to Marx, forms of planned and public economy can be traced back up to primitive human-gatherer societies, but it is only with the modern era that this theory proposed itself as the alternative response to capitalism.[36] This latter commodifies land, means of production and work to create profit, but this can be seen as opposite to the fabric of society. Some scholars thus started pointing out that the problem of capitalism was private property, since they maintained that even if we control and 'tame' private property with the rule of law, the fact that some individuals own the means of production unavoidably leads to the exploitation of those who do not own them.[37]

Capitalism was thus seen as contrary to human needs such as creative work, diversity, solidarity and satisfaction of needs. As a response, socialism aimed at structuring an economic system more compatible with these economic needs. At first, socialism

---

[34] Hill, L. E. (1964), "On Laissez-Faire Capitalism and Liberalism'.", *The American Journal of Economics and Sociology*, 23 (4), 393-396.

[35] Ganti, T. (2014), "Neoliberalism.", *Annual Review of Anthropology*, 43, 89-104.

[36] Saitta, D. J. "Marxism, prehistory, and primitive communism.", *Rethinking Marxism*, 1 (4), 145-168.

[37] Brenkert, G. G. (1979), "Freedom and private property in Marx.", *Philosophy & Public Affairs*, 122-147.

was more a utopian ideal. Analyzing workers' poor conditions, some scholars – such as Shaker's Christian socialism or the Hutteriti in the United States - maintained that the source of workers' problems was that they were working in large factories exploited by their employers. On the contrary, the solution was to be found in small communities that would have resolved material scarcity by structuring societies on a commune spirit. Hence, this first period lacked a proper economic theory and was mainly based on utopian ideas.[38]

The first glimpses of an economic theory that promoted equality as a way to achieve a meritocratic society arose with the anarchist Pierre-Jospeh Proudhon, or with anti-capitalist scholars such as Robert Owen and Charles Fourier.[39] Yet, it was Henri de Saint-Simon who first coined the term "socialism" as the alternative system to capitalism who could have granted equal opportunities to the people.[40] Finally, socialism became a proper economic theory thanks to the famous work of Karl Marx and Friedrich Engels "Das Kapital" (Capital),[41] where it is possible to find the basis of the main socialist economic concepts, such as:

- *Marxist theory of value*: capitalism produces a multitude of goods, the value of which is mainly determined by the amount of work required to manufacture it;

- *Historical ownership relationship:* capitalism changed the ownership of the means of production, since whereas peasants used to own the tools of their job, urban workers were employees who have to sell the only thing they own, namely their work;

- *Commodity fetishism and economic exploitation:* workers are the source of economic value and the bourgeoisie, who own the means of production, exploits this value by transforming into profit the plus value coming from workers.

- *Capital accumulation:* capitalism is inherently led to continuously accumulate wealth by gaining from investments' returns and by profiting from workers' plus value. For this reason, capitalism must continuously find new markets and opportunities to expand itself world-wide and to repeat the accumulation process.

- *Crisis and centralization:* capital accumulation cyclically finds social and economic barriers that lead to periods of crisis which often result in further centralization of the means of production in the hands of fewer capitalist;

---

[38] Bestor A. (2018), *Backwoods Utopias: The Sectarian Origins and the Owenite Phase of Communitarian Socialism in America, 1663-1829*, University of Pennsylvania Press, Pennsylvania.

[39] Prichard, A. (2013), *Justice, order and anarchy: The international political theory of Pierre-Joseph Proudhon,* Routledge, London.

[40] Simon, W. M. (1956), "History for utopia: Saint-Simon and the idea of progress.", *Journal of the History of Ideas* 17 (3), 311-331.

[41] Marx K. (2019 [1867]), *Das Kapital (Capital) A Critique of Political Economy*, Benediction Classics, Oxford.

In this framework, class conflict is an inherent characteristic of the economic system that according to Marx could be fixed only with a revolutionary movement aimed at the abolishment of private property so as to favor public property as the means of production. After Marx, other scholars not necessarily connected to socialism – such as J.S.Mill and J.M.Keynes – acknowledged that capitalism was unstable and that if the economic system was to 'tame' social conflict and to produce better results both in the different economic fields and in the market, it required some form of public intervention.[42] This debate on the connection between public intervention and market liberty has been a central feature of political economic debate over the last century, even though there currently are almost no countries framed on an integral socialist model.

Nowadays, we identify a **socialist economy** as a system where commodities are produced directly to be used, rather than to be sold to create profit. A central feature of the socialist economy is that it is **'planned'** which means that economic inputs are assigned directly by using resources to produce value according to the needs. This is opposite to what happens in a market economy where value is assigned indirectly by letting the market and economic cycles decide the inputs. A planned economy requires the public ownership of the means of production, even though this varies from a complete ownership by the state (statalism) to mixed forms of ownership by workers' cooperatives and a common property by all society.

Socialist industries do not encompass hierarchical relationships, but should be based on workers' self-government where each worker has the same decisional power over collective decisions as others.' Yet, most historical examples of socialist countries, such as the Soviet Union or Yugoslavia, framed the management of their factories on a rigid bureaucracy that implemented the will of the state, thus leading to the debate related to whether or not such states were actually economically socialist or "collectivist bureaucrats."[43]

Aim of socialism is thus to 'neutralize' the capital by tying investments and capital to a social planning aimed at eliminating the economic cycle and the overproduction crisis typical of economies that rely on private property. In this way, socialist theorists maintain that workers could obtain more equality, freedom to access the resources they need to live and they would not be exploited of the value produced by their work. Over the last century, there have been several attempts to implement socialist economy in practice, even though most of them encompass certain capitalist features such as salaries given to employees and forms of partial free market.

---

[42] Taylor Q. (2016), "John Stuart Mill, Political Economist: A Reassessment", *The Independent Review*, 21 (1), 73-94.
[43] Verdery, K. (1996), *What was socialism, and what comes next?*. Princeton University Press, Princeton.

Most of the social historical examples were structured on an economy planned by a central government who decided the kind and amount of commodities that had to be produced, as it was the case in the Soviet Union, in the Vietnamese socialist republic or in Cuba. This economic regime reached its peak in the 80s, when almost 1/3 of the total world population lived underneath such economic regimes, even though all these economies together generated only 15% of world's GDP. However, with the dissolution of the Soviet Union in 1991, countries steadily changed their economies to more liberal forms, such that nowadays only a few countries – Cuba, North Korea, China – adopt this economic regime and aside from North Korea, this socialism is more liberal than the central planned version of the Soviet Union.[44]

3.2 Political-Economic Systems

Since the dissolution of the Soviet Union, the vast majority of the countries in the world has adopted various forms of capitalism and this has created different debates. The first aspect that has often been debated in political economy is the connection between capitalism and democratic systems. A **capitalist democracy** is a country that has both a democratic government – a rule of law, democratic elections and that guarantees political liberty - and a capitalist economy with an emphasis on free markets and private enterprises.[45]

These political systems usually have a welfare system to make sure that citizens' basic rights are guaranteed, but at the same time they emphasize economic liberty and they rely on free-markets to create the innovation and competitiveness required for a prosperous social and economic development. Overall then, several scholars in social sciences – such as Przeworski, Lipset, Huber, Sen and many others – have studied the connection between democracy and economic development, finding that while it is not possible to maintain that economic development causes democratization, there is a positive correlation between democracies and economic development.[46]

Most western societies have adopted mixed forms of democratic capitalism. On the contrary, other regimes have implemented more stringent economic policies. This is the case of **authoritarian states** where there is no political plurality and where governments dispose of a strong central power that they use to reduce the rule of law, the separation of powers and many other democratic liberties. Even though there are

---

[44] Sabry, M. I. (2017), *The Development of Socialism, Social Democracy and Communism: Historical, Political and Socioeconomic Perspectives*, Emerald Group Publishing, Bingley.

[45] Weingast & Wittman 2006; 603-618.

[46] Baum, M. A., Lake D.A. (2003), "The Political Economy of Growth: Democracy and Human Capital", *American Journal of Political Science*, 47 (2), 333-347.

different forms of these regimes - some may be dominated by a military, while others may be based on a religious theocracy or on the control of a strong political party - all these typologies have in common the fact that they hold a strict control over the economic system.[47]

This control over society is even more stringent in **totalitarian states** – such as the Nazi regime and the Soviet Union - where every aspect of the people's lives is under control of a central power. Therefore, while an authoritarian state hinders democratic liberties but it may guarantee certain freedoms to its citizens, there is no independent organization in a totalitarian state. For example, whereas there are still many authoritarian countries around the world, North Korea is the only actual totalitarian regime left.

---

[47] Somndrol P.C. (1991), "Totalitarian and Authoritarian Dictators: A Comparison of Fidel Castro and Alfredo Stroessner", *Journal of Latin American Studies*, 23 (3), 599-620.

Chapter 3: Politics and Economic Models

1) Rules are used to _____.

   a. decide who gets power and influence

   b. decide who gets material resources and how

   c. govern the country

   d. determine who will win or lose future power struggles

2) The market controls economic decisions in a(n) _____ economy.

   a. socialist

   b. capitalist

   c. authoritarian

   d. totalitarian

3) In the United States, businesses have substantial freedom from government interference, but the government will step in and regulate the economy from time to time to guarantee individual rights. The United States uses which type of economic system?

   a. socialism

   b. laissez-faire capitalism

   c. communism

   d. regulated capitalism

4) In socialist economies, control over economic decisions is exercised by _____.

   a. the market

   b. the government

   c. supply and demand forces

   d. a vote by the people

5) A capitalist economy is an economic system that relies on the _____ to determine who should have material goods.

   a. government

   b. people

   c. top businesses

   d. market

6) Some countries in Western Europe utilize a hybrid system that gives individuals more control over their personal lives and a government that supports equality, which is a form of _____.

   a. capitalist democracy

   b. Marxist utopia

   c. totalitarianism

   d. authoritarian capitalism

7) A political system in which the state holds all the power over the social order is known as _____.

   a. a republic

   b. an authoritarian government

   c. a capitalist government

   d. a pure democracy

8) In non-authoritarian systems, _____.

   a. there is no government at all

   b. the government regulates people's behavior but grants considerable freedoms

   c. the government has total control over people's behavior

   d. the government has all the power

9) A _____ government combines an authoritarian government with a socialist economy.

   a. totalitarian

   b. anarchic

   c. democratic

   d. monarchical

10) Which is a characteristic of a democratic government?

   a. The government rules over subjects.

   b. There is usually one central head that is in charge of all laws and regulations.

   c. The government dictates how its people can behave.

   d. The citizens have considerable power to make the rules that govern them.

11) The absence of a government and laws is a characteristic of _____.

   a. totalitarianism

b. anarchy

c. authoritarianism

d. democracy

12) A person who believes that there should be no government or laws whatsoever is most likely a(n) _____.

a. communist

b. socialist

c. capitalist

d. anarchist

13) The principle that serves as the basis for democracy and allows people to have a hand in the rules that govern them is known as _____.

a. authoritarianism

b. socialism

c. popular sovereignty

d. totalitarianism

14) Individuals who must submit to a government authority under which they have no rights are _____.

a. elitists

b. citizens

c. democrats

d. subjects

15) True or False: Rules are directives that determine how resources are allocated, and they determine how we try to get the things we want.

16) True or False: In a socialist economy, the market controls economic decisions.

17) True or False: In a laissez-faire capitalist society, there are no restrictions on the market at all, making the economy subject to wild swings up and down.

18). True or False: Politics is the system or organization for exercising authority over a body of people.

19) True or False: Those who live under an authoritarian-style government are known as citizens.

20) True or False: A totalitarian government combines an authoritarian government with a socialist economy.

21) True or False: Powerful national government, collectivism, and a belief in social hierarchies are fundamental to American political culture.

22) True or False: An economic conservative would favor lower taxes and limited government regulation of the economy.

23) True or False: Having control over the political narrative does not give anyone an advantage or a disadvantage.

24) True or False: Prices represent the equilibrium point at which the quantity of goods supplied by producers equals the amount required by consumers.

25) True or False: Henri de Saint-Simon was the first to coin the term "socialism" as the alternative system to capitalism who could have granted equal opportunities to the people.

Discussion questions

1. Define capitalism. Identify countries with a capitalist economy. What are the common characteristics these countries share?

2. Define socialism. Identify countries with a socialist economy. What are the common characteristics these countries share?

3. True or False: China has a capitalist economy. Why? Why not?

4. Define state capitalism. Identify countries with a state capitalist economy.

5. Since the dissolution of the Soviet Union, the vast majority of the countries in the world has adopted various forms of capitalism. Why? Explain the reasons.

6. What is a capitalist democracy? Is there a connection between capitalism and democracy?

Video Resources

USA.gov Channel https://www.youtube.com/usagov1

Icount https://icount.com/

PBS Frontline http://www.pbs.org/wgbh/pages/frontline/watch/

TED Talk - Eric X. Li: A Tale of Two Political Systems https://www.ted.com/talks/eric_x_li_a_tale_of_two_political_systems

The Collision of Capitalism and Democracy https://sc4.idm.oclc.org/login?url=https://sc4.idm.oclc.org/login?url=http://digital.films.com/PortalPlaylists.aspx?wID=97865&xtid=70940

Heaven on Earth: The Rise and Fall of Socialism Series https://sc4.idm.oclc.org/login?url=https://sc4.idm.oclc.org/login?url=http://digital.films.com/PortalPlaylists.aspx?seriesID=12584&wID=97865

Marx Reloaded https://sc4.idm.oclc.org/login?url=https://sc4.idm.oclc.org/login?url=http://digital.films.com/PortalPlaylists.aspx?wID=97865&xtid=52228

Website Resources

20th century US Capitalism and Regulation (Khan Academy) https://www.khanacademy.org/humanities/us-history/history-survey/us-history-survey/v/20th-century-capitalism-and-regulation-in-the-united-states

Communism: Karl Marx to Joseph Stalin https://europe.unc.edu/iron-curtain/history/communism-karl-marx-to-joseph-stalin/

American Socialists www.americansocialists.org

Data and Statistics about the United States https://www.usa.gov/statistics

A Chronology of US Historical Documents www.ushistory.org/documents/

Follow the Money http://www.followthemoney.org/

Political Resource Directory http://politicalresources.com/

The Internet Classics Archive classics.mit.edu

The Online Library of Liberty http://oll.libertyfund.org/

FEDERALISM

What is federalism? Federalism is the division of governmental power among the various public jurisdictions. In antiquity, government was much more unitary or "top-down" in its execution and delivery. Before power-sharing arrangements became common, political systems had been either unitary systems or confederal systems. Power was usually exercised in a *one-way direction*. A **unitary government** is a national polity governed as a single unit. The idea is to have the central government exercising all or most political authority. A **confederation** is a group of independent states or nations that yield some of their powers to a national government. A Confederation differs from a unitary government by the way the subsidiary states much more sovereign authority. During the period of American history when the country was governed under the Articles of Confederation (1781 to 1789), the individual states had more autonomy but also less cohesion with neighboring states. Critics of that regime claimed that the absence of a weak central government left the young republic vulnerable to crises without mediation or judicial arbitration. Shay's Rebellion, a tax revolt that took place in Massachusetts, was considered the crisis that ended the United States's attempt at confederate governance.

America turned away from a unitary government style and tried a Confederation style of government for 10 years. The United States has used the federal form of governance since 1789 and the ratification of the United States Constitution. American federalism is not just the division of powers between the federal government and the states but is further nuanced by local governments. In America, the three Some of the powers that the federal government possesses it also shares with the states. These are called **concurrent powers**. Federalism is a system of implementing public policy across multiple layers of government. The process of testing and spreading ideas across multiple levels of government from federal, state, and local levels is known as diffusion.

Diffusion is the spreading of policy ideas from one city or state to others. An example of diffusion comes whenever local governments borrow policies. If New York City were to construct an ordinance that fined litterers $100 per offense, and San Francisco copied and administered the same policy, then it was a diffusion of New York City's original concept.

4.1 The Federalist Papers and Federalism

The Federalist Papers are a collection of 85 newspaper editorials written in support of the Constitution under the pseudonym of Publius, whose real identity was three Federalists: Alexander Hamilton, James Madison, and John Jay. The word 'federalism' does not appear in the Constitution of the United States. It has been adopted and became manifest within the governmental structures as inspired by The Federalist Papers. James Madison, writing as Publius, addressed the concept of Federalism in The Federalist Papers.

There are many different topics in The Federalist Papers. In Federalist No. 39, Madison defines "republic" and establishes three rules which must apply:

1. What is the foundation of its establishment? Only the possess *ultimate* sovereignty over the government.
2. What are the sources of its power? The elected officials chosen by the people should not break the rules or abuse their power.
3. Who has the authority to make future changes? When someone is chosen to rule the country, he or she should only be in that position for a certain amount of time and must be held accountable (through impeachment if necessary) if found to have committed high crimes or treason.

The republic defined by Madison consists of the different elements of the government leadership. A Madisonian republic is a system of government as defined by these three stipulations where the citizens elect representatives to make decisions for them. This constitutes most civic officials within the three branches of government: the executive, the judicial, and the legislative. There are still some offices that are *not* directly accountable to the people. This includes justices on the Supreme Court of the United States as well as United States senators prior to the passage of the 17th Amendment. Federalists like Madison believed that there needed to be a balance of direct election (popular vote) versus internal appointment by informed elites.

Madison, along with the other framers, was aware of two methods of arranging the government: confederate or federal. The Articles of Confederation was the country's original attempt at confederacy, which was a loosely assembled body of state governments prior to the ratification of the Constitution. The second version of government is called federal, national, or consolidation. It is also known as a unitary system.

Madison's essays proposed a five-component model for the American federal system. The first component was the method of ratification. The establishment of the Constitution was not a mere proclamation or decree by central authorities. Rather it was voted upon by the various member states before becoming the supreme law of the land. The second component was the sources of power for national officers. Here Madison emphasized how the bodies of Congress (House & Senate) as well as the presidency should arise. The presidency, for example, would be subject to direct election by the people, but administered as a function of the states through the Electoral College. The third component considers the apportionment of representatives based on the census. This determines how many representatives there are per state. This third component was the establishment of the representative as a national officer. The people thus gained a national representation. The fourth component referred to a fixed number of senators; two per state. People are not represented in the Senate, the states are. The Senate reinforces the federal nature of the Constitution. Madison's fifth component was the power of the presidency. The president's power is derived from elections and governed through the Electoral College system. As was mentioned before, the popular vote of the citizens is involved with determining the president, but it is the Electoral College (based on the size of the state and its apportionment of senators and representatives) that ultimately elects the president.

4.2 Federalist Paper 10 and Factions

Federalist No. 10 was published on November 23, 1787, under the pseudonym "Publius." It addresses the question of how to reconcile citizens with interests contrary to the rights of others or the interests of the greater community. During the late 18th century, the concept of factions bothered the founding fathers. Madison saw factions within society as inevitable due to the nature of man. As long as humans hold differing opinions, have differing amounts of wealth, and own differing amounts of property, they will continue to form alliances with people who are most like them. The result is that they may work against the public interest and infringe upon the rights of others. Madison warns against these dangers.

Federalist No. 10 continues a theme begun in Federalist No. 9, "The Utility of the Union as a Safeguard Against Domestic Faction and Insurrection." Scholars and jurists contend that Federalist 9 and Federalist 10 are an authoritative interpretation and explication of the Constitution. The question of faction undergirds the development of modern interest groups and the role in which minority groups are protected from majority opinions.

In addition to the problem with factions, Federalist No. 10 continues the discussion of the question broached in Hamilton's Federalist No. 9. Hamilton there addressed the destructive role of a faction in breaking apart the republic. The role in which people form groups and allegiances dictate how effective a republic will be. The question Madison answers, then, is how to eliminate the negative effects of factions. Can a faction exist without the consequences to the republic? Madison defines a faction as many citizens, whether amounting to a minority or majority of the whole, who are united and actuated by some common impulse of passion, or of interest, adverse to the rights of other citizens, or to the permanent and aggregate interests of the community. In Madison's definition, he identifies the most serious source of faction to be the diversity of opinion in political life which leads to dispute over fundamental issues such as what regime or religion should be preferred.

Distribution of property was at the core of the debate during Madison's time. At the heart of Madison's fears about factions was the unequal distribution of property in society. The reality of property ownership was that some people owned property and others owned nothing, and Madison felt that people would form different factions that pursued different interests based on such a gap in ownership.

Recognizing that the country's wealthiest property owners formed a minority and that the country's unpropertied classes formed a majority, Madison feared that the unpropertied classes would come together to form a majority faction that gained control of the government. This fear of the minority rising became part of the framing of the American Constitution. Specifically, Madison feared that the unpropertied classes would use their majority power to implement a variety of measures that redistributed wealth in a disordered fashion. In short, Madison feared that a majority faction of the unpropertied classes might emerge to redistribute wealth and property for populist purposes and to the dismay of the ruling class, which would inevitably result in conflict.

4.3 Madison's Arguments for Faction Limitation

Madison first assessed two ways to limit the damage caused by factions: remove the causes or control the effects. He then described the two methods of removing the causes of factions: first, destroying liberty, which would work because liberty is to faction what air is to fire. The second option would be to create a society of homogeneous opinions and interests, which is difficult but not impossible. Madison particularly emphasized that economic stratification prevents everyone from sharing the same opinion. He concluded that the damage caused by factions can be limited only by controlling the effects.

Madison further contended that a person may offer two ways to check majority factions: (1) prevent the existence of the same passion or interest in a majority at the same time or, (2) render a majority faction unable to act. Madison concluded that a small democracy cannot avoid the dangers of a majority faction because small size means that undesirable passions can very quickly spread to a majority of the people, which can then enact its will through the democratic government without difficulty. A republic is different from a democracy because its government is placed in the hands of delegates, and, as a result, can be extended over a larger area. The idea is that, in a large republic, there will be more fit characters to choose from for each delegate.

4.4 Federalist 51 and Checks and Balances

The notion of checks and balances became fundamental in the formation of government. Federalist No. 51 is titled: "The Structure of the Government Must Furnish the Proper Checks and Balances Between the Different Departments." It was another essay by James Madison. This document was published on February 8, 1788, under the pseudonym Publius. Federalist No. 51 addresses a means by which appropriate checks and balances can be created in government and advocates a separation of powers within the national government One of its most important ideas, an explanation of check and balances, is the often-quoted phrase, "Ambition must be made to counteract ambition." In government, it is well known that people will seek to be self-promoting. Madison's idea was that the politicians and the individuals in public service in the United States would all have proclamations and ideas that they would work hard to enact-- this is true for Madison's time as well as now. The solution to ensure that laws and strong ideas were not enacted by a small group of partisan individuals was to use a federalist system where each level of government had different branches, each branch having the authority to impact the operation of the other branches. One of the primary ways that Federalist Paper 51 was able to encourage checks and balances was to tie it to the concept of liberty and an aversion to centralized tyranny. The concentration of power into one branch or level of government is antithetical to liberty. Whenever one branch or institution (of any sort) gets too much power, they become corrupted and tyrannical. As Lord Acton reminds us: "power corrupts; absolute power corrupts absolutely." Checks and balances can be a remedy to the corruption of power.

The system of checks and balances, as espoused by Madison and philosophers like John Locke and Jean-Jacques Rousseau, was designed to allow an independent function of the various branches of government within certain constraints. For example, the legislative branch would draft laws that would have to be signed (or vetoed) by the president. The Supreme Court could strike down the laws if deemed unconstitutional. The president appointed members of the court, but only by an approval vote of the Senate. It was a way to avoid allowing any one branch to gain too much influence and power.

4.5 Changes in Federalism Over Time

The balance of power between states and the national government changes over time. Because the balance of power between state and national government was clearly left open to some interpretation by the founders, it left a lot of power to the Supreme Court for interpretation. Looking at federal/state power relations over time, we can see two trends:

1. Changes like industrialization, urbanization, and advances in science and technology have led citizens to look to the government at all levels for assistance, protection, and security.
2. There is an undeniable shift of power over time from the states to the national government, particularly since the culmination of the Civil War, but some of it as early as the ratification of the Constitution.

There have been some key moments where power has shifted from the states to the federal government. John Marshall's tenure as Chief Justice of the Supreme Court (1801–1835) marked a drastic shift of power from the states to the federal government. **Marshall** was the third Chief Justice of the Supreme Court. He believed in the Federalist vision of a strong national government. One of the groundbreaking cases heard under his tenure was *Marbury v. Madison*. ***Marbury v. Madison*** (1803) gave the Supreme Court the power of **judicial review** to determine if congressional laws, state laws, or executive actions are constitutional. This groundbreaking change in the role of the judiciary extended the role of checks and balances to the judicial branch with stronger enforcement.

A second key moment that shifted the power from the states to the federal government was the extension of the "Necessary and Proper Clause" in *McCulloch v. Maryland* (1819). The result of this case allowed that clause to be interpreted broadly to include many powers that were not in the Constitution.

The third key moment that shifted the power from the states to the federal governments was *Gibbons v. Ogden*. The extension of the Interstate Commerce Clause and the right to regulate commerce emanating from *Gibbons v. Ogden* (1824) opened the door to federal regulation of commerce, broadly understood to mean most forms of business. The landmark decision in which the Supreme Court of the United States held that the power to regulate interstate commerce, granted to Congress by the Commerce Clause of the United States Constitution, encompassed the power to regulate sea navigation.

4.6 Federalism: Then and Now

Nowadays, advocates of national power tend to be Democrats whose ideology leads them to believe, like the Federalists, that national power is not a threat to individual liberties. Republicans tend to be more like the Anti-Federalists in their distrust of national power and their preference for keeping important decisions at the state level. Republicans have long advocated *devolution*, or the returning of power to the states. Their enthusiasm for that position changes somewhat when they are in control of the federal government. When Republicans control Congress and the executive, many of them are less wary of the reach of the national government because it is doing their bidding. Similarly, when Democrats are out of power, they look to the states to enact their agendas. Today the battle over federalism seems to have less to do with its old framework of limited government versus big government and more to do with the battle for power between two highly polarized parties.

During the first 150 years of the United States, the country practiced something called Dual Federalism. **Dual Federalism (1789-1933)** is when you have a clear division of governing authority between national governments and state governments. One example of this is layer cake federalism, which is when you have a clear division between the authority of the state government.

During the 1930s, President Franklin D. Roosevelt's New Deal programs involved a strengthening and combination of federal/state functions. This included new regulatory agencies such as the Tennessee Valley Authority (TVA). This concept became known as Cooperative Federalism. **Cooperative Federalism (1933-1981)** is the mingling of governing authority between different levels of government.

President Ronald Reagan (1981-1989) changed how American federalism operated. It was coined **New Federalism**. **New Federalism** was a version of Cooperative Federalism but with less oversight by the federal government. It left more control to the state and local levels. New Federalism was characterized by the administering of Block Grants from the federal government to local governments. This was a way of transferring federal funds to local jurisdictions.

During the Obama administration, President Barrack Obama became known for Progressive Federalism in 2009. **Progressive Federalism** known as modern federalism is when the national government has broad goals but relies on local and state innovation to make sure they are met.

4.7 Tools Used in Modern Federalism

The modern tools used in federalism today are tied to the types of funding and programs that the federal government grants the state governments. One type of tool used by the federal government to fund state programs is a block grant. A **Block grant** gives funds that come with flexibility for the states to spend the money as they wish within broad parameters. Block grants were first introduced in 1966 as a channel for the federal government to give money to specific areas they wanted to improve. These examples in the 1960s included transportation and education. A second tool used by the federal government to fund the state governments is a categorical grant. A **categorical grant** is a grant of money with specific instructions on how it is to be spent. Finally, a third type of funding tool used by the federal government is an unfunded mandate from the federal government to the states. An **unfunded mandate** is when Congress will tell the states to do something but provide no funds for administering the policy. Unfunded mandates include local, state, and federal requirements not in synergy. For the unfunded mandate, there are federal laws or regulations that the local or state government must pay in order to enact a new law.

As one can tell, federalism has taken many shapes and forms in our country's history. There has been a general decline in the influence of the states, but the institutions of government remain similar to what was conceived by the founders of the Constitution. The United States has evolved considerably since the Articles of Confederation and the old debates over the various Federalist Papers. Things are different and they will undoubtedly change more with the passing of time. What will be the future for federalism and power sharing in America?

Chapter 4: Federalism

1) The complex interplay between state, local, and national governments stretches all the way back to the debates between:

   a. Federalists and Whigs.

   b. Federalists and Anti-Federalists.

   c. Republicans and Democrats.

   d. Anti-Federalists and Whigs.

2) Which form of government favors a central government exercising all or most political authority?

   a. unitary

   b. confederation

   c. loosely coupled federation

   d. federal

3) When the federal power is weak, providing defense and economic benefits, one can consider it an

   a. confederation

   b. federation

   c. republic

   d. democracy

4) Which level(s) of government is/are responsible for regulating business?

   a. federal

   b. state

   c. local

   d. federal and state

5) The hybrid developed by the delegates at the Constitutional Convention was a _____ system.

   a. confederal

   b. federal

   c. unitary

   d. socialist

6) Which of the following is not a weakness of a confederation?

   a. more local control over policy

   b. weak central authority

   c. a variety of contradictory state actions

   d. unclear individual rights

7) Public education would be a good example of what kind of power or powers?

   a. federal

   b. state

   c. concurrent

   d. local

8) Which of the following is not an advantage of federalism?

   a. coordination across levels of government

   b. protecting individual rights

   c. providing sources of innovation

   d. responsiveness to local needs

9) Which of the following is not a disadvantage of federalism?

   a. coordination

   b. individual rights

   c. poor policies

   d. inequalities across layers

10) Which of the following is not a granted power to Congress?

   a. organizing state elections

   b. handling US foreign policy

   c. establishing post offices

   d. raising an army

11) What is the name for a power that is explicitly found in the United States Constitution?

   a. enumerated

   b. necessary and proper

   c. implied

   d. informal

12) powers could be thought of as those implied by but not explicitly named in the Constitution.

    a. Inherent

    b. Enumerated

    c. Expressed

    d. Concurrent

13) Which amendment to the Constitution provides the foundation for states' rights?

    a. Fourth

    b. Tenth

    c. Twelfth

    d. Fourteenth

14) The Tenth Amendment is most likely favored by

    a. big-government advocates.

    b. those favoring dual federalism.

    c. small-government advocates.

    d. those with a strong liberal ideology.

15) The Tenth Amendment relates to and demonstrates best which type of powers?

    a. reserved

    b. concurrent

    c. inherent

    d. implied

16) Which of the following is not an example of a reserved power?

    a. organizing state elections

    b. coining money

    c. public education

    d. public health

17) Being able to use one's driver's license in any state is an example of the _____ clause.

    a. necessary and proper

    b. full faith and credit

c. supremacy

d. inherent powers

18) Which clause of the Constitution says that each state should recognize and uphold laws passed by any other state?

a. necessary and proper

b. full faith and credit

c. supremacy

d. inherent powers

19) Building railways, borrowing money, and regulating business are examples of ː powers.

a. police

b. reserved

c. inherent

d. concurrent

20) _____ federalism argues for the clear division of governing authority between national and state governments.

a. Dual

b. Cooperative

c. Coaptive

d. New

21) If Virginia law conflicts with federal law, which clause argues for federal law to be superior?

a. supremacy

b. full faith and credit

c. elasticity

d. inherent powers

22) The _____ clause says that the national government may wield powers "necessary and proper" to support its function.

a. supremacy

b. full faith and credit

c. elasticity

d. inherent powers

23) Which of the following is not an example of a concurrent power?

   a. education

   b. transportation

   c. taxation

   d. national defense

24) Block grants provide funds for

   a. elections

   b. any use

   c. specific use

   d. urban growth

25) Which of the following is a key feature of New Federalism?

   a. grants in aid

   b. heavy use of block grants

   c. limited state income tax

   d. increased income tax

26) is defined as the transfer of authority from national to state or local governments.

   a. Supremacy

   b. Devolution

   c. Elastic

   d. Power-seeking theory

27) Who are more likely to prefer state control of an issue?

   a. Republicans

   b. Democrats

   c. Socialists

   d. Communists

28) The states and federal government are _____ in progressive federalism.

   a. partners

   b. competitors

   c. separate

   d. alienated

29) Through the Court's interpretation of the necessary and proper clause, which institution of government is most affected?

    a. the presidency

    b. Congress

    c. the bureaucracy

    d. independent commissions

30) Which Supreme Court case extended to individuals the right to challenge federal statutes on the grounds that they interfere with powers reserved to the states?

    a. Medellin v. Texas

    b. Citizens United v. Clinton

    c. Gonzales v. Oregon

    d. Bond v. United States

31) Feelings of nationalism help maintain the federal balance by instilling loyalty to which level(s) of government?

    a. federal

    b. state

    c. local

    d. all of the above

32) The Supreme Court's review of a law passed by Congress best demonstrates which American government principle related to federalism?

    a. checks and balances

    b. supremacy clause

    c. nationalism

    d. unfunded mandates

33) Federalism operates along a _____ dimension.

    a. vertical

    b. horizontal

    c. lateral

    d. multidimensional

34) Which group best demonstrates civic voluntarism?

    a. members of Congress

b. local school board members

c. district court judges

d. local police officers

35) What two layers of government interacted to define dual federalism?

a. national and state

b. state and local

c. national and local

d. national and the nonprofit sector

36) Which "cake" metaphor was introduced during the New Deal?

a. layer cake

b. Bundt cake

c. marble cake

d. none of the above

37) A large, diverse and fragmented nation can be bound together through

a. nationalism

b. federalism

c. voting

d. borders

38) A reason for historical shifts in the Supreme Court can be traced to

a. state courts

b. the bureaucracy

c. the party in power

d. the president

39) Federalism is the relationship between different levels of

a. government

b. people

c. bureaucracies

d. states

40) Powers necessary for the president to fulfill their duties but not named in the Constitution are known as _____ powers.

   a. inherent

   b. concurrent

   c. diffused

   d. mixed

41) Congress's authority to establish a national bank exemplifies its powers.

   a. concurrent

   b. inherent

   c. reserved

   d. granted

42) The "_and proper clause" provides Congress's power over issues not explicitly found in the Constitution.

   a. necessary

   b. useful

   c. immediate

   d. utilized

Discussion Questions

1) Does federalism result in greater competition between state and local governments? Why, and in what areas might it?

2) What is the foundation for states' rights?

3) In what policy areas is there a clear distinction for national responsibility? Are there any recent actions by political officials that may refute this?

4) Why are the courts necessary in discussing federalism?

5) Discuss the question of concurrent powers.

6) Discuss the advantages and disadvantages of federalism.

Video Resources

Federalism in Education Made Simple http://www.youtube.com/watch?v=Ebf1HLiZeyY

Federalism in the United States - Khan Academy https://www.khanacademy.org/humanities/us-government-and-civics/us-gov-foundations/us-gov-relationship-between-the-states-and-the-federal-government/v/federalism-in-the-united-states

Federalism - Bill of Rights Institute https://billofrightsinstitute.org/videos/federalism-homework-help

Federalism in the United States - C Span Classroom www.c-span.org/classroom/document/?7105

Chief Justice Roberts on the Role of the Supreme Court http://www.cspanclassroom.org/Topics/FE/Federalism.aspx

The Rise of Nationalism in 2017 https://www.youtube.com/watch?v=cH3I8nFyp6g

Website Resources

James Madison's Federalist no. 10 and the American Political System http://cstl-cla.semo.edu/renka/renka_papers/madison.htm

Timeline of Federalism in the United States http://www.education.ne.gov/SS/CSSAP%20Modules/CSSAP%20First%20Phase%20Modules/federalism/timeline.html

Understanding Federalism https://www.archives.gov/legislative/resources/education/federalism

Federalism - Political Science - Research Guides at University of British Columbia http://guides.library.ubc.ca/politicalscience/federalism

Cornell University Law School Legal Information Institute http://www.law.cornell.edu/wex/federalism

The definition of a nationalist https://www.cnn.com/2018/10/23/politics/national-ism-explainer-trnd/index.html

Nationalism Has Gotten a Bad Reputation. But It's What America Needs Right Now http://time.com/5431089/trump-white-nationalism-bible/

CHAPTER 5

THE DECLARATION OF INDEPENDENCE AND THE UNITED STATES CONSTITUTION

The United States political culture resulted from the influence of English political culture and Western philosophical tradition. Since the United Colonies of America were English provinces, England has historically played an essential role in shaping American economics and culture. The ultimate political enforcer in Colonial English America was the British monarchy, which based its legitimacy on kings' divine rights. The English King was God's legitimate representative on Earth.

Since the independence period, the United States has developed a new political culture that still serves as inspiration for the rest of the world. At the time, there was no model to follow for the United States Founders. The process of writing the constitution required creativity, originality, and clarity. The Founders chose Thomas Jefferson to write the United States Declaration of Independence. The ideas of John Locke served as an inspiration to write the political document. Both legally and politically speaking, the national constitution was the founding document for the United States democracy.

5.1 The roots of the United States political culture

As a former colony, the nation was a political subject of the ruling country—England. America was economically dependent on England, and the United Colonies had cultural ties to it as well. The economic relationship between the mother country and its colonies was called *mercantilism*. England provided protection and settlement costs to the colonists. The colonies sent prime resources and cuts of the profits from their trade back to the mother country. The center of power denied colonists access to the lucrative markets in which England competed.

The ultimate political enforcer in Colonial English America was the British monarchy. England followed the *divine right of kings*, which had its roots in a political culture that understood the power to be vested in the king because he was God's legitimate representative on Earth. This situation put a significant burden on the colonists to produce a counternarrative to justify political independence that did not make them all sinners. As the American colonists began to consider themselves a separate cultural and political entity, the idea of struggling for independence started to look like a desirable and viable option for some American-born Englishmen.

More than anything, the Americans developed a new way of looking at the world during the independence days. The social contract theory was essential to the development of the United States as an independent country. This theory principally emerged and took shape from the writings of the British philosophers Thomas Hobbes and John Locke. In a *social contract*, power is to be held by all citizens, each of whom gives up some of their rights to the government in exchange for the right to use safely and securely the power citizens retained.

The recently-formed government based its legitimacy on the consent of those governed. If the government did not adequately protect and guarantee their remaining rights, subjects had the right to rebel and establish a new government. A government that does not secure the remaining rights of citizens lacks legitimacy.

British political philosopher Thomas Hobbes believed that free men had the right to subject themselves to a ruler who would protect them. The government was an all-powerful entity, and its subjects had no right to push back against its power. On the other hand, John Locke believed that the social contract was conditional upon rights' protection. Governed subjects could revoke the social contract if the government failed to safeguard their rights.

Of all the political thinkers who influenced American beliefs about government, the most relevant was assuredly John Locke, who wrote nearby in time that the founders of the United States were contemplating independence. The ideas of Locke were hugely popular in the United Colonies of America. When discussing the influences of the political philosophy of John Locke, one should start by analyzing and focusing on the theory of natural law and rights. However, one should consider that the natural law concept existed long before Locke and was an integral principle of his philosophical theories. The natural law is a way to express universal moral truths that apply to all people. Universal moral law likely served as a preceding influence of the United States Constitution.

In many more than one pamphlet, the United States writers and thinkers cited Locke on natural rights and the social and governmental contract as well; they referred to Montesquieu and Delolme on the character of British freedom and the institutional prerequisites for its fulfillment; Voltaire on the evils and disasters of clerical oppression; Beccaria on the change of criminal law; Grotius, Pufendorf, Burlamaqui; and Vattel on the laws of nature and nations, and the standards of civil government. The pervasiveness of such citations is, on occasion, astonishing.[48]

The most significant early contrast was between natural and generally applicable laws and those conventional, which operated only in those places where specific particular customs existed. Simply put, this is a contrast between a universal moral right and a law created by society depending on culture and historical tradition. This distinction is known as one of the main differences between natural law and positive law.

Natural law also differs from divine law. Divine law is from the Christian tradition and customarily referred to those laws that God had directly revealed through visionary prophets and other enlightened writers. One can discover natural law by reason alone. Natural law applies to all people. On the contrary, one can get in touch with divine law only through God's special revelation, and it is only applicable to those whom the revelation God disclosed. For Locke, the biblical law did not apply to the modern human being[49].

5.2 The Declaration of Independence

The Founders chose Thomas Jefferson to write the *Declaration of Independence.* The ideas of John Locke served as an inspiration to write the document. Locke, born in 1632, is among the most influential political philosophers in history. In the *Two Treatises of Government*, Locke supported the claim that men are by nature free and equal against those that said that God had made all people naturally subject to a divinely-legitimate monarch. He argued that humans have natural rights, such as the right to life, liberty, and property.

The rights to life, liberty, and property are universal and natural. These rights have a foundation independent of the cultural and consuetudinary law built on any particular society's traditions. Locke stated that all men are naturally free and equal as part of the justification for understanding the legitimate political government that results from the social contract. This social contract is a condition in which people in the state of nature conditionally transfer some of their rights to the government, which subjects expect to provide stable and comfortable enjoyment of their lives, liberty, and property.

---

[48] Bailyn, Bernard. *The Ideological Origins of the American Revolution*, 1967. Massachusetts: Belknap Press.
[49] For an in-depth analysis of Locke's influence in United States independence, see Bailyn.

The Declaration of Independence is a political document about changing the rules about what makes power legitimate and who should reasonably hold it. The historical record represents the social contract between the government and the U.S. people. By relying on the social contract, the Declaration of Independence stated that Americans had *inalienable rights* that subjects could not give up to the government.

One should acknowledge that the American Constitution created the modern notion of citizens distinct from subjects. Even if related, both terms are not equivalent. The United States constitution writers laid blame on George III for breaking a political contract he barely understood. This incident was one of the main circumstances that legitimated the Americans' rebellion. It also attempted to convince the leaders of other colonial powers like Spain and France that they had nothing to worry about since supposedly they were not tyrants like George, King of Great Britain, and Ireland. Not every person in the new country was a citizen with full political rights. The task of creating a new government was not as easy as they had hoped, and it took more than one try to get things done right.

5.3 The United States Constitution

The constitution is the framework for the legal system of the United States. Depending upon the constitution's definition and since some Nation-States do not have a formal central constitution like the United States, one can argue that the United States Constitution is the oldest codified constitutional text still in use today. The United States Constitution is divided into Articles and Amendments. Congress Representatives have updated the American Constitution over the years, and courts continue to argue the text's applications. Both legally and politically speaking, the national constitution was the founding document for the United States democracy.

The Preamble of the United States Constitution—the document's famous first fifty-two words— introduces everything to follow in the Constitution's seven articles and twenty-seven amendments. It proclaims who is adopting this Constitution: "We the People of the United States." It describes why the country adopts the Constitution— the purposes behind the enactment of America's governing charter. Furthermore, it explains the principles adopted, as the United Constitution, a single authoritative written text, serves as the land's fundamental law.

While accurate, the word "preamble" does not quite capture the full importance of this provision. "Preamble" implies that these words are merely an opening rhetorical flourish or frill without meaningful effect. To be sure, "preamble" usefully conveys the idea that this provision does not itself confer or delineate powers of government or rights of citizens, outlined in the substantive articles and amendments that follow in the main body of the constitution's text.

5.4 The Articles of Confederation

Before the Civil War, the two leading and legislative power-affecting doctrines of American Constitutional Law were the Doctrine of Vested Rights and the Police Power Doctrine, both complementary to each other. The first one presumably flourished before the rise of the Jacksonian Democracy style in the United States. The Doctrine of the Vested Rights is the more fundamental doctrine[50].

The United States Constitution has a foundation in the Articles of Confederation. The founders' primary duty was to write a constitution or political rulebook that would determine who would have power, how that power would be limited, and how the new government functioned. The first constitution has been historically known as the *Articles of Confederation*. Because the states viewed themselves as sovereign, they decided to limit their new constitution to a "firm league of friendship" amongst states rather than a complete union entity. This change was about the establishment of a *United States Confederation.* Economic troubles, drought, and crop failures meant that there were heavy demands for relief from state governments.

The Articles of Confederation provided new restrictions on the government's power. The national government was not allowed to take some measures under the Articles of Confederation, such as draft soldiers' power. Drafting soldiers allowed for a robust military force; whoever, not allowing a draft made it challenging to coordinate a response to a threat from a foreign power. The Articles of Confederation stopped citizens' taxation, making the Federal government dependent on the states for funds. The Articles could not regulate interstate commerce; consequently, it left the states to create their own markets, economic rules, and more. Furthermore, the Articles forbid establishing a central monetary system and having different currencies in each state.

The last draft of the Articles of Confederation, which framed the new country's government's basis, was acknowledged by Congress in November 1777 and submitted to the states for endorsement. It would not become the tradition that must be adhered to until every one of the thirteen states had endorsed it. Within two years, all except for Maryland had done so. Maryland contended that all domains west of the Appalachians, to which a few states had laid case, should instead be held by the public government as open land to help every state. When the remainder of these states, Virginia, surrendered its property claims in mid-1781, Maryland affirmed the Confederation Articles. Half a month later, the British capitulated. Americans aspired their new government to be a republic, wherein people, not a monarch or ruler, held power and chose agents to oversee as per law and order.

---

[50] Corwin, Edward. "The Basic Doctrine of American Constitutional Law." *Michigan Law Review,* vol. 12, no. 4, 1914, pp. 247–276. JSTOR, www.jstor.org/stable/1276027.

Many feared that a country as large as the United States would not be managed successfully as a republic. Those voices also stressed that even an administration of delegates elected by the people might become too powerful and overbearing. Subsequently, public administrators created a confederation as an entity in which independent, self-governing states form a union to act together in defense areas. Unfortunate of supplanting one abusive public government with another. Nonetheless, the Articles of Confederation's composers made collusion of sovereign states held together by a feeble focal government.[51]

The result of the problems with the Articles led to economic problems. When economic chaos arose, so did Shay's Rebellion. Shay's Rebellion was a march of angry farmers demanding debt relief in western Massachusetts. This rebellion drove some of the founders to meet in Annapolis in 1786 to discuss fixing the dysfunctional Articles. Later, some at the gathering in Annapolis decided the Articles were too broken to fix, and thus they decided to create a whole new Constitution instead.

5.5 The Constitutional Convention

The drafting of a new national constitution began with the Constitutional Convention of 1787. The most significant fracture came between two groups, the first known as the Federalists and the second as the Anti-Federalists. The Federalists were those who wanted a more robust national government. The prospect of a stronger government less threatened the Federalists because they mainly were representatives of large states who felt they could control national government power. Over time, they were known as the Federalists because they preferred to get rid of the Articles' confederal system, where the states ultimately held power and moved to a federal system, where power would be shared between states and national government.

There were multiple plans put forth at the Constitutional Convention as proposals for the new government. One plan put forward was a bicameral legislature by Virginia. The *Virginia Plan* was a comparatively strong but limited government whose signature institution would be a *bicameral legislature* (meaning it would have two chambers). The representation in both chambers would be based on population and taxes paid. On the other hand, the Anti-Federalists were against a robust national government on principle and out of fear. They would have preferred to tweak the Articles to make them more valuable and practical. Mostly, representatives of smaller states feared a more robust government would roll over them, and the big states would always get their way. The *New Jersey Plan* wanted a slightly upgraded

---

[51] Corwin, 33-44.

Articles of Confederation—a single chamber of the legislature where every state cast one vote, with a weak executive and a nonexistent court system, but some additional powers for the national government.

The solution to this political crisis was the agreements on compromises. The **Great Compromise** was "great" because it effectively worked to bring the two sides together. However, it was more remarkable for the Federalists than the Anti-Federalists since the outcome exceeded its initial expectations. The Federalists truly benefited from the negotiation results. The Compromise the two groups agreed on called for a bicameral legislature that split the difference between the two political sides. Parliamentary representation was based on the state's population in the House of Representatives. Every state received two members, regardless of population, in the Senate.

The result of the Great Compromise was the *Three-Fifths Compromise* indicates that, when determining representation, the population count would be made "by adding to the whole Number of Free persons … three-fifths of all other persons." Both the Great Compromise and the Three-Fifths Compromise reduced the national government's popular control by countering it with state control and significantly empowering smaller, rural states.

The concerns of southern states to boost their power vis-a-vis the north had another lasting effect on the United States Constitution: we do not elect the United States president by direct popular vote. Instead, we have the Electoral College. In this settlement, the states had more power to choose the president. The number of electors a state gets in the Electoral College (that is, the number of votes that a state can cast for president) is determined by the total number of representatives that that state has in both houses. The South fought a direct popular presidential election because actual population totals would have determined the presidency in some cases.

5.6 Basic Constitutional Principles

The American founders had created a document that was path-breaking in its innovative approach to human governance. Several nations have throughout the years used the United States Constitution as an inspiration, but at the time, there was no model for the American founders to follow. The writers of the national constitution were original and have inspired other states throughout history. *James Madison* was the genius behind the United States Constitution. His fundamental idea was to design a system that takes human nature *as it is* (self-interested, greedy, and ambitious), not as you want it to be. James Madison wanted to create an internal mechanism based on the idea that human nature will produce fair laws and public policy because of it, not despite it.

Basic principles of the United States provided by the national constitution are to have separation of powers[52], checks and balances, and federalism. The United States Constitution gives the three branches of government their own powers, shared powers, and checked powers. In some countries, these functions are not separated (i.e., a *parliamentary system*).

Separation of powers is the government's division vertically into three branches: legislative, executive, and judicial. This power division gives each layer and branch independent status with some of its constitutional power.

The founders thought a presidential system would better protect against abuses of power. In the United States, we have a *presidential system*: the executive and the other two branches are constitutionally distinct. The three are given their own powers according to the United States Constitution. *Checks and balances* give each layer and branch just enough power over the others in its system that their jealousy will guard against the others' over-reach. Simply put, the *legislative branch* is the lawmaking component, the *executive branch* is the law-enforcing component, and the *judicial branch* is the law-interpreting component. *Federalism* divides the government horizontally into layers: national and state.

5.7 Constitutional Powers

The United States Constitution provides powers to the Federal government and the states. The constitutional provisions fostered federalism's development. Article I Section 8 (*enumerated powers*) spells out exactly what Congress (and hence the national government) is allowed to do, including coining money and managing interstate commerce.

The *necessary and proper clause* coming at the end of the enumerated powers indicates Congress can do anything "necessary and proper" to carry out its duties suitably. The United States constitution's necessary and proper clause defines the Congress's authority to exercise the necessary and proper powers it needs to carry out its designated functions. This power or clause of the United States Constitution also goes by a similar name, *the elastic clause,* because it stretches the national government's authority to include or imply anything written in the United States Constitution's text. In practice, this clause generally strengthens the national government at the expense of state power.

The *Tenth Amendment to the United States Constitution* indicates that any powers not explicitly given to the national government are reserved to the states. It ultimately depends on what the Court says, and the Court changes its mind repeatedly. Who gets

---

[52] On the separation of powers in the United States constitution, see Corwin.

the advantage? It is pretty much a tie; the balance of national state power again depends on judicial interpretation.

In Article VI of the Constitution, the *supremacy clause* states that the constitutional text itself and national laws made under it are the land's law. This clause found in the Constitution defines the national government's authority. The supremacy clause says that the national government's authority prevails over state or local government claims provided that power was given to the federal government. This idea found in the United States Constitution provides the federal government's implied powers, and when laws between States and Federal governments clash, the Federal Government's laws are supreme and take priority over the state's laws. Who gets the advantage? If national law clashes with state law, national law almost always wins if the federal government chooses to impose its will.

The founders were well aware of the tension between the states themselves as a threat to national stability. The United States Constitution's framers developed a formal way to balance federal vs. state rights. The *Constitution's full faith and credit clause* (Article IV, Section 1) says that the states have to respect the other states' legal proceedings and public acts. An example of the full faith and credit clause includes one's driver's license, which must be accepted across state lines as a valid form of identification. The *privileges and immunities clause* (Article IV, Section 2) indicates a state cannot deny a citizen of another state the rights its citizens enjoy.

The balance has changed over time, but the national government has often gained power at the states' expense. Battles over federalism are typically fought in the states, except for the Civil War. The history of federalism proves that national and state governments have periodically checked each other over time.

Chapter 5: Declaration of Independence and Constitution

1) The document America considers its "owners' manual" is

   a. the Declaration of Independence.

   b. the Articles of Confederation.

   c. the Constitution.

   d. the Magna Carta.

2) The document that takes the ideas of the Declaration of Independence and turns them into laws and institutions is

   a. the Articles of Confederation.

   b. the Magna Carta.

   c. the Mayflower Compact.

   d. the Constitution.

3) There are _____ articles in the United States Constitution and _____ amendments in the Bill of Rights.

   a. 7, 10

   b. 7, 27

   c. 10, 17

   d. 7, 26

4) Article 7 requires _____ states to ratify the Constitution of 1787.

   a. all

   b. thirteen

   c. six

   d. nine

5) All of the following are features that propelled the framers toward the Constitutional Convention of 1787, except

   a. representation.

   b. violent borders.

   c. social mobility.

   d. abolitionism.

6) In England, in the eighteenth century, the notion that members of Parliament should be guided by their sense of "the general good" regardless of the district they represented was known as

a. constituency service.

b. trustee representation.

c. delegate representation.

d. "better men" representation.

7) One Act of Parliament the colonists found particularly repugnant required them to house British troops in barns and warehouses; it was called the

a. Stamp Act.

b. Redcoat Accommodation Act.

c. Quartering Act.

d. English Occupation Act.

8) The Boston Massacre was precipitated by the

a. Impoundment Act.

b. Tea Party.

c. Townshend Act.

d. Amistad.

9) Due to continued requirements for the colonists to house, or "quarter," British soldiers at colonists' expense wrote into the Bill of Rights

a. the Fifth Amendment.

b. the Fourth Amendment.

c. the Third Amendment.

d. the Second Amendment.

10) The key statement of American political philosophy is

a. the Constitution.

b. the Emancipation Proclamation.

c. the Mayflower Compact.

d. the Declaration of Independence.

11) The colonists favored the representation model where the legislature members responded to constituents' desires, known as

    a. the trustee model.

    b. the parliamentary model.

    c. the delegate model.

    d. the politico model.

12) The Declaration of Independence was adopted on

    a. July 4, 1774.

    b. July 4, 1775.

    c. July 4, 1776.

    d. July 4, 1787.

13) The Declaration of Independence details all of the following American ideals except

    a. life, liberty, and the pursuit of happiness.

    b. capitalism and the protection of private property.

    c. all men are created equal.

    d. people form governments to protect rights that they are "endowed" with and cannot be taken away.

14) The political philosopher that had an enormous impact on revolutionary America and the framers' thinking was

    a. Tocqueville.

    b. Robespierre.

    c. Hobbes.

    d. Locke.

15) The second half of the Declaration of Independence lists twenty-seven

    a. God-given rights.

    b. principles of government.

    c. grievances against King George III.

    d. principles of democracy.

16) Identify the three complaints against the English Crown that dominate the Declaration of Independence.

    a. representation, occupying army, loss of an independent court

b. representation, taxes, loss of an independent court

c. taxation without representation, the tax on tea, and British impressments of American sailors

d. taxation without representation, the quartering of soldiers, and the Stamp Act

17) The Declaration of Independence states that liberty is a right that is

a. quite important.

b. fundamental to happiness.

c. unalienable.

d. subject to the whims of governments—it can be taken away.

18) In 1776, for the first time in world history, the American colonists claimed that government

a. must be limited.

b. must protect private property.

c. derives its power from the consent of the governed.

d. must be subject to frequent elections.

19) The Founding Father who stated: "that laws and institutions must go hand in hand with the progress of the human mind" was

a. George Washington.

b. James Madison.

c. Thomas Jefferson.

d. John Adams.

20) The Articles of Confederation were approved by the First Continental Congress in

a. 1620.

b. 1776.

c. 1777.

d. 1787.

21) Under the Articles of Confederation, ___ votes were required on important matters.

a. thirteen

b. seven

c. four

d. nine

22) Among the severe obstacles to the new government under the Articles of Confederation,

a. Congress could not raise taxes and had no money of its own.

b. Virginia dominated all policy discussions.

c. The southern states were in open rebellion.

d. North Carolina had brokered treaties with foreign powers.

23) The provision that all thirteen states must approve any changes to the Articles of Confederation

a. facilitated the amendment process.

b. made it difficult to conduct foreign affairs.

c. gave the states too little power.

d. made it virtually impossible to amend the Articles.

24) A major lesson learned from our experience under the Articles of Confederation

a. was that a strong confederation of states was impossible.

b. was that a weak central government left the nation vulnerable.

c. was the need for a Supreme Court.

d. was the alliance between Rhode Island and South Carolina.

25) The constitutional deliberations were

a. open to the public

b. very quick

c. secret

d. attended by delegates from only eight states

26) The Articles showed the founding fathers that a weak government could

a. support rights

b. fail to protect rights

c. create new rights

d. abuse power

27) The Founders adopted a federal system

a. because they hoped King George III would approve.

b. because they were inspired by John Locke, who advocated such a division of powers.

c. because the division of sovereignty between a strong central government and regional governments is a basic principle of all democratic governments.

d. as a compromise between those who wanted a strong central government and those who wanted to retain strong state governments.

28) Which of the following is not a difference between the Virginia Plan and the New Jersey Plan?

a. The Virginia Plan created stronger state governments.

b. The New Jersey Plan created a single legislature, whereas the Virginia Plan called for a bicameral legislature.

c. The Virginia Plan strengthened the national government, whereas the New Jersey Plan weakened the national government.

d. The New Jersey Plan had multiple chief executives, whereas the Virginia Plan created a one-person executive.

29) The Great, or Connecticut, Compromise

a. provided strong powers to state governments.

b. established a legislature with equal state representation in the Senate and proportional representation in the House of Representatives.

c. limited the importation of slaves until 1808.

d. created a confederacy of state governments.

30) Some delegates at the Constitutional Convention were concerned that an executive would be

a. too powerful.

b. too weak.

c. too subject to "the whims of the people."

d. someone who was not an American.

31) The delegates did not want people electing the president because they felt people

a. would be swayed by political parties

b. would not vote

c. had enough information or wisdom

d. did not want to elect the president

32) Why did the framers not give the popular-vote winner the presidency?

   a. They did not trust the judgment of voters.

   b. Women could not vote.

   c. The country had a bad history of electing corrupt politicians.

   d. The Electoral College was more efficient.

33) The number of electors in a state is based on

   a. the number of people in the state.

   b. the number of voters in the state.

   c. the number of senators plus the number of members of the House of Representatives.

   d. the number of members in the state legislature.

34) For each power described in the Constitution for a branch of government,

   a. there is an appropriation process independent of the other branches.

   b. there is "countervailing" power.

   c. there is a federal agency.

   d. there is a way for the other branches to destroy that branch.

35) The president is the commander in chief, but Congress has the power to declare war. This situation is an example of

   a. the imperial presidency.

   b. the imperial Congress.

   c. checks and balances.

   d. judicial neutrality.

36) How did the Founders treat slavery in the Constitution?

   a. It was not important.

   b. It was very divisive, so they had to tackle it head-on.

   c. They were unified in their desire to eliminate it.

   d. It was very divisive, so they did not mention it directly.

37) The practice of counting slaves as fractional "persons" for representation in the House of Representatives is known as

   a. The "Not-Quite" Compromise.

   b. The Three-Fifths Compromise.

c. The Two-Thirds Compromise.

d. The Three-Quarters Compromise.

38) During the Constitutional Convention, the state with the highest percentage of slaves out of the total population, at 43 percent, was

a. Virginia.

b. Massachusetts.

c. Texas.

d. South Carolina.

39) If the institution of slavery had not been protected in the Constitution,

a. the southern states would have walked out.

b. Massachusetts would have immediately abolished slavery.

c. North Carolina would have seceded from the Union.

d. Texas would have never been admitted to the Union.

40) The first three words of the Constitution are

a. "Fourscore and seven . . . "

b. "In order to . . . "

c. "We the People . . . "

d. "My fellow Americans . . . "

41) In 1787, a member of the House of Representatives had around 30,000 constituents. Today that number is approximately

a. 50,000.

b. 150,000.

c. 350,000.

d. 700,000.

42) A large-scale program like Social Security is constitutionally legitimate because

a. Congress can write any law it deems "necessary and proper."

b. there is a need to protect older people.

c. older people vote.

d. the executive branch has extensive powers to make laws under Article 2.

43) Far and away, the most extended and most detailed section of the Constitution is
   a. the First Amendment.
   b. Article 1.
   c. Article 2.
   d. Article 3.

44) Constitutionally, members of the US House of Representatives must be____ years of age.
   a. 18
   b. 25
   c. 30
   d. 35

45) Constitutionally, members of the US Senate must be____ years of age.
   a. 18
   b. 25
   c. 30
   d. 35

46) All of the following are powers granted to Congress under article 1, section 8, of the Constitution except
   a. the power to declare war.
   b. the power to command the armed forces.
   c. the power to collect taxes.
   d. the power to coin money.

47) The necessary and proper clause
   a. allows Congress to regulate commerce.
   b. allows Congress to control the money supply.
   c. gives Congress a great deal of creative leeway.
   d. it has defined boundaries.

48) According to article 1, section 9 of the Constitution, habeas corpus may not be suspended unless
   a. Americans gather to protest for the overthrow of the government.
   b. an election takes place.

c. a majority of Congress votes to suspend.

d. in cases of rebellion or invasion, public safety requires it.

49) Originally, each state decided how it choose its electors for the Electoral College, but now

a. every state has the minority party select them.

b. Twenty-seven states have the people make a choice.

c. Seventeen states have the people make a choice.

d. all states have the people make a choice.

50) Treaties made by presidents are constitutionally valid if

a. two-thirds of the Senate approves.

b. two-thirds of the House of Representatives approve.

c. three-quarters of the Senate approve.

d. three-quarters of the House of Representatives approve.

51) The case in which Chief Justice John Marshall established judicial review, giving the Supreme Court the power to overturn Congress's act, was

a. Wickard v. Filburn.

b. Brown v. Topeka Board of Education.

c. Marbury v. Madison.

d. Barron v. Baltimore.

Discussion Questions

1) What weaknesses were inherent in the Articles of Confederation?

2) How did the ideas that inspired the colonists to rebel shape the Constitution and the Bill of Rights?

3) What were the arguments put forth by the Federalists and the Anti-federalists? Which arguments do you support?

4) How do Americans change the Constitution? Is the Constitution a living document?

Discuss the Articles of Confederation, focusing on how the government functioned with a centralized administration. Be sure to highlight how power was distributed then and what it means for current views of states' rights. From our modern viewpoint, why does it seem inevitable that the Articles did not survive? What did the Articles teach us about government?

5) Does democracy work? One way to frame the rest of the course, especially from this text's viewpoint, is to ask the "big" questions and explore them thematically throughout the course using the Constitution as the fulcrum.

Video Resources

The Declaration of Independence - Khan Academy www.khanacademy.org/humanities/us-history/road-to-revolution/the-american-revolution/v/the-declaration-of-independence

The Preamble to the Constitution - Khan Academy www.khanacademy.org/humanities/us-government-and-civics/us-gov-foundations/us-gov-ideals-of-democracy/v/preamble

Key Constitutional Concepts - Annenberg Classroom www.annenbergclassroom.org/resource/key-constitutional-concepts/

The Declaration of Independence and the Birth of America https://jackmillercenter.org/declaration-independence-birth-america/

Mr. Smith Goes to Washington, 1939

John Adams (HBO Films) 2010

A More Perfect Union: America Becomes a Nation, 1989

The Crossing, 2000

Amistad, 1997

Website Resources

The Supreme Court and Supreme Court Cases http://oyez.com/

Annotation of the Bill of Rights https://www.scribd.com/document/238698937/the-bill-of-rights-annotated

History of the Constitution of the United States http://www.archives.gov/exhibits/charters/constitution_history.html

A Collection of Websites on the Constitution and Early American History http://www.loc.gov/rr/program/bib/ourdocs/Constitution.html

United States House of Representatives http://www.house.gov/

United States Senate http://www.senate.gov/

The White House http://www.whitehouse.gov/

The Library of Congress http://www.loc.gov/index.html

CHAPTER 6

CIVIL LIBERTIES

6.1 Introduction to Civil Liberties

What is the difference between civil rights and civil liberties? It is the word *civil*—having to do with the non-political life of citizens—that gives the phrases *civil rights* and *civil liberties* specific and different meanings. In democracies and other non-authoritarian societies where, at least some political power is held by citizens, both civil liberties and civil rights are essential to operational societies. Civil liberties are individual rights that come from the *limitation of* government power. Civil rights *empower the government* to give us group rights. You could say civil liberties are about equal protection *from* the law and civil rights are about the equal protection *of* the laws.

So, what do civil liberties and civil rights actually mean in order to differentiate from one another? **Civil liberties** are the individual freedoms that limit government. These rights are guaranteed by the Bill of Rights and the text of the Constitution itself. Some others, like the right to privacy, come from Supreme Court decisions that have interpreted the Constitution. **Civil rights** are the freedom of groups to fully participate in the public life of a nation. These groups are defined by some particular characteristic—like race, gender, or sexual orientation—that is beyond their members' control. Rather than limiting government, the protection of civil rights often *empowers the government* to act.

6.2 Rights Equal Power

Giving citizenry rights empowers the people. Rights confer power on people and limitations on government. When a person has the ability to claim a right, it makes one a citizen, not a subject. The ability to deny rights gives citizens power over each other.

The ability to use government to fight back against those who would deny their fellow citizens rights is also a form of power.

6.3 Where do our rights come from?

If we believe we have rights because the government, the Constitution, the Bill of Rights or any other amendments grant them to us, then those rights can also be taken away. These rights differ from **natural rights**, which are the inalienable rights conferred by "Nature and Nature's God" that no government can take away.

The rights of American citizens provided by the Constitution and the Bill of Rights are limited in two main ways. First, they become limited when they clash with other people's rights. Second, is when they conflict with collective societal values. Solving rights conflicts often involve compromise. These conflicts are resolved by different aspects of government such as Congress, the President and the bureaucracy, the courts, and the people.

6.4 The Bill of Rights

The Bill of Rights established the fundamental constitutional rights afforded to every American. These important rights are included in the Bill of Rights. These rights are:

- Amendment 1: Establishment clause, free exercise of religion, free speech, free press, right to assemble.
- Amendment 2: Right to bear arms necessary for a well-regulated militia.
- Amendment 3: You can't be forced to house soldiers during peace.
- Amendment 4: No unreasonable searches and seizures.
- Amendment 5: Grand jury indictment for capital crimes; no double jeopardy, self-incrimination, or deprivation of property without due process of law.
- Amendment 6: Right to a speedy trial and counsel.
- Amendment 7: Jury trials for civil cases where the value in controversy is over $20.
- Amendment 8: No cruel or unusual punishment or excessive bail.
- Amendment 9: The rights listed in the Constitution does not limit the possession of other rights.
- Amendment 10: All rights not given to the national government are reserved to the states.

The founders struggled with having a Bill of Rights. Alexander Hamilton argued in *Federalist* #84 that a Bill of Rights might be redundant, because the founders' intent was to create a government that was already powerless to do the things the Bill of Rights ruled out. All of the founders feared a powerful government; they just differed on ways to limit it. The Federalists thought they had created internal mechanisms—separation of powers, checks and balances—that would keep the government from over-reaching. The Anti-Federalists wanted to spell out restrictions on the government—limiting powers the Federalists didn't think the Constitution conferred.

The Bill of Rights limited the national government's power. On its face, the Bill of Rights applies to the national government and specifically to Congress. But most Americans don't interact with the federal government or commit federal crimes. States may have their own Bill of Rights within their own state constitutions, but states are not required to guarantee these rights and there are no regulations about what their state constitutions should cover.

The power of the states is checked or held accountable by the federal government. Americans are not helpless if a state denies them a basic right. **The Fourteenth Amendment** was originally drafted and intended to stop southern states from denying former slaves their citizenship rights after the Civil War. Using a process called **incorporation**, the Court was able to fold the national right into required state protections via the Fourteenth Amendment. Language in the Fourteenth Amendment can be interpreted to mean that no state can deny a citizen any of the rights the federal government guarantees. With incorporation, the Supreme Court expanded the national power at the expense of the state, changing the balance of federal power.

6.5 Civil Liberties—Understanding the First Amendment

The basic civil liberties of Americans include all the rights the founders felt were necessary to keep the states in check. The most important of those rights they packed into the First Amendment, because they wanted to indicate their primary importance. The reason that this amendment covers so many rights is that, for the founders, these were all fundamental to a fully functioning democracy.

The First Amendment prohibits Congress from establishing a religion or interfering with the exercise of religion, abridging the freedom of speech or the press, or interfering with the right of the people to assemble. These prohibitions have been made applicable to the states through the Fourteenth Amendment. The freedoms, however, are not absolute and encompass different boundaries that have been established by judicial interpretation.

6.6 Freedom of Religion.

Freedom of religion was important to the founders. The founders' main task was to write a constitution, or rulebook, that would determine how the new government was to function, who would have power, and how that power would be limited. The Articles of Confederation gave the foundational importance to the writing of the Bill of Rights because religious freedom was at the forefront of the founders' minds. Many of the original colonists had fled England to avoid an established church in the first place.

The First Amendment has two clauses that establish freedom of religion. The First Amendment provides "Congress shall make no law respecting an establishment of religion or prohibiting the free exercise thereof".

Establishment Clause

First, the **Establishment Clause** was designed to limit Congress and ensure that Congress shall make no law respecting an establishment of religion. The role of the state is to accommodate all religions. Unfortunately, this first amendment guarantee can be divisive. **Accommodationists** are people who want to support "all" religions equally. This is opposed to **separationists**: people who want a separation between church and state. Americans and, indeed, members of the Supreme Court, are divided on whether we need to keep church and state entirely separate, or whether it is okay to allow some state recognition and support for religion as long as it accommodates all religions. What is a constitutional issue—how far church and state can be intermingled—has become a cultural clash that it is almost impossible to solve to everyone's satisfaction.

The first step is to determine if the law has a religious preference. When determining if a law or government program violates the Establishment Clause and includes a preference for some religious sects over others, the law or program will be subject to a compelling interest analysis and ask if it is **narrowly tailored** to promote a **compelling interest**. In *Board of Education v. Grumet*, the Supreme Court struck down a state law that created a public school district whose boundaries were intentionally set to match the boundaries of a particular Jewish neighborhood. Since the government had no other interest rather than one that was furthered by "religious favoritism", the Court held it failed to exercise governmental authority in a religiously neutral way.[53] Therefore, if there is a preference and the law is not crafted in a religiously neutral way, it will receive the compelling interest test.

---

[53] *Board of Education v. Grumet*, 512 v. 687 (1994).

Secondly, if there is no religious preference, and the compelling interest test is not used, then the law is subject to the Lemon Test. The **Lemon Test** was established in *Lemon v. Kurtzman* to provide a constitutional understanding on how much the government can establish a religion. The law or program will be valid under the Establishment Clause if it:

1. Has a **secular** purpose
2. Has a **primary effect** that neither **advances** nor **inhibits** religion; and
3. Does not produce excessive government **entanglement** with religion.[54]

"Secular", as opposed to sacred, means not having a religious, spiritual or temporal basis. If the government maintains a holiday-Christmas Times display that does not appear to endorse one religion and includes holiday decorations, such as a Christmas tree or a Santa Claus figure, the court will hold that the display has a **secular purpose** based on the history of government recognition of holidays.[55]

If the law **advances** or **inhibits** a particular religion or specific religious group, then that law will be invalid. But if a law favors or burdens a larger segment of society that happens to include religious groups, it will generally be upheld. For example, the IRS may provide deductions and other financial benefits to churches and other religious donations because the **primary effect** of the benefit does not only include religious organizations- but it also applies to all charitable organizations that happen to include religious groups.[56]

It is hard for the Court to decide what "excessive entanglement" means. **Excessive entanglement** can mean too much government involvement. There are times when government action can cross paths with private religions. It becomes excessive when government action crosses into religious action that they can run afoul of other people's actions or the state's obligation to exercise its police power to protect the health, well-being, and security of all citizens. For example, if a public school allows members of the public and private organizations to use school property when classes are not in session and a religious organization utilizes the space and the meetings are not run by school personnel, there is no excessive government entanglement.[57] The government was not a significant actor.

---

[54] *Lemon v. Kurtzman*, 403 U.S. 602 (1971).
[55] *County of Allegheny v. ACLU*, 492 U.S. 573 (1989).
[56] *Hernandez v. Commissioner of Internal Revenue*, 490 U.S. 680 (1989).
[57] *Good News Club v. Milford Central School*, 533 U.S. (2001).

Free Exercise Clause

The freedom from an establishment of a religion afforded the free exercise of religion for the founders. Because the government cannot establish one or more religions
means people have the freedom to practice any religion. The **Free Exercise Clause**
states that Congress shall make no law… prohibiting the free exercise thereof.[58] The
trouble with those words spelling out religious freedom protection is that they contain
an inherent contradiction. Any effort to establish one of the founders' denominations
as the official state religion would have doomed the new country from the start. When
political differences are reinforced with religious differences, every conflict is infused
with profound meaning and compromise is impossible. When a government can put
the power of an Almighty behind its laws, it is very hard to resist it if it over-reaches.

The Free Exercise Clause prohibits the government from punishing, denying benefits to or imposing burdens on someone on the basis of the person's religious beliefs.
For many years the Supreme Court had suggested that the government had to show
it had a compelling reason to infringe on religious practice. But in 1990 it reversed
course and put the burden of proof back on religious groups to show that the state
regulation has violated the groups' rights. However, the test for such impermissible
government action remains unclear as the Court has never found an interest that was
so compelling that it would justify punishing or regulating a religious belief.

The Court has directed that the Free Exercise Clause prohibits the government
from punishing conduct merely because it is religious or displays religious belief.[59] A
law that is designed to suppress actions only because the actions are religiously motivated is not a neutral law and would be invalid. A city law that prohibits a precise type
of animal slaughtering for a particular religion violates the Free Exercise clause because
the law was not neutral and did not prohibit all animal slaughtering.[60]

But the states can prohibit or regulate conduct in general, and this is true even if the
prohibition or regulation happens to interfere with a person's religious practices. The Free
Exercise Clause does not require exemptions from criminal laws or other regulations. A
law that regulates conduct of all persons can be applied to prohibit the conduct of a person
despite the fact that his or her religious beliefs prevent him or her from complying with the
law. For example, the prohibition against the use of peyote was permissible if it applied generally to all persons, even if individuals require use of peyote during religious ceremonies.[61]

But what is a religious belief?

---

[58] U.S. Const. Amend I.
[59] *Employment Division v. Smith.*
[60] *Church of the Lukumi v. Babalu Aye, Inc. v. Hialeah*, 508 U.S. 520 (1993).
[61] *Employment Division v. Smith.*

The Supreme Court has not defined or laid out elements for what constitutes a religious belief. However, it has made clear that religious beliefs do not require recognition of a supreme being[62] and need not arise from a traditional, or even an organized, religion.[63]

6.7 Why freedom of expression is a BIG deal

As important to the founders in limiting government as freedom from an established religion was **freedom of expression**. Freedom of expression includes speech, press, and **freedom of assembly**, the right to join together with other persons for expressive or political activity. While freedom of speech and press are mentioned in the First Amendment, freedom of association is not mentioned but is still protected by the First Amendment. The freedom of speech protects the free flow of ideas, a most important function in a democratic society. A regulation or law that tries to forbid speech of specific ideas (**content regulation**) is more likely to violate the free speech doctrine. It is usually unconstitutional for the government to prohibit speech based on its content. In ***Brandenburg v. Ohio***, the Court held that the government could not prohibit political speech, or speech with political content, unless it is linked to immediate lawless behavior[64]. However, **conduct regulation**, which is content-neutral and regulates how the speech is conducted, is more likely permitted (*i.e.,* law prohibiting billboards for purposes of traffic safety).

Speech and communication, and its conduct from which it is expressed, can take many forms and, if that conduct is intended to express an idea, can still be protected under the First Amendment much like content speech. In *Masterpiece Cakeshop v. Colorado Civil Rights Commission*, a cake shop owner refused to sell a wedding cake to a same sex couple, claiming, in part, requiring him to create the cake would violate his First Amendment right to free speech by compelling him to exercise his artistic talents to express a message with which he disagreed. The Court did not rule on the speech claim but agreed with the Court of Appeals holding that preparing a wedding cake is not a form of protected speech or would force the cake shop owner to adhere to and express an ideological point of view. In their concurring opinion, Justices Kagen and Breyer, note and insinuate that cake making is certainly a conduct for which speech is expressed, which is generally permitted. However, the Justices noted that "the Court has recognized a wide array of conduct that can qualify as expressive,

---

[62] *Torcaso v. Watkins*, 367 U.S. 488 (1961).
[63] *Frazee v. Illinois Department of Employment Security*, 489 U.S. 829 (1989).
[64] *Brandenburg v. Ohio*, 395 U.S. 444 (1969)

including nude dancing, wearing a military uniform and conducting a silent sit-in" and cake making also be a type of protected speech conduct if it intends to express an idea. Here the Justices suggest that conduct, like making a cake, can be protected speech if the cake maker uses his artistic talent of cake making as an expression of value, or opinion. [65]

Freedom of expression is important predominantly for the right to criticize the government. Denying free speech sets a dangerous precedent—if we can stop our opponents from speaking out today, they might stop us from speaking out tomorrow. So, if free speech is so important, why do we ever limit it?

The Supreme Court has at various times ruled that speech (and symbolic speech) can be limited. As indicated above, very few restrictions on the content of speech are tolerated. The Court allows them only to prevent grave injury. The following is a list of the reasons for which the Court has allowed content-based restrictions on speech:

- For purposes of national security during war (**sedition**)
- Because it is **obscene**
- Speech that is inherently likely to incite immediate physical retaliation (**fighting words**)
- Because it maliciously damages a reputation (**libel** when printed; **slander** when spoken)

To determine what is unprotected speech, the Court has come up with a series of tests, many of which have introduced even more ambiguity. The **clear and present danger test** was meant to distinguish speech that was immediately harmful from that posed only a remote threat.[66] The **imminent lawless action test** protected speech unless it was directed to producing or inciting imminent lawless action and is likely to produce or incite such action.[67] The *Miller* test defines standards for obscenity and asks whether the work lacks "serious literary, artistic, political, or scientific value".[68] The **prior restraint test** prohibits censoring and refusing to allow the publication of something, even though it very well might fail one of its tests after publication. The Supreme Court has been fairly steady on its refusal to engage in prior restraint.[69] Only a national emergency could justify such censorship.

---

[65] *Masterpiece Cakeshop v. Colorado Civil Rights Commission*, 138 S. Ct. 1719 (2018).
[66] *Scheneck v. United States*, 249 U.S. 47 (1919).
[67] *Brandenberg v. Ohio*, 395 U.S. 444 (1969).
[68] *Miller v. California*, 413 U.S. 15 (1973).
[69] *Near v. Minnesota*, 283 U.S. 697 (1931)

6.8 Electronic communication makes it vastly more complicated.

In addition to the wide variety of types of speech discussed above, electronic communication can also be a type of speech. The question as to whether media companies can limit access to the internet is evolving. The role of **net neutrality** is the way the Internet works now on the principle that service providers cannot speed up or slow down access for customers or make decisions about the content they see or the apps they download. The Supreme Court is constantly, and likely indefinitely, interpreting the Free Speech Clause to keep up with new types of speech created through new technology.

6.9 Civil Liberties—Understanding Due Process Rights

What are due process rights? **Due process rights** are the rights that give Americans some protections against being railroaded into jail by the police and the courts, especially for political purposes. The founders devote half the Bill of Rights to this subject to protect the citizens from a police state. A chief fear of the founders was a government so strong that its leaders could use the police power and the judicial system for political purposes. These protections provide that the government shall not take a person's life, liberty, or property without due process of law. Due process contemplates fair procedures, which at least require at least an opportunity to present objections to the proposed action to a fair, neutral decision maker, like a judge. There are two separate clauses protecting due process: (1) The Due Process Clause in the Fifth Amendment (applies to the federal government) and (2) The Due Process Clause in the Fourteenth Amendment (applies to state and local governments).

6.10 What do the due process rights include?

Article I provides that Congress cannot suspend habeas corpus, pass a bill of attainder, and pass an ex post facto law. Congress cannot suspend a person's right to be brought before a judge. The writ of **habeas corpus** is the right from unlawful imprisonment and includes the right to be brought before a judge and informed of the charges and evidence against you. The due process rights of people cannot be violated by acts of Congress unduly targeting them by passing a bill of attainer. A **bill of attainder** is a law directed at an individual or group that accuses and convicts them without a trial. The due process of people is so important that Congress was precluded from making laws to incriminate people for actions previously committed. An **ex post facto law** is a law that makes a criminal act (not civil regulation, such as denial of a professional license) illegal that was innocent when done, or "after the fact", hereby not allowing an accused to make an informed decision about the legality of his or her actions before he or she acts.[70] The right to be brought before a judge, informed of the law and charges and receiving a trial, ensures a due or appropriate judicial process before a conviction.

Due process rights include civil liberties. The **exclusionary rule** prohibits evidence from being introduced at a criminal trial if it was obtained by violating your civil liberties protected under the Constitution. The main purpose of the exclusionary rule is to deter the government, usually the police, from violating a person's civil liberties and constitutional rights. If the government cannot use evidence obtained in violation of a person's rights, it will be less likely to infringe on the person's rights.

The right to self-protection in a police arrest is guaranteed under the Fifth Amendment which provides that no person "shall be compelled to be a witness against himself…".71 This has been interpreted to establish a guarantee against compelled incrimination. Miranda rights come from the case that established that you have the right to be told that you possess these rights and guarantees.72 Miranda rights are a set of warnings that must be given to an accused person that is in custody prior to any police interrogation. In order for the accused statement's to be later admissible in court, the accused must be clearly informed that: (1) he or she has the right to remain silent, (2) anything he or she says can be used against him in court, (3) he or she has the right to an attorney, and (4) if he or she cannot afford an attorney, one will be appointed.

While the above are some examples, additional civil rights and liberties include a right to be told why you are being arrested, a right to not be tried twice for the same crime, a right to an attorney and the right to resist questioning.

6.11 Civil Liberties—Understanding the Right to Privacy

What is the right to privacy? While one can argue that the founders created a limited government and never intended it to be powerful enough to infringe on the private lives of Americans, none of them thought it a serious enough threat to put it into the document itself. The right to privacy is a judicial creation of the Supreme Court in the 1965 case of *Griswold v. Connecticut*.[73] In this case the Court declared that the Constitution does guarantee a "zone of privacy" within a "penumbra" of existing fundamental constitutional guarantees and amendments. Since there was no actual

---

[70] U.S. Const. Art. I §9 prohibits the federal government and U.S. Const. Art. I §10 prohibits the states from passing ex post facto laws.

[71] U.S. Const. Amend. V.

[72] *Miranda v. Arizona*, 384 U.S. 436 (1966).

[73] *Griswold v. Connecticut*, 381 U.S. 479 (1965).

right to privacy mentioned in the Constitution or any of the amendments, the justices "found" such a right to be implied in the Bill of Rights. These specific rights for privacy emanated from:

- The First Amendment protection of one's beliefs and speech
- The Fourth Amendment protection against unreasonable searches and seizures
- The Fifth Amendment protection against self-incrimination
- The Ninth Amendment's promise that one's rights weren't limited to the ones enumerated in the document

The Supreme Court extended this right to privacy marriage, sexual relations, abortion, childrearing and LGTBQ rights in later decisions. The right to privacy has become controversial because, through constant interpretation of the Constitution, the Court creates new rights not explicit in the Constitution. The disagreement arises because the precedent set in *Griswold* was the basis for the landmark, and most controversial, decision in *Roe v. Wade*, which held the right to privacy includes the right to abortion with some limitations.[74] Although contraception may not be all that controversial when considered today (unless we are talking about the provision of health care), abortion still definitely is decades after the *Roe* decision.

The conflict over the right to privacy brings us back to Hamilton's *Federalist* #84. Underlying this controversy is an interesting constitutional issue: whether the Constitution should be read literally as the founders wrote it or whether it can be read flexibly in the light of contemporary circumstances. The first position is exactly the argument that Hamilton feared would be made if a Bill of Rights were to be attached to the Constitution. The right to privacy has become a target of those who argue that position.

The method in which the court systems interpret the Constitution can be either strict constructionists or judicial interpretivists. **Strict constructionists** are scholars and judges who believe that the Constitution should be read just as it was written. **Judicial interpretivists** are those who believe that the founders could not have anticipated all the changes that make the world today different from theirs and, therefore, that judges should read the Constitution as the founders would write it in light of modern-day experience. Strict constructionists generally interpret the Constitution to limit rights to privacy, while judicial interpretivists recognize the evolving right to privacy as implied in the Constitution.

---

[74] *Roe v. Wade*, 410 U.S. 113 (1973).

The method in which a justice interprets the Constitution determines how rights are created from the constitution. The political significance of this argument today can give people new civil rights and liberties or take them away. Since individual interpretations of the Constitution have such clear policy implications, Supreme Court confirmation hearings have often become battlegrounds as well. Reproductive rights are not the only ones that fall under the right to privacy. Supporters of LGBTQ rights tried to use the right to privacy to fight laws that criminalized homosexual behavior but were initially unsuccessful. Slowly, the Court recognized the LGBT community has some protections under the right to privacy by holding unmarried couples (largely LGBTQ couples since same sex marriage was illegal at the time) had the same right to obtain contraception as married couples.[75] The movement has had setbacks in 1986 when the Court held that the Constitutional guarantees don't prohibit states from criminalizing sex between people of the same sex. In *Bowers v. Hardwick*, the Court held that the right of privacy recognized in cases such as *Griswold* and *Roe* does not prevent the criminalization of homosexual conduct between consenting adults.[76] The opinion of the Supreme Court pendulum swung again in 2003 and reversed their prior decision and held that the due process clause gave people "the full right to engage in private conduct without government intervention…[and there is] no legitimate state interest which can justify its intrusion into the individual's personal and private life."[77]

A landmark decision in 2015 held that the fundamental right to marry under the right to privacy is guaranteed to same-sex couples in *Obergefell v. Hodges*.[78] While the law is slowly moving in the direction to eventually provide full equal protection for the LGTBQ community, it is likely that real change will be incremental, and the movement has a long way to go.

---

[75] *Eisenstadt v. Baird*, 405 U.S. 438 (1972).
[76] *Bowers v. Hardwick*, 478 U.S. 186 (1986).
[77] *Lawrence v. Texas*, 539 U.S. 558 (2003).
[78] *Obergefell v. Hodges*, 576 U.S. 644 (2015)

Chapter 6: Civil Liberties

1) _____ are the limits on government so that people can freely exercise their rights.

   a. Civil liberties

   b. Civil rights

   c. Selective incorporation

   d. Civil controls

2) Civil require government action to help secure individual rights.

   a. rights

   b. liberties

   c. freedoms

   d. laws

3) Civil _____ restrict government action to protect individual rights.

   a. rights

   b. liberties

   c. freedoms

   d. laws

4) Initially, the Bill of Rights protected against violations of citizens' rights from government(s).

   a. state

   b. federal

   c. state and federal

   d. state and local

5) The Barron v. Baltimore case demonstrates the selective incorporation of what civil liberty?

   a. seizing property

   b. search and seizure

   c. right to bear arms

   d. free-exercise clause

6) _____ incorporation is defined as extending protections from the Bill of Rights to the state governments, one right at a time.

   a. Concurrent

   b. Majority

   c. Selective

   d. Applicable

7) For what process is the Fourteenth Amendment often the basis?

   a. concurrent incorporation

   b. majority incorporation

   c. applicable incorporation

   d. selective incorporation

8) The Fourteenth Amendment is known as the _____ clause.

   a. due process

   b. clear and present danger

   c. free-exercise

   d. necessary and proper

9) In what year did the Supreme Court make a classic statement of civil liberties?

   a. 1940

   b. 1941

   c. 1943

   d. never

10) What case provides for the selective incorporation of the free exercise of religion?

   a. Miranda v. Illinois

   b. Benton v. Maryland

   c. Cantwell v. Connecticut

   d. Powell v. Alabama

11) What case provides for the selective incorporation of the right to free speech?

   a. Miranda v. Illinois

   b. Benton v. Maryland

   c. Gitlow v. New York

   d. Powell v. Alabama

12) What case provides for the selective incorporation of the right to remain silent?

    a. Miranda v. Illinois

    b. Benton v. Maryland

    c. Gitlow v. New York

    d. Powell v. Alabama

13) What case provides for the selective incorporation of the right to counsel in felony cases?

    a. Miranda v. Illinois

    b. Gideon v. Wainwright

    c. Gitlow v. New York

    d. Powell v. Alabama

14) Which of the following rights is not found in the Constitution or Bill of Rights?

    a. bear arms

    b. abortion

    c. cruel and unusual punishment

    d. free speech

15) Which Supreme Court case granted women a right to contraceptives?

    a. Griswold v. Connecticut

    b. Gideon v. Wainwright

    c. Gitlow v. New York

    d. Powell v. Alabama

16) Which Supreme Court case established a woman's right to choose?

    a. Gideon v. Wainwright

    b. Roe v. Wade

    c. Gitlow v. New York

    d. Powell v. Alabama

17) Roe v. Wade overturned a(n) law banning abortion.

    a. Texas

    b. South Carolina

    c. Alabama

    d. Mississippi

18) In what year was the Roe v. Wade decision rendered?

    a. 1982

    b. 1973

    c. 1994

    d. 1984

19) In 1980, the Court a congressional ban on federal funding for abortions.

    a. upheld

    b. overturned

    c. did not address in the ruling

    d. none of these

20) With the Planned Parenthood v. Casey decision, the Court left much discretion in abortions to (the) government(s), so long as they did not go against the Roe decision.

    a. state

    b. federal

    c. local

    d. none of these

21) The Planned Parenthood v. Casey decision established a judicial ,_guiding principles that help governments make judgment calls.

    a. standard

    b. rule

    c. opinion

    d. regulation

22) A judicial can be found in the Roe v. Wade case.

    a. standard

    b. rule

    c. opinion

    d. regulation

23) The state that passed the law struck down by Roe v. Wade was

    a. Oklahoma

    b. California

    c. Texas

    d. Arkansas

24) What right did the Lawrence v. Texas case address?

    a. privacy

    b. right to bear arms

    c. free exercise

    d. A cruel and unusual punishment

25) Which case relates to same-sex couples?

    a. Gideon v. Wainwright

    b. Lawrence v. Texas

    c. Gitlow v. New York

    d. Powell v. Alabama

26) Which of the following is not one of the clauses relating to freedom of religion?

    a. free exercise/practice

    b. necessary and proper

    c. establishment

    d. none of these

27) Where are the rights related to freedom of religion found?

    a. First Amendment

    b. Second Amendment

    c. Eighth and Ninth Amendments

    d. Fourth Amendment

28) Which clause says that the government may not interfere in religious practice?

    a. free exercise/practice

    b. necessary and proper

    c. establishment

    d. none of these

29) To which clause relates the wall of separation permitting religious freedoms?

    a. free exercise/practice

    b. necessary and proper

c. establishment

d. none of these

30) Which Court case said starting the school day with a prayer violated the establishment clause?

a. Williams v. Ohio

b. Engel v. Vitale

c. Lemon v. Kurtzman

d. none; the Court ruled it is constitutional

31) The case set a test for judging what government actions are permissible relating to the establishment clause.

a. Lemon

b. Engel

c. Williams

d. Miranda

32) Which of the following is not part of the Lemon test?

a. secular purpose

b. neither advancing nor inhibiting religion

c. not excessively entangling government in religion

d. none; these are all parts of the Lemon test

33) Which of the following is allowable, thus not violating the freedom of religion?

a. children reciting "under God" during the Pledge of Allegiance

b. prayer at graduation

c. public school minute of silent prayer or meditation

d. Christmas displays with secular displays as well

34) Which faith has been predominant in the United States since its founding?

a. Catholicism

b. Jewish

c. Islam

d. no predominant religion

35) Of what perspective on judging violations of the establishment clause is the Lemon test an example?

    a. accommodation

    b. strict separation

    c. strict entanglement

    d. none of these

36) Which test applies to the free exercise clause?

    a. Lemon

    b. Engel

    c. Sherbert

    d. Miranda

37) In the Sherbert case, the Court ruled denying unemployment benefits to someone who was fired for refusing to work on Saturdays for religious reasons was

    a. constitutional.

    b. unconstitutional.

    c. the right thing to do.

    d. none of these

38) Which Court case replaced the Sherbert test with a neutrality test?

    a. Lawrence v. Texas

    b. Employment Division v. Smith

    c. Miranda v. Illinois

    d. Ohio v. Smith

39) speech is hostile statements based on someone's personal characteristics.

    a. First-degree

    b. Second-degree

    c. Culturally insensitive

    d. Hate

40) When the right to speak out clashes with other rights, like protecting minorities from abusive language, free speech usually

    a. wins.

b. loses.

c. ties.

d. fails to be upheld.

41) In what amendment is the right to free speech guaranteed?

    a. First

    b. Third

    c. Sixth

    d. Seventh

42) Freedom of speech holds a position among rights.

    a. deferential

    b. subsidiary

    c. preferred

    d. none of these

43) The Alien and Sedition Acts relate to which individual freedom?

    a. freedom of speech

    b. freedom of religion

    c. unreasonable search and seizure

    d. no quartering of troops

44) Under the Alien and Sedition Act criticizing the government would lead to

    a. new legislation

    b. changes in laws

    c. right to assembly

    d. prosecution

45) What test was the result of the Schenck v. US case?

    a. necessary and proper

    b. clear and present danger

    c. constitutional determination of legitimacy

    d. none of these

46) Which Supreme Court justice articulated the clear and present danger test?

    a. Holmes

    b. Roberts

    c. Warren

    d. O'Connor

47) To which civil liberty applies the clear and present danger test?

    a. speech

    b. bear arms

    c. cruel and unusual punishment

    d. right to a grand jury

48) Which of the following is not a form of protected symbolic speech?

    a. burning the flag

    b. banners advocating drugs at schools

    c. wearing armbands to school

    d. burning a cross to express views

49) What Court case formed the basis for the test for obscenity in regulating free speech?

    a. Mapp v. Ohio

    b. Miller v. California

    c. Engel v. Vitale

    d. Michigan v. Jones

50) It is generally to prove slander or libel against a public official than an average citizen.

    a. less difficult

    b. more difficult

    c. about the same difficulty

    d. none of these

51) For slander or libel against a public official, what must be proven in the speech?

    a. knowledge

    b. malice

    c. poor fact-checking

    d. none of these

52) In what amendment is the right to bear arms found?

    a. Second

    b. Third

    c. Fifth

    d. Seventh

53) What government was at issue in a recent (2008) Supreme Court decision, which struck down a rule restricting guns to people's homes?

    a. Illinois

    b. Virginia

    c. District of Columbia

    d. South Carolina

54) What case provided for the incorporation of the Second Amendment to lower-level governments?

    a. McDonald v. Chicago

    b. DC v. Heller

    c. Michigan v. Arnold

    d. Mapp v. Ohio

55) Which amendment does not apply to the rights of the accused?

    a. Fourth

    b. Fifth

    c. Seventh

    d. Eighth

56) Relating to the accused's rights, the courts are generally moving away from individual protections and toward law enforcement powers.

    a. enhanced

    b. limited

    c. neutral

    d. none of these

57) Which country leads in the number of incarcerated individuals?

    a. Italy

b. Denmark

c. Mexico

d. US

58) Which case provides the foundation for the exclusionary rule?

a. Mapp v. Ohio

b. Miranda v. Arizona

c. Lawrence v. Texas

d. Roe v. Wade

59) Which amendment does the exclusionary rule relate to most prominently?

a. First

b. Third

c. Fourth

d. Seventh

60) The rule says that evidence obtained in an illegal search may not be introduced in a trial.

a. exclusionary

b. limited approach

c. limited inclusion

d. false pretense

61) The case out which came the exclusionary rule was

a. Roe v. Wade

b. Griswold v. Connecticut

c. Barron v. Baltimore

d. Mapp v. Ohio

62) The Fourth Amendment is generally referred to as preventing

a. trials without attorneys.

b. reading of rights well after arrest.

c. unlawful search and seizure.

d. none of the above

63) Which amendment relates to the rights of individuals at trials?

    a. Fourth

    b. Fifth

    c. Seventh

    d. Ninth

64) A citizen's right to a grand jury before a trial is found in what amendment?

    a. Fourth

    b. Fifth

    c. Seventh

    d. Ninth

65) A(n) jury is one that does not decide on guilt or innocence but only on whether there is enough evidence for the case to go to trial.

    a. grand

    b. arraignment

    c. attainment

    d. golden

66) "You have the right to remain silent" is a famous introduction to what warnings, based on the interpretation of the Fifth Amendment?

    a. Miranda

    b. Mapp

    c. Lawrence

    d. None of the above

67) Through the Miranda decision, if a police officer acquires evidence before reading Miranda's warnings, such evidence _____ be admitted in Court.

    a. could

    b. sometimes could

    c. could not

    d. none of the above

68) On what amendment is based one's right to an attorney in felony cases?

   a. Fourth

   b. Fifth

   c. Sixth

   d. Ninth

69) Originally, one's right to an attorney was only provided in what kind of case?

   a. civil

   b. capital

   c. felony

   d. misdemeanor and above

70) Which case granted citizens' rights to an attorney in all felony cases?

   a. Gideon v. Wainwright

   b. Powell v. Alabama

   c. Lawrence v. Texas

   d. Jones v. Ohio

71) Debates surrounding the death penalty center around which amendment?

   a. Sixth

   b. Seventh

   c. Eighth

   d. none of the above

72) The Eighth Amendment is typically associated with

   a. unlawful search and seizure.

   b. quartering of troops.

   c. cruel and unusual punishments.

   d. states' rights.

Discussion Questions

1) Define civil liberties.

2) Where is the right to privacy found? Why is it not in the Constitution?

3) Explain the importance of the Fourteenth Amendment.

4) What issues does the right to privacy surround? Discuss current issues facing the Court relating to a person's right to privacy.

5) Discuss the two clauses relating to the right to practice religion.

6) Explain the rights of the accused.

7) Why are some rights, such as speech, sometimes limited? What are the tests for the limitations of some of these rights? Are these hard-and-fast "tests"?

Video Resources

Civil Rights & Liberties: Crash Course Government: #23 Civil Rights and Civil Liberties https://www.youtube.com/watch?v=kbwsF-A2sTg

The Birth of a Nation (1915) https://www.youtube.com/watch?v=ebtiJH3EOHo

Civil Liberties | The National Constitution Center http://constitutioncenter.org/interactive-constitution/learning-material/civil-liberties

Korematsu and Civil Liberties www.annenbergclassroom.org/resource/korematsu-civil-liberties/

Milk (2008)

Website Resources

Civil Liberties Monitoring Project http://www.civilliberties.org/

US Department of Homeland Security http://www.dhs.gov/topic/civil-rights-and-civil-liberties

Stanford Journal of Civil Rights & Civil Liberties http://sjcrcl.stanford.edu/home.html

American Civil Liberties Union www.aclu.org

Civil Liberties and Civil Rights http://www.ushistory.org/gov/10.asp

C H A P T E R   7

CIVIL RIGHTS IN AMERICA

Chapter summary

Not all people have always had equality under the law in the United States of America. The dilemma of equal protection is vital to ensure that some people in America do not have more rights afforded them than others. Discrimination occurs when the government treats its citizens differently and usually takes the form of denying a benefit or imposing a burden or penalty on a group of persons simply because of a societal dislike for that social class. The deal is to know what kinds of discrimination are permitted and what kinds are not.

Slavery abolitionists and women's rights, and African American civil rights movements set a precedent in American political history. Three civil rights amendments to the United States Constitution, the Fifteenth, Nineteenth, and Twenty-Sixth— prevent both the states and the federal government from abridging citizens' right to vote based on race, sex, and age. Their tactics to engage people around spreading their ideas and their tricks to influence public opinion and the policymaking process still serve as inspiration these days. The rights gained have significantly improved the quality of life for many in America, especially for minorities. Boycotting and desegregation practices are still prevalent among human rights activists.

7.1 Introduction to Civil Rights in America

Civil rights are constitutionally supported, which guarantees that government officials will treat citizens equally and base their decisions on merit rather than race, gender, or other personal characteristics. In the United States of America, it is unlawful for a school or university to discriminate against a student based on its identity and background. In the 1960s and 1970s, many states still had separate schools where only students of a certain race or gender could study and afford a career. Over time, the courts ruled that these policies violated students' civil rights who could not be admitted because of those discriminatory rules.

Although the United States Constitution, as written in 1787, did not formally include a *Bill of Rights*, the idea was proposed and discussed. United States Constitution framers decided to dismiss the bill during the final week of the Constitutional Convention. They dismissed it because there were more important issues to address since the union was still weak and national unrest was still likely to happen. Besides, they perceived that they already had appropriately covered rights concerns in the American Constitution's main body.

The United States' founding principles are liberty, equality, and justice. Throughout its history as an independent country, not all its subjects have enjoyed equal access to rights and opportunities, nor have they been considered citizens by law. Discrimination can take many forms, from *segregation to forced mass sterilization policies*, based on sex, income, race, ethnicity or country of origin, religion, sexual orientation, or physical or mental abilities. Federally-funded sterilization programs took place in 32 states continuously through the 20th century in America; for around 70 years, California led the country in the number of sterilization procedures performed on men and women. For much of United States history, most of its people have been deprived of civil and fundamental rights, and sometimes of citizenship itself.

The struggle for equality and civil rights for all continues today since many subjects still encounter prejudice, violence, injustice, and negative stereotypes that lead to exclusion, discrimination, and marginalization.

7.2 Constitutional Source

The Equal Protection Clause of the Fourteenth Amendment only applies to the states and provides that "[no state shall] deny any person within its jurisdiction the equal protection of the laws".[79] There is no equivalent counterpart in the United States Constitution applying to the federal government. Therefore, the language of the Fourteenth Amendment is limited to state action.

Nevertheless, the Supreme Court has held that the federal government's grossly unreasonable discrimination violates the *Due Process Clause of the Fifth Amendment*, where the language applies to the federal government. Thus, there are two equal protection guarantees for each state and federal government. While the protections stem from different constitutional sources, the Court applies the same standards in interpreting those protections and determining appropriate discrimination.

---

[79] For more information, see the Constitution of the United States, Amend. XVI, Sec. 1.

When the Court tries to answer what is permitted governmental discrimination, it applies three different standards based on the classification of persons involved: (1) *suspect classifications or fundamental rights*, (2) *quasi-suspect classification*, and (3) any other classification of persons.

7.3 Discrimination based on Suspect Classifications

The Supreme Court has held that specific kinds of government actions that discriminate against individuals are inherently suspect and, therefore, must automatically be subject to the strictest judicial scrutiny. This stipulation means the government must have a valid reason to discriminate and has the burden of proof, or the party must prove that their actions are constitutional. The Court determined that there are generally four suspect classifications of people: race, religion, national origin, and alienage. However, this is not a complete list, and as the law develops, the current classifications could be modified, and they may later add more classifications.

Suppose a law or governmental action discriminates against persons that belong to a suspect classification. In that case, the Court will review the law under the most rigorous review called strict scrutiny. Strict scrutiny means asking if the law is necessary to achieve a compelling state interest. If strict scrutiny is applied, the law or government action will be struck down unless the government proves and demonstrates to the Court the crucial or necessary reason for the discriminatory action to accomplish a vital or compelling governmental interest or result.

Instances whereby the government classifies or uses an individual's race and national origin when applying the law, have been closely reviewed by the Court over the last century. During World War II, Franklin Roosevelt issued an executive order requiring people of Japanese descent, two-thirds of whom were citizens, to be relocated and placed in internment camps, where they stayed until the order was suspended in 1944. The order was challenged on equal protection grounds and reached the Supreme Court in 1944. In *Korematsu v. United States*, the Supreme Court decided that laws that treat people differently because of race are highly suspicious, making race a suspect classification.[80] In the majority opinion, Former Associate Justice of the Supreme Court of the United States Hugo Black declared "all legal restrictions which curtail the civil rights of a single group are immediately suspect. That is not to say that all such restrictions are unconstitutional; it is to say that courts must subject them to the most rigid scrutiny. Pressing public necessity may sometimes justify the existence of such restrictions; racial antagonism never can".

---

[80] See Kenney, Karen L, and Friedman, Richard D. *Korematsu V. the United States: World War II Japanese-American Internment Camps*. Minneapolis: ABDO Pub, 2013. Print..

Since the government action, the executive order has used individual's race and national origin; the Court had to apply *strict scrutiny* when asking if the action was constitutional. In Korematsu, it was the only clear racial discrimination case upheld despite applying strict scrutiny. The Court found placing the Japanese Americans in the camps was necessary to achieve *national security's compelling interest*. The Court held there was a compelling state purpose in national security. However, this holding was vital because it set a precedent and legal standard of review that legislators have used to evaluate laws that had discriminated against based on race and national origin.

Becoming a suspect class sounds like a good thing since it means that laws that discriminate against one's group get the strictest level of scrutiny. Nevertheless, it has proven to be a double-edged sword for racial groups because it tends to strike down laws that discriminate against one and laws that discriminate in one's favor. The efforts that groups have had to gain higher levels of scrutiny applied to the laws that treat them differently have been grueling. Moreover, even when the outcome is successful and discriminatory laws get annulled, only de jure discrimination formally is ended, while de facto discrimination may still be prevalent.

In United States constitutional law, when a court finds that a law infringes a fundamental right, it will also apply the strict scrutiny standard to hold it until the government can demonstrate that the law or regulation is necessary to achieve a *compelling state interest*. The United States Constitution protects certain fundamental constitutional rights and civil liberties.[81] If rights are denied to everyone, it is a substantive due process problem. If they are denied to some individuals but not to others, it is an equal protection problem. In either case, the standard of strict scrutiny will be applied.

Various privacy rights, including marriage, sexual relations, abortion, and child-rearing, are fundamental rights. Thus, regulations affecting these rights are reviewed under the strict scrutiny standard and upheld only if necessary to protect a compelling interest.

7.4 Discrimination based on Quasi-Suspect Classification

Laws that discriminate according to gender do not get the same level of scrutiny applied to race and other suspect classifications. *Quasi-suspect classifications* are based on gender and legitimacy (such as legitimate and illegitimate children), and representatives review them with a less rigorous analysis. When analyzing government action based on quasi-suspect classifications, the Court will apply the intermediate standard and strike down

---

[81] Even if lawyers and political scientists use to make a distinction between civil liberties and civil rights, they have interpreted the United States Constitution to protect both.

the law or government action unless it is substantially related to a significant government interest. As with strict scrutiny, *intermediate scrutiny* also places the burden of proof on the government.

First, when a law creates a gender classification, intermediate scrutiny will apply. As stated in *United States v. Virginia*, "parties who seek to defend gender-based government action must demonstrate an exceedingly persuasive justification for that action." (Ginsburg and Supreme Court Of The United States). *The important governmental interest* used to justify discrimination based on gender must be genuine, meaning it has to be reliable and cannot be overly broad or generalized. When, in *United States v. Virginia*, a state military school's policy of admitting only men was challenged, the state attempted to justify it, claiming that it offers a diversity of *educational approaches*. Also, that females would not be able to meet the male-only military school's physical requirements.

The Supreme Court found these arguments unconvincing. There was no evidence that that the single-sex school was established or maintained with a view of fostering diversity of educational opportunities, and there was some evidence that some women could meet the school's physical requirements. The state's argument of a vital governmental interest was not genuine and had no evidence to prove their claims were valid.

Intermediate scrutiny is not as hard to overcome as strict scrutiny. Therefore, there are more examples of where the Court has upheld classification or discrimination based on gender. A state law that excluded normal pregnancy and childbirth from state disability benefits was upheld that the law did not create a classification based on gender. The program's purpose was to create classifications based on the risk of disability, and normal pregnancies did not create such a risk.[82]

The Court has also reviewed discrimination against men. Laws punishing males but not females for statutory rape were upheld because the Court found the classification to be substantially related to the vital interest of preventing minors' pregnancy.[83] While other laws that preferred males over females to act as an administrator of an estate[84] or only authorize wives to be eligible to receive alimony[85] were struck down because there was no substantial relationship to a significant government interest.

---

[82] For more information, see Stewart, Potter, and Supreme Court Of The United States. *U.S. Reports: Geduldig v. Aiello*, 417 U.S. 484. 1973. Periodical. Library of Congress, www.loc.gov/item/usrep417484/.

[83] See Rehnquist, William H, and Supreme Court Of The United States. *U.S. Reports: Michael M. v. Sonoma County Superior Court*, 450 U.S. 464. 1980. Periodical. Retrieved from the Library of Congress, www.loc.gov/item/usrep450464/.

[84] See Supreme Court Of The United States. U.S. Reports: Reed v. Reed, 404 U.S. 71. 1971. Periodical. Retrieved from the Library of Congress, www.loc.gov/item/usrep404071/.

[85] See Brennan, William J., Jr, and Supreme Court Of The United States. *U.S. Reports: Orr v. Orr, 440 U.S. 268. 1978*. Periodical. Library of Congress, www.loc.gov/item/usrep440268/.

7.5 Discrimination based on Other Groups' Classifications

All other classifications are reviewed under the rational basis standard and will be upheld unless they bear no rational relationship to any conceivable legitimate government interest. Nevertheless, if the government has no interest in discriminating against a group of persons other than a societal fear or dislike of them, the classification will not meet the standard. The understanding is that for any class of persons that is not a suspect or quasi-suspect class defined by the Court, then the rational basis standard will apply.

The Court has held that several classifications are not suspect. Age is not a suspect class. Thus, the government action based on age will be upheld if there is a conceivable rational basis for the classification. Laws that force police officers to retire at age 50, even though physically fit as a young officer, or judges to retire at age 70 do not violate the *Equal Protection Clause*. Mental disabilities are also not suspect classifications. The Court struck down a zoning ordinance that prohibited a group of mentally disabled persons from sharing a residential home because the only reason to deny them the benefit was their mental condition. The government has no legitimate interest in prohibiting mentally disabled persons from living together.[86]

Utterly because a law or governmental action results in discrimination is not sufficient to trigger strict or intermediate scrutiny or the rational basis test, the government's law or action must be intentional. The intent is shown in three different ways: (1) *facial discrimination*, (2) *discriminatory application*, or (3) *discriminatory motive*. Once the Court has determined that there was an intent to discriminate, the Court will then apply and look at the law through one of the strict standards of review.

Facial discrimination is when a law includes classifications that make evident social distinctions based on race and gender on its "face" or within its terms. In *Strauder v. West Virginia*, the Supreme Court considered a law that provided that only white males can serve as jurors[87]. In such cases, the Court can then apply the appropriate standard of review for racial and gender classifications. Another indicator of facial discrimination is *de jure discrimination*, which is discrimination by laws. De jure segregation, or legalized segregation of Black and White people, was present in almost every aspect of life in the South during the Jim Crow era: from public transportation to cemeteries, from prisons to health care, from residences to libraries. Under segregation laws that, on their face, created racial classifications, Black and White people were to be separated, purportedly to minimize

---

[86] See White, Byron Raymond, and Supreme Court Of The United States. *U.S. Reports: Cleburne v. Cleburne Living Center*, 473 U.S. 432. 1984. Periodical. Library of Congress, www.loc.gov/item/usrep473432/.

[87] See Strong, William, and Supreme Court Of The United States. U.S. Reports: Strauder v. West Virginia, 100 U.S. 303. 1879. Periodical. Library of Congress, www.loc.gov/item/usrep100303.

violence. De jure segregation, or "Jim Crow," lasted from the 1880s to 1964. *Jim Crow laws* were efficient in perpetuating the idea of "white superiority" and "black inferiority."

In contrast, *de facto discrimination* results from life circumstances, habits, customs, or socioeconomic status. De facto segregation is the direct manifestation of de jure segregation. While the Court eventually held laws that segregated races were unconstitutional, it could not change its people's hearts and minds. If people did not want to be in the presence of another ethnicity or race, they could certainly make this a reality. So, de jure segregation was implemented by law, de facto segregation, shared understandings, and personal choice.

Second, *discriminatory application* applies when a law appears neutral and fair on its face but is applied differently to different groups of people and cultures. If the persons challenging the governmental action can prove that the government officials applying the law had a discriminatory purpose, representatives will likely annul the law. In *Yick Wo v. Hopkins*, a law prohibited people from operating a laundry mat in wooden buildings but gave local governmental officials discretion to grant exceptions[88]. At that time in history, the laundry mats in that area were owned almost exclusively by people of Chinese descent. The governmental officials ended up only granting the exceptions to non-Asian laundromat owners. The law had a discriminatory application based on the suspect classification of race and national origin and was annulled.

Sometimes, a law or government action will appear neutral and fair on its face and its application but will have a discriminatory impact on a particular class of persons. Such law will be found to involve a prohibited classification (and be subject to the level of scrutiny appropriate to that classification) only if a court finds that the law-making body enacted the law for a discriminatory purpose. It can be challenging to prove that the government had a discriminatory purpose when passing a law. In *McCleskey v. Kemp*, the statistics and historical facts showing that black defendants in capital cases are much more likely to receive the death penalty than white defendants in similar cases. However, the statistical evidence was not enough to prove that the state had a discriminatory motive or purpose when convicting the black defendants. Moreover, the convictions, the governmental action were upheld. It takes more than statistical evidence to prove a discriminatory purpose.

It is important to remember that the Equal Protection and Due Process Clauses only prohibit state or government action. Furthermore, while private actors are not subject to the *Equal Protection Clause*, they may be subject to other laws preventing discrimination. For example, the federal Age Discrimination in *Employment Act* prohibits

---

[88] For more information and insights, see Matthews, Stanley, and Supreme Court Of The United States. *U.S. Reports: Yick Wo v. Hopkins*, 118 U.S. 356. 1885. Periodical. Library of Congress, www.loc.gov/item/usrep118356.

age discrimination for people who are age 40 or older. Similar laws prohibit workplace discrimination based on disability, race and national origin, genetic information, pregnancy, religion, and sex. These laws were passed by Congress and enforced by the *Equal Employment Opportunity Commission.*

7.6 The Case of Race

It is essential to understand the origins of discrimination to understand the journey and development of civil rights. Why do some people call slavery America's original sin? The narratives that white slave-owners used to justify slavery created an image of an inferior race that required white mastery. These tales established a set of stereotypes of African Americans that continue to haunt the nation. Researchers have evidenced stereotypes' lingering effects in the relatively recent cases and development of law discussed above. While slavery has not been prevalent in the United States for over a century, racial stereotypes are still prevalent today.

As slavery persisted in the country's beginnings, the landmark decision in *Dred Scott v. Sandford*[89], which held African Americans were not citizens and could not be free, increased tensions between the North and South and helped incite the anti-slavery movement. The Supreme Court came up with the principle of separate but equal. This decision created a two-class system in America. The Civil War did not settle the issue of slavery in the United States. The American Civil War (1861–1865) was fought mainly over slavery, and even the conclusion of that event did not put the issue to rest. Immediately following the war and the passage of the *Thirteenth Amendment* of the United States Constitution banning slavery, white southerners tried to seize back the power they had lost, bypassing state and local laws.

The laws passed after the Civil War limited the rights of African Americans. The arena of national legislative politics was closed to African Americans after the North turned to its own affairs following the Civil War Amendments' passage. Black codes were known as state and local laws that denied freed blacks the right to vote, go to school, and own property. The era of Jim Crow laws began. To shut down the black codes, the Northern-dominated Congress passed the Fourteenth and Fifteenth Amendments that granted citizenship and the right to vote to African Americans. *Jim Crow laws* were passed by white southerners that tried to re-create the power relations of slavery by running around the amendments designed to give blacks citizenship rights. These were forms of de jure discrimination that created a segregated society.

---

[89] See Taney, Roger Brooke, and Supreme Court Of The United States. *U.S. Reports: Dred Scott v. Sandford, 60 U.S. 19 How. 393. 1856.* Periodical. Retrieved from the Library of Congress, www.loc.gov/item/usrep060393a/.

While the Civil War attempted and failed to remedy the societal damage of slavery, Congress and the Supreme Court were also slow with their efforts. Decades after the Civil War, in *Plessy v. Ferguson*[90], the Supreme Court still did not provide equal treatment of all citizens and came up with the principle of separate but equal use of public facilities by different races and put the seal of constitutional approval on segregation. This established a two-class system in America.

In the 1930s, the NAACP began to use a law school-centered strategy to undermine Plessy slowly. The separate but equal view held a standard that separate facilities were legal if they were equal. Of course, this was not equal at all. This circumstance gestured that the courts would not be a profitable arena for blacks to fight in either. In 1910, African Americans who refused to accept the Jim Crow second-class citizenship organized the National Association for the Advancement of Colored People.

The NAACP's calculation was that to most Americans, law schools would be a less threatening area for desegregation than primary education, but one where the justices of the Supreme Court were particularly well suited to find arguments against segregation to be persuasive. In Brown v. Board of Education, the Court finally reversed its prior ruling, holding that segregation itself was unequal and the separate but equal doctrine that had prevailed in the legal community for more than half a century was unconstitutional.[91]

Even after the Brown decision, the right to equality was fought with boycotts to address systematic discrimination. One year after the Brown decision, when Rosa Parks refused to vacate her bus seat for a white man in Montgomery, Alabama and launched the bus system boycott, African Americans realized that their purchasing power could be a considerable political weapon[92]. This circumstance was to be followed by the quick realization that television's new technology could bring their plight out of isolation in the South to the whole country's attention.

The battle for equality was also fought with public opinion. The civil rights movement was fought in the arenas of public opinion and, finally, in Congress. In 1964 and 1965, civil rights legislation, initiated by President John Kennedy and then pushed through Congress by President Lyndon Johnson after Kennedy's assassination, removed most of the legal barriers to integration. Southern Congress members staged a filibuster to prevent a vote on the Senate's legislation, voting against their party's president. Most notably, the Civil Rights Act of 1964 prohibited segregation in public places based on race, religion,

---

[90] See Supreme Court Of The United States. *U.S. Reports: Plessy v. Ferguson, 163 U.S. 537. 1895*. Periodical. Retrieved from the Library of Congress, www.loc.gov/item/usrep163537/.

[91] See Warren, Earl, and Supreme Court Of The United States. *U.S. Reports: Brown v. Board of Education, 347 U.S. 483. 1953*. Periodical. Library of Congress, <www.loc.gov/item/usrep347483/.

[92] See Krutz, Glen S. *American Government 2e.*, 2019. Internet resource. especially chapter 5, for an in-depth analysis on how boycotts were used to address systematic discrimination in the United States.

or national origin. It also created the Equal Employment Opportunity Commission that enforces laws that prohibit discrimination in the workplace. The civil rights movement was the combination of all these strategies used to alleviate African Americans' plight.

Did the civil rights movement eradicate de facto discrimination as well as de jure? One irony of all the legislative changes was that it ended the de jure discrimination in the South but pointed out the shortcomings of legal change as a method to redress de facto segregation in the North. Segregation in the North arose from long-term economic patterns and demographic changes that left African Americans in the city centers and succeeding waves of newly assimilated white immigrants in the suburbs. De facto discrimination cannot be remedied by fixing laws. It requires an effort to fix the outcomes, which strikes many Americans as fundamentally unfair. Despite the hard-won changes in laws, demeaning racial narratives were still woven into the American story and still determined how African Americans were treated and fared in rules and institutions based on white privilege.

Does the United States still have a race problem? Racial discrimination endures as one of American politics' defining issues, especially as demographic change forces whites to grapple with sharing minority status with other racial groups. Systemic racism is built into the American system to give whites preference and stacks the deck against people of color. The battle for equal rights does not end with African Americans. People of color who have had to fight for equal treatment by the law also include Native Americans, Latinos, and Asians. The assimilation of European immigrants has traditionally been about their ability to fit in; the assimilation of people of color has depended on the willingness of the white population to give up racist narratives to accept them.

The government has a compelling interest in remedying past discrimination against a racial or ethnic minority. Thus, if a court finds that a governmental agency has engaged in racial discrimination, it may exercise affirmative action, a race-conscious remedy to help end the discrimination and ease the effects. A remedy of this type is permissible under the *Equal Protection Clause* because it is narrowly tailored to further the compelling interest to eliminate discrimination. For example, when it has been proven that a public employer engaged in persistent racial discrimination, a court may order relief that establishes a goal for hiring or promoting minority persons to eliminate the effects of the past discrimination.

7.7 The Case of Gender

The women's rights movement began in Seneca Falls in 1848. Sexism, like racism, is pervasive, often unrecognized, and has deep cultural roots. The women's rights movement is commonly dated from the Seneca Falls (NY) Convention of 1848, where the first woman's rights convention was held. The widely accepted narrative that kept wealthy white women out of public life was that they were too good and pure for the rough and tumbled corruption of public life. As with the racial equality movement, the women's suffrage movement was also gradual and spanned several decades.

Women fought for equality across all levels of government. On the western frontier, women worked side by side with men to carve a life out of the wilderness. The state-level effort promised more but slower success for women's rights. By 1912, women could vote in states that accounted for 74 electoral votes for the presidency. The *Nineteenth Amendment* (1920) gave women the right to vote. More equal rights would have required the passage of the *Equal Rights Amendment*. It was never ratified by the states but still discussed in current political platforms.

Modern legislation has called for equality for women. The *Lilly Ledbetter Fair Pay Act of 2009* requires equal pay for equal work. Women often make less money than men for the same work. The glass ceiling is the concept that women are still a minority in places where power is wielded. *Cultural attitudes* toward women are changing (e.g., the #MeToo movement) and will continue to change.

7.8 Sexual Orientation and Gender Identity

Unlike race and gender, the movement for equal protection for LGBTQ (lesbian, gay, bisexual, transgender, and queer or questioning) is still in its beginnings. It has only gained momentum in the last couple of decades. The movement seeks to accomplish what the race and gender movements have only recently achieved- guarantees for federal and state civil rights and protections against discrimination.

The Court addressed the first step in considering LGBTQ rights in *One, Inc. v. Olsen*, which primarily expanded the right of free speech by establishing that material published for a gay audience was not inherently obscene.[93] The movement had had setbacks in 1986 when the Court held that the *14th Amendment's Due Process guarantee* does not prohibit states from criminalizing sex between people of the same sex. The opinion of the Supreme Court pendulum swung again in 2003 and reversed their prior decision and held that the due process clause gave people "the full right to engage in private conduct without government intervention…[and there is] no legitimate state interest which can justify its intrusion into the individual's personal and private life". (Kennedy and Supreme Court of The United States, Lawrence et. al. Texas)

A landmark decision in 2015 held that the fundamental right to marry under the right to privacy is guaranteed to same-sex couples in *Obergefell v. Hodges*. While the law is slowly moving toward providing complete equal protection for the LGBTQ community eventually, real change will likely be incremental. The movement still has a long way to go.

---

[93] See Supreme Court Of The United States. *U.S. Reports: One, Incorporated, v. Olesen, 355 U.S. 371. 1957.* Periodical. Library of Congress, www.loc.gov/item/usrep355371/.

Chapter 7: Civil Rights

1) When did Congress outlaw sex discrimination in the Civil Rights Act?
   a. 1964
   b. 1966
   c. 1965
   d. 1968

2) What are rules issued by the president that have the force of law but do not require congressional approval?
   a. presidential orders
   b. executive orders
   c. White House decrees
   d. none of the above

3) What was the Compromise of 1850?
   a. Permitted territories to vote on whether they would be slaves or free.
   b. Local governments would decide whether they would be slaves or free.
   c. Slavery was allowed only in the western states.
   d. all of the above

4) Which 1857 Supreme Court case ruled that the federal government did not have the power to give black men rights rights?
   a. Brown v. Board of Education
   b. Dred Scott v. Sandford
   c. Roe v. Wade
   d. none of the above

5) Which war in American history caused more Americans to lose their lives than in all the other American wars put together?
   a. World War I
   b. Civil War
   c. Korean War
   d. Vietnam War

6) The Fifteenth Amendment excluded which group?

   a. women

   b. blacks

   c. Chinese

   d. none of the above

7) Southern state and local governments reacted to slaves' freedom by passing

   a. anti-sovereignty codes.

   b. nonwhites codes.

   c. black regulations.

   d. black codes.

8) For a time, Congress supported the former slaves. In an effort known as ___, it tried to rebuild the South around a racial justice vision.

   a. the Fourteenth Amendment

   b. Reconstruction

   c. the Civil Rights Act

   d. none of the above

9) Did the Civil Rights Act of 1866 guarantee African Americans the same rights as white Americans?

   a. property rights

   b. right to participate in politics

   c. limited private racial discrimination in hotels, restaurants, and theaters

   d. all of the above

10) ___ were allegedly a requirement that voters were literate. In reality, they were a way to restrict black suffrage.

   a. Literacy tests

   b. Intelligence tests

   c. Black voters' tests

   d. none of the above

11) In the Civil Rights Cases of 1883, the Supreme Court struck down the Civil Rights Act of 1875, ruling that Congress did not have the authority to stop

private discrimination. In what year did Congress finally find a way around this barrier?

a. 1901

b. 2011

c. 1964

d. 1887

12) The white majority built a system of segregation known as ___.

a. Ku Klux Klan

b. James Crow

c. Jim Crow

d. none of the above

13) In what year did the Supreme Court rule, in Plessy v. Ferguson, that there was nothing inherently discriminatory in separating the races?

a. 1843

b. 1851

c. 1896

d. 1954

14) The percentage of southern students in integrated schools eight years after Brown v. Board of Education was

a. 74

b. 6

c. 1

d. none

15) What was the plot of the 1915 movie Birth of a Nation?

a. Social equality for all in America.

b. Lust-filled black men

c. The framers of the Constitution.

d. The Puritans' quest for religious freedom.

16) Beginning in the 1920s, many African Americans left southern agriculture and moved to more lucrative factory jobs in the northern cities—a journey known as the

a. Northern Migration.

b. Extradition.

c. Great Migration.

d. Great Movement.

17) In 1909, black leaders formed the NAACP. What does this abbreviation stand for?

a. National Association for the Advancement of Celebrated People

b. National Association for the Advancement of Christian Patrons

c. National Association for the Advancement of Colored People

d. National Association for the Advancement of Christian People

18) In 1961, activists came up with a new tactic. Groups of young people rented Greyhound buses as ___ to protest segregated interstate bus lines and terminals.

a. Desegregation Riders

b. Freedom Riders

c. Freedom for Blacks

d. freedom activists

19) Which of the following activists was instrumental in the success of the civil rights movement?

a. Martin L. King

b. Rosa Parks

c. A. Philip Randolph

d. all of the above

20) Martin L. King delivered his famous "I Have a Dream" speech in ___ in Washington, DC.

a. 1963

b. 1968

c. 1995

d. 1866

21) The Civil Rights Act was passed in what year?

a. 1991

b. 1962

c. 1964

d. 1865

22) Congress passed the Voting Rights Act in what year?

   a. 1965

   b. 1992

   c. 1967

   d. 1866

23) What is the American ideal often expressed as equality of opportunity?

   a. Give every individual a fair chance at achieving success with the aid of government assistance.

   b. Give every individual a fair chance at achieving success if they can access seed money from parents.

   c. Give every individual a fair chance at achieving success if they are talented and hardworking.

   d. all of the above.

24) When did the new approach of affirmative action emerge in America?

   a. The 1850s and the 1860s

   b. The 1960s and the 1970s

   c. The 1970s and the 1980s

   d. The 1980s and the 1990s

25) Which of the following could a woman do in the early nineteenth century?

   a. vote

   b. serve on a jury

   c. enter into a contract

   d. none of the above

26) When was the first convention for woman suffrage, held at Seneca Falls, that grew directly from the abolition movement?

   a. 1848

   b. 1891

   c. 1898

   d. 1937

27) By 1916, an influential political campaign had won full suffrage in fifteen states and partial suffrage in twenty-three others. Women voted in every state of the West and Midwest except

a. Utah.

b. Wyoming.

c. Idaho.

d. New Mexico.

28) Have Latinos taken many of the black civil rights movement tactics and adapted them to their own needs. Did they organize which of the following organizations in 1929?

a. League of United Hispanic American Citizens

b. League of United Latin American Citizens

c. United Latin American League

d. Hispanic League of Freedom

29) Congress passed the _____ in 1882 barring _____ immigrants and declaring them ineligible for citizenship.

a. Japanese Exclusion Act . . . Japanese

b. Chinese Exclusion Act . . . Chinese

c. Vietnamese Exclusion Act . . . Vietnamese

d. Korean Exclusion Act . . . Korean

30) After the Pearl Harbor attack in 1941, President Roosevelt ordered the army to round up Japanese Americans and place them in internment camps. What did they lose as a result of this act of injustice?

a. their liberty

b. their jobs

c. their property and their bank accounts

d. all of the above

31) In 1831, the Supreme Court ruled that Indian tribes were ___.

a. domestic indigenous tribes

b. domestic dependent nations

c. independent countries

d. none of the above

32) The civil rights protests inspired some Native Americans, just as they did so many other groups, to organize a political movement. Which is one such movement?

a. American Indian Sovereignty

b. American Indian United

c. American Indian Movement

d. American Indian Justice

33) Section 504 of the 1973 Rehabilitation Act benefited the disabled. Which piece of legislation did this bill borrow from?

a. the Civil Rights Act of 1964

b. the Constitution

c. the Bill of Rights

d. Civil Rights Act of 1866

34) The movement for same-sex rights began with a riot. In 1969, police raided a ___ gay bar named the Stonewall Inn.

a. San Francisco

b. New York City

c. Los Angeles

d. Salt Lake City

35) When did the American Psychiatric Association remove homosexuality from its list of mental disorders?

a. 1949

b. 1961

c. 1973

d. 1999

36) The freedom to participate in the community's full life is also known as

a. civil liberties

b. legal rights

c. executive mandates

d. civil rights

37) Once civil rights aure won, what is the next job of the public?

    a. protecting them

    b. codifying them

    c. ignoring them

    d. there is no next step

38) One way to view the history of civil rights is as a(n)

    a. easy path

    b. slow march

    c. steady march

    d. fast run

39) Which of the following is a civil right?

    a. voting

    b. using public facilities

    c. equal economic opportunity

    d. all of the above

40) One way to view the history of civil rights is as

    a. expanding and contracting

    b. moving forward rapidly

    c. moving forward slowly

    d. moving backward slowly

Discussion Questions

1) Does de facto discrimination still exist today—and, if so, how much?

2) America has made astonishing progress since the days of the civil rights movement; however, significant inequalities remain. What are some of these inequalities?

3) Discuss how Hispanic people come from many different places, each with its own interests and concerns. For example, Cuban Americans are not as concerned with immigration issues as Mexican Americans.

4) Analyze why, unlike Latinos or African Americans, Asian Americans do not form a majority in any electoral districts except Hawaii, although some California districts may soon come close.

5) Discuss the policy of "Indian removal."

6) Discuss the social problems of American Indians. Indian poverty rates are approximately three times as high as the national rates and stand at 32.2 percent—well above any other American group. Analyze what the US government can do to relieve this dilemma.

Video Resources

USA.gov Channel https://www.youtube.com/usagov1

Icount https://icount.com/

PBS Frontline http://www.pbs.org/wgbh/pages/frontline/view/

Freedom Rider http://www.pbs.org/wgbh/americanexperience/freedomriders/watch

Stonewall Uprising http://www.pbs.org/wgbh/americanexperience/films/stonewall/

We Shall Remain http://www.pbs.org/wgbh/amex/weshallremain/

A Class Apart http://www.pbs.org/wgbh/americanexperience/films/class/

Selma (2014)

The Fight for a Right (2014) www.youtube.com/watch?v=ZOX36uYgMys

Racism, School Desegregation Laws and the Civil Rights Movement in the United States www.youtube.com/watch?v=U9ACS4PgDFA

The Civil Rights Movement: A Cultural Revolution www.memphis.edu/benhooks/documentaries/aculturalrevolution.php

Website Resources

Movement Bibliography: Online Books, Audio, Films & Videos Photos and Images http://www.crmvet.org/biblio-e.htm

Voices of Civil Rights http://www.loc.gov/exhibits/civilrights/

Civil Rights Digital Library http://crdl.usg.edu/?Welcome

The Founder's Constitution http://press-pubs.uchicago.edu/founders/

Political Resources Online http://politicalresources.com/

Online Library of Liberty http://oll.libertyfund.org/

CHAPTER 8

THE LEGISLATIVE BRANCH

Chapter summary

To successfully prevent the national government, or any group within it, from becoming exceedingly powerful, the United States Constitution divided the government into three branches with different powers and attributions. Congress can pass laws, but its power to do so can be checked by the United States president, who can veto potential legislation so that it ultimately cannot become a law.

Most of Congress's work activities and work take place in *legislative* committees. The House of Representatives has 20 permanent committees. The Senate has 21, and there are four joint committees with members from both chambers. These congressional committees have purview over specific issues, and they identify potential issues that could be subject to legislative review. Some areas in which these committees jurisdiction include agriculture, foreign affairs, budgets, and finance. House members from states with significant sectoral interests, such as agriculture, will likely seek these specific committees' positions.

To sit in the United States Congress, almost every member has to run for election and beat their opponent. The Seventeenth Amendment outlines how representatives should fill a vacancy caused by death, resignation, or removal from office should.

8.1 Introduction – What is the Legislative Branch?

The *legislative branch* is one of the three branches of the United States government as outlined by the Constitution. The legislative comprises the two chambers of Congress, the House, and the Senate. The legislative government branch produces the laws, declares war, and regulates taxes, among other duties.

One hundred elected representatives, two from each state, compose the *United States Senate*. It is the Senate's upper chamber and has more powers than the House, such as the power to impeach the United States President and confirm Cabinet positions, Supreme Court Justices, and other positions. Since it has more specific powers and has fewer members than the House, politicians have a more sought-after position. Citizens elect *Senators* to six-year terms with elections staggered, so approximately 1/3 of the Senate is up for election every even-numbered year.

The *House of Representatives* is the lower chamber of Congress, and it has 435 elected members. Unlike the Senate, the House is divided proportionally based on the population size of each state. The seven states with the lowest population have only one representative, while the most populous state, California, has 53 representatives in the House. The House also has powers that are unique to it, including impeaching federal officers and electing a United States President in the event of an Electoral College tie. A *Representative* serves a shorter term than a Senator, only two years, and is up for election every even-numbered year.

8.2 How the Constitution Established Congress

The Constitution outlines the role of Congress in Article I. Article I, Section I, states:

> "All legislative Powers herein granted shall be vested in a Congress of the United States, which shall consist of a Senate and House of Representatives."

One of the key design elements from the Founding Fathers was making Congress bicameral. A *bicameral legislature* is a legislative body that has two chambers. When discussing the government's structure under the United States Constitution, the delegates from Virginia called for a bicameral legislature consisting of two Houses. Delegates from small states objected to the Virginia Plan, which ultimately prevailed.

Another proposal, the New Jersey Plan, called instead for a unicameral legislature with one House, in which each state would have one vote. Consequently, smaller states would have the same power in the national legislature as larger states. Notwithstanding, the larger states argued that they should be allotted more legislators to represent their interests because they had a more significant population. (Corwin, 48)

The two chambers of Congress in the United States were created with different characteristics to represent different interests to protect any region or state from getting too much power. Each state has equal representation in the Senate, while in the House, states with a higher population have more seats and thus more voting power. The House of Representatives has developed a more robust and structured leadership than the Senate. Because its members serve two-year terms, they regularly answer their constituency's demands when running for election or reelection. Even House members of the same party in the same state will occasionally disagree on different issues because of their specific districts' particular interests. The House can be highly partisan at times. In contrast, members of the Senate are furthest from the demands and scrutiny of their constituents. Because of their longer six-year terms, they will likely see every House member face their constituents multiple times before they have to seek reelection.

The foundation of Congress and the Constitution's contents resulted from the bitter battle between Federalist and Anti-Federalist factions. The Federalists supported a strong federal government, while the Anti-Federalists wanted more power in the states' hands. In the Constitution's passage, the Federalists ultimately prevailed, but Congress's structure was a source of compromise. While not all Anti-Federalists agreed between the House's proportional representation and the Senate's equal representation, they also created state legislatures to compromise with Anti-Federalists.

Another compromise to Anti-Federalists was who elected members of the Senate. While the voting public elected members of the House, state legislatures initially elected their state's senators. This setting gave the state legislatures more power over federal policy. State legislatures elected senators until the Seventeenth Amendment's ratification in 1913, which changed senators' election to a popular vote by voters in the state.

The Senate and the House were made with two different structures so that they would represent different constituencies. Each member of government has a *constituency*, the individuals and groups whose interests the elected official represents. Senators represent their whole state when they go to Congress, and until 1913 they were closely tied to political interests in their state's legislature. Each House member represents a district in their state. For example, California has 53 distinct districts. Under this original design, representatives were supposed to represent the people and their opinions, while senators were representatives of their state and legislature.

The two chambers of Congress also have different qualification requirements and restrictions. A senator has to be at least 30 years old, a United States citizen for at least nine years, and be a resident of the state they are running to represent. A representative only has to be 25 years old, be a United States citizen for seven years, and live in the state they politically represent.

8.3 How Congress Does Its Job

To adequately perform the duties given to Congress by the Constitution, the legislative body's structure has various leadership roles. Throughout United States history, the division of power for congressional leadership positions has evolved. Partisanship, narrow margins between the two parties, and the rise in leadership positions' power have marked and shaped modern congressional politics. The Speaker of the House and the Senate majority leader, the majority party's congressional leaders, have all-powerful tools at their disposal to conveniently punish party members who defect on a particular vote.

Most of Congress's work activities and work take place in *legislative committees*. The House of Representatives has 20 permanent committees. The Senate has 21, and there are four joint committees with members from both chambers. These congressional committees have purview over specific issues, and they identify potential issues that could be subject to legislative review. Some areas in which these committees jurisdiction's include agriculture, foreign affairs, budgets, and finance.

Initially, Senate committee membership was determined either by a vote by the full Senate or appointments by the committee's presiding officer. In 1846, the Senate changed its rules on committee appointments in order to streamline the process. Today, each party's leadership determines Senate committee membership and submissions to the floor for approval. Similarly, in the House, Democratic and Republican leadership determine which representatives to submit for committee membership approval. This situation gives each party's leadership significant power to keep incoming and incumbent Congress members in line with the respective party's vision.

In Congress, four main types of committees perform different roles and specialize in specific public policy areas. *Standing committees* are permanent as laid out in the House and Senate rules that have specific legislative jurisdiction. In this type of committee, members review and recommend legislative measures and monitor government agencies relevant to their jurisdiction. The Senate has 16 standing committees with 67 subcommittees, and the House has 20 standing committees with 97 subcommittees.

Select or special committees are established for a limited time, often to conduct investigations or research. If an emerging issue does not fall under a standing committee's purview or crosses multiple committees' jurisdiction, a select committee will be set up. While they put these committees in place for a limited time, they can renew them by their respective chambers, and sometimes they become permanent standing committees.

Conference committees are used to reconcile bills passed in both the House and the Senate. The conference committees are appointed on an ad hoc basis when a bill passes the House and Senate in various forms. Congress members sometimes skip these committees in the interest of expediency, in which one of the chambers relents to the other.

Lastly, *joint committees* are composed of members of both the House and the Senate. Joint committees are permanent and mainly perform housekeeping duties or conduct studies rather than doing legislative work. Leadership on these committees alternates between the Senate and the House.

The most influential role in the Senate is the *Speaker of the House*. This position was established in Article 1 Section II of the Constitution, but the office's power has grown significantly in the modern era. The Speaker is the House's presiding officer, the lower chamber of Congress's administrative head, and the majority party's head in the House. The Constitution does not call for the Speaker to have a partisan role, but the role has developed significantly over the years. The Speaker of the House is also third in line for the presidency.

The leader of the majority party in the Senate is known as the *Senate Majority Leader*. Unlike the Speaker of the House, the United States Constitution does not set this position. They are the majority party's head in the Senate and derive their power from their party and various Senate precedents. While the Senate Majority Leader does not enjoy as much formal power as the House's Speaker, they serve as the chief spokesperson for their party in the Senate. The leader of the party with fewer members in the Senate is known as the Senate Minority Leader. The Constitution established the Vice President as President of the United States Senate.

8.4 Congress's Role in the System of Checks and Balances

The Founding Fathers established the federal government as a system of checks and balances so no single branch of government, person, or political interest would become too powerful. The framers of the Constitution created such a system to satisfy the concerns of those who feared an overly strong central government. In this vein, Congress plays a crucial role and has some power over the executive and judicial branch, and vice versa.

Congress has three key ways to check the executive branch, and they give the legislative branch power to balance the President's power. The first and most important is *congressional oversight*. This provision refers to Congress's powers to oversee the executive branch and numerous federal agencies. Congress can review and keep an eye on various federal programs, administrative activities, and policies. The power to create an investigative committee, hold legislative hearings, and set budgets also fall under this category. The Constitution does not explicitly state that Congress has these powers; instead, these powers have been built up over time under the principle of implied powers.

One of the most visible powers of Congress in the modern presidency has been the power of impeachment. Congress has the sole power to impeach a government official and remove them from office. The House has the power to impeach government officials. The Senate can take up the House's impeachment, hold a trial, and vote in the Senate to convict and remove the impeached official from office. The Constitution explicitly gives Congress the power to impeach federal officials, and it also gives the legislative branch the power to bar impeached and convicted officials from running for office.

The House has passed articles of impeachment 21 times, three times against a sitting president. Presidents Andrew Johnson, Bill Clinton, and Donald Trump have all been impeached by the House, and the Senate later acquitted all. President Richard Nixon resigned in 1974 rather than face certain impeachment and a likely conviction in the Senate after the Watergate scandal. President Donald Trump is the only federal official to be impeached twice, and he was acquitted both times.

The final important check Congress has on the executive branch is advice and consent, the Senate's role of confirming presidential appointments, including Supreme Court appointments, Cabinet officials, and ambassadors. The Constitution only grants this power to the Senate and not the House, and it is outlined in Article II Section 2 Clause 2. Initially, the Founding Fathers disagreed about the Senate's role in advising the President on nominations. In modern American politics, this power mostly plays out in high-profile congressional hearings with a majority of senators needed to approve appointments. A two-thirds majority of the Senate is also required to approve international treaties signed by the President.

Not only does Congress check and balance the power of the executive branch, but they also have powers to do the same with the judicial branch. Some of these powers are also within the above powers to check the executive, such as approving or denying judicial appointments and impeach and remove federal judges from office.

One of the leading powers that Congress has to check the judicial branch's power is to amend the Constitution. As the highest court in the land, the Supreme Court takes cases and gives rulings based on the justice's interpretation of the legislation or executive order constitutionality. As the federal courts use the Constitution as the basis for their legal rulings, the ability to amend the Constitution through the legislative process is one of Congress's most important powers.

Congress also has significant organizational power over the judicial branch. The United States Constitution grants Congress the power to determine how many Supreme Court Justices sit on the court and establish inferior courts. The Constitution only required the Supreme Court, but Congress has established a vast and powerful judicial branch with many inferior federal courts. Congress established the district courts system in the Judiciary Act of 1789. Today, there are 94 district courts in the country. Congress also established the 13 courts of appeals.

Furthermore, Congress can also pass laws that circumvent the courts' rulings. While one has traditionally assumed that the Supreme Court has the final say on applying the law regarding new legislation, congressional overrides have become more common in the modern era. William Eskridge Jr. and Matthew Christiansen found that congressional overrides grew dramatically between 1967 and 1990. While they have decreased after the Clinton impeachment, they remain a relevant tool for Congress to override the judicial branch.[94] Former Supreme Court Justice Ruth Bader Ginsburg asked Congress to override the Supreme Court's ruling in 2013 and said, "Congress has, in the recent past, intervened to correct this Court's wayward interpretations of Title VII."[95]

While Congress has significant power to check the executive and judicial branches, these two branches also have been granted the ability to check and balance the legislative branch. The President's most important check on Congress is the power to veto legislation, thus directing the legislative agenda. However, this power is not ultimate, and Congress can reject a presidential veto by a two-thirds vote. The judicial branch primarily checks Congress's power through judicial review. One of the Supreme Court's primary roles is to review the legality of legislation passed by Congress.

8.5 How Congress Makes the Law

How does Congress go about performing its most important duty, making laws through passing legislation? Both the Senate and House are constrained by the Constitution and norms that have been built up over time. Political interests may influence Congress members, who also have different commitments to their state or district's particular interests. Specifically, in the House, where representatives face reelection every two years, Congress members are constrained by electability concerns. With all this said, Congress is the place all new federal legislation has to go through, and it performs an essential role in American democracy.

Congress members are often drafting and working on bills for years before they reach the floor of Congress, and many bills go through a long and arduous process before they become the law of the land. Bills do not necessarily originate from Congress

---

[94] Eskridge and Christiansen state that, before 1975, the United States Congress regularly overrode Supreme Court decisions interpreting federal statutes, but this mostly was an occasional phenomenon. The big turning point in United States history of statutory overrides was the 94th Congress (1975-1976), where the post-Watergate representatives overrode twenty Supreme Court decisions. Amid political polarization, the 1990s was the golden age of overrides. Eskridge Jr., William N., and Matthew R. Christiansen. "Congressional Overrides of Supreme Court Statutory Interpretation Decisions, 1967-2011." *Texas Law Review*, vol. 92, 2014, doi:https://digitalcommons.law.yale.edu/cgi/viewcontent.cgi?article=5895&context=fss_papers.

[95] For more information, *see* Supreme Court. Vance v. Ball State University. 24 June 2013.

members, as political interest groups, think tanks, policy groups, and more pitch ideas to congresspeople regularly. Whether a member of Congress presents himself with a bill or ideates and finetunes the whole piece of legislation, the next step for a bill is to be introduced in either Congress's chamber.

The bill's *sponsor* is the representative or Senator who first brings the bill to Congress. In addition to the bill's primary sponsor, other senators and representatives who sign on supporting the legislation in this early phase are cosponsors.

Next, the bill is sent to a relevant committee or multiple committees if the bill spans multiple jurisdictions. The committee then assigns the bill to a subcommittee, where representatives kill most legislation. Here the senators or representatives on the committee discuss and hold hearings on the bill and either decide to kill the bill through inaction or make amendments to the bill and send it to the floor for a chamber-wide vote.

If the bill makes it to a vote in the House or Senate for a debate and vote, a simple majority supporting it will send it to the other chamber for approval. The two chambers have some minor differences in how a bill comes out of committee and debating on the floor. In the House, the House Committee on Rules decides for approval before representatives can debate it on the House floor. A bill in the Senate will be put to open debate, but it can be subject to a *filibuster*.

Unlike in the House, which got rid of the filibuster in 1842, the Senate filibuster allows a senator as much as they want to slow down a bill's passage and take floor time away from it. The practice is a Senate rule and not in the Constitution, and it has become increasingly used in the modern era. The longest filibuster by a single senator was Strom Thurmond's unsuccessful 24 hour and 18-minute attempt to stop the 1957 Civil Rights Act. Thurmond also participated in a 60-day filibuster by multiple senators attempting to stop the 1964 Civil Rights Act. The only way to stop a filibuster is by *cloture*, a vote which requires 60 senators.

Once sent to the other chamber, it faces a similar cycle where relevant committees hold hearings on the bill and make potential amendments before approving it or killing the bill. A bill can pass one chamber of Congress but be voted down or killed through inaction, and both chambers have to agree on the final version of the bill. Once both the House and the Senate approve a bill, they send it to the President for signature and approval. A president can either sign the bill, approve it, make it law, or veto it. United States presidents have historically used the line-item veto and signed statements to influence the laws they will sign. While a presidential veto will often kill the legislation, Congress can override a veto if two-thirds of each chamber votes to override the President.

While this is the standard procedure for a bill to become a law, there are multiple ways that congressional leadership or a congressperson can bypass committee hearings to fast-track legislation through various congressional rules not outlined in the Constitution. If a Congress member asks for unanimous consent to put a bill on the agenda and nobody votes against it, a bill can bypass committees. The Senate Majority Leader can also use Senate Rule XIV to bypass committee hearings.[96]

There are also ways for the Senate to bypass the traditional rules around the filibuster by using *reconciliation*. While bills in the Senate require a 60-vote supermajority to avoid a filibuster, the Senate can use reconciliation to pass legislation by a simple majority on bills related to spending, revenue, and the federal debt limit. The Senate can do this three times a calendar year, one per subject.

Another modern development in Congress is *omnibus legislation*; unrelated legislation packaged together for a single vote. Due to their large size and scope of multiple subjects, many congresspeople do not have enough time to read and understand the bill. In modern politics, this creates what is known as "pork," unrelated and sometimes controversial spending that gets attached to bills that will quickly pass. For example, many criticized elements within the various stimulus package deals during the coronavirus pandemic as senators filled omnibus bills with unrelated spending.

8.6 How Congress is Challenged and How Congresspeople Represent Voters

Modern Congress is shaped and constrained by the Constitution, the precedence set over hundreds of years, and present-day political realities.

First, in that list, the Constitution contains the foundation for Congress, both its powers and limitations. The founding fathers shaped the legislative branch's structure after the Constitution's predecessor, the Articles of Confederation, left the then unicameral legislature with some shortcomings. As it lacked power and was challenging to have all the relevant members meet with an impending war with Britain looming, the Founding Fathers saw it necessary to change Congress while submitting it to a system of checks and balances.

While the Constitution set the Congress foundations, the political body has gone through many changes since its inception. As the country has expanded, so has

---

[96] On pieces of noncontroversial legislation, Senate leaders and representatives might use one of two informal processes called clearance and hotlining to determine the feasibility of expeditious or immediate consideration of a measure. The process of passing noncontroversial measures may include bypassing a Senate committee or truncating committee action, even though a committee might well have played a key role in the development of the measure sought to be passed or in the measure's clearance. For more information, see Koempel, Michael L. "Bypassing Senate Committees: Rule XIV and Unanimous Consent." *Congressional Research Service*, fas.org/sgp/crs/misc/RS22299.pdf.

Congress, making the balance of power between big and small states all the more delicate to balance. The country's demographics have changed immensely since the Constitution called for proportional representation in the House of Representatives; one should before calculate by counting each slave as three-fifths of a person for population counts.

This situation leads to the modern political constraints that Congress has. The body is supposed to represent everyone in the country. With diverging political interests and growing corporate power, Congress members are beholden to a wide variety of political groups.

As a rule of thumb, Congress has to answer three constituencies: the voters who elected them, the nation, and their party. In Congress, the people who elect congress-people all reside in the same state. These politicians are supposed to focus on the *representation* of this group mainly. This political representation means a congressperson has to look out for the constituents' interests in their state or district. Each state is divided into *congressional districts* by their state legislatures. Each member of the House of Representatives represents one of these congressional districts.

In modern politics, congresspeople attempt to represent their constituents in several ways. The first form is *policy representation*, the passing policy that will benefit the people's interests in their constituency. A particular policy proposal may be prevalent in a congressperson's constituency, and voting for its passage is a form of political representation. Secondly, members of Congress often represent their district or constituency by *allocative representation*. These conditions work by a congressperson securing funds for allocating to their district or state that will materially benefit their voters. In section 11.5, "pork" is mentioned, and this is one of the most prominent forms of allocative representation. This obligation also works through *earmarks*, providing taxpayer dollars to projects related to a specific district. Congresspeople also represent their constituents by doing *casework* and solving problems faced by people living in their district and through *symbolic representation*, representing the district and its people at public events.

Congress also passes legislation that impacts the nation as a whole. By the process of *national lawmaking*, Congress passes legislation meant to benefit the entire country. However, it is often perceived as real contractions between the national interest and a congressperson's district or state's interests. Nationally popular legislation can be hamstrung by individual congress people's decision to vote against the popular will in favor of constituents in their district. The tension between national and local interests is inherent in Congress's structure. In case a congressperson does not represent their constituents' interests, they enjoy an *incumbency advantage*. The sitting congressperson is more likely to be elected under these conditions.

Senators and representatives are also beholden to their political parties. Many United States Founding Fathers opposed political parties at the outset of the nation, and President George Washington did not belong to a party. The Constitution does not mention political parties at all. In the Federalist Papers, Founding Fathers James Madison and Alexander Hamilton wrote about the dangers they perceived in political parties. Nevertheless, the pipedream of non-partisan politics quickly dissipated, and parties formed on Federalist and Anti-Federalist lines. While the American political party system has been through multiple iterations, a two-party system has reigned after Washington's presidency.

While the Founding Fathers were concerned about political parties, Congress was established without considering the implications of a two-party partisan system. Throughout the history of Congress and the United States, there have been ebbs and flows in *partisanship*. If a politician is notably partisan, they will fall in line with the direction of his party. If political parties differ on significant, key issues, *political polarization* leads to high levels of partisanship. They perceived that the public's increasing polarization levels were also prevalent within the political parties and Congress. In *hyper-partisanship times*, party members stick strictly to their party line, leading to a *gridlock* in the legislative branch. If there is a divided legislative branch, where each party controls one chamber, and parties have high partisanship and polarization levels, legislators can pass very scarce meaningful legislation through Congress.

The Pew Research Center found in 2014 that Democrat and Republican voters had become significantly more polarized in previous decades.[97] Beginning in the 1980s and escalating since then, the Democratic and Republican parties began to polarize in Congress. The moderate members in each party started diminished, while more ideologically motivated candidates began to win election to the House and later the Senate. Consequently, the Democrats in Congress generally turned more liberal, and the Republicans became more conservative than before. The moderates from each party, who had earlier been able to work together, were politically edged out. It became more likely that the party opposite the President in Congress might be more willing to question his initiatives, whereas, in the past, it was uncommon for the opposition party to publicly stand against the United States president in foreign policy affairs.

If the legislative branch is divided or the President is from a different party than both chambers, Congress often has to rely more on *bipartisanship* to pass legislation.

---

[97] *See* Pew Research Center, for an insightful analysis of this trend. Republicans and Democrats seem to be more divided along ideological lines, and partisan antipathy is deeper and more extensive than at any point in the last two decades. Political Polarization in the American Public. Pew Research Center, 12 June 2014, www.pewresearch.org/politics/2014/06/12/political-polarization-in-the-american-public/

The two parties often work together to craft legislation and compromise on issues. However, bipartisanship does not solve all the tension and constraints within Congress. Local versus national interests still would play a significant role. All in all, the different levels of representation and how Congress is organized play crucial constraints on Congress's ability to pass sweeping legislation.

8.7 Elections

To sit in Congress, almost every member has to run for election and beat his opponent. The Seventeenth Amendment outlines how representatives should fill a vacancy caused by death, resignation, or removal from office should. In the House, a special election always has to be held when a vacancy occurs. However, the Constitution leaves vacancies in the Senate to state legislatures, so some states' governors are required to appoint someone to fill a Senate vacancy rather than hold a special election.

Other than the difference when a vacancy occurs, Senate and House elections also have other distinctions. Senate elections are more straightforward as every state receives two senators, and these borders do not change. Every six years, a senate seat is up for election, so a sitting senator or a challenger has plenty of time to prepare for an election. In the House, they regularly redraw districts to reflect demographic changes as each district has to have about the same number of residents living in the area. Representatives are also up for reelection every two years, so they often have to campaign and raise money more regularly.

One of the most critical determinants of House elections is how districts are drawn and redrawn. The districts are drawn based on preset rules and political lines. Districts are drawn based on United States Census results held every ten years, mandated by Article I, Section 2, of the United States Constitution. The Constitution sets out that Congress members will use this data every ten years to finalize *congressional apportionment*, dividing up to the now 435 seats in the House.

The number of representatives may fluctuate based on state population. For the 2016 and 2020 presidential elections, there were 538 electors in the Electoral College, and a majority of 270 electoral votes were needed to win the presidency. Once the President of the Senate has read the electoral votes during a special joint session of Congress in January, the presidential candidate who received the majority of electoral votes is officially named President of the United States.

While the Census might seem apolitical, it often becomes a politicized and controversial topic. If someone does not return their census form, he will not be counted. Republicans have long attempted to exclude undocumented immigrants from the

Census,[98] and President Donald Trump pushed hard to include a citizenship question on the 2020 Census. The Democratic Party has pushed statistical estimation to represent better who lives in each district, including undocumented immigrants, which would theoretically benefit the Democrats. If a state increases its population relative to other states, it will increase its share of seats in the House and political power.

There are other manners in which the two parties attempt to tip the congressional district system in their favor. *Redistricting* is one of the most politicized ways that the House's make-up is determined, which is the process of redrawing congressional district lines based on the Census results so that all districts remain about equal in population. Every ten years, the state legislature has the final say on how they will redraw districts, and in the end, the majority party in the state legislature has the most significant say. This provision makes state legislatures quite influential in determining the look of Congress. These districts are subject to *gerrymandering*, a highly politicized process that redistricts the congressional lines to benefit one party over another. This situation leads to bizarre congressional districts drawn to include voting populations that the majority party in the state legislature believes will benefit their party. The name gerrymandering originates from Massachusetts Governor Elbridge Gerry, who redrew a district in 1812 to resemble a salamander.

Historically, *gerrymandering* has been used in the United States to change districts' racial composition to marginalize racial minorities. This process of racial gerrymandering was made illegal in the Voting Rights Act of 1965. However, the Supreme Court had to intervene in several cases in the 1990s to overturn *redistricting* and drawing on racial lines. Now districts are often redrawn to benefit one party, known as partisan gerrymandering. Some have argued that this is an extension of racial gerrymandering and still marginalizes racial minorities and other groups. The Supreme Court has ruled that this type of gerrymandering is a political question with a 5-4 ruling on a conservative-liberal line.

8.8 Does Congress Look Like and Represent America?

While anyone over a certain age and a United States citizen can run for Congress, there are high barriers to running and winning a successful campaign. In 2016, the average winning Senate campaign spent $10.4 million, and the average winning House

---

[98] One should also consider that, weeks before the 1980 census formally began, the Federation for American Immigration Reform launched its campaign to exclude unauthorized immigrants from population counts, See Lo Wang, Hansi. "Immigration Hard-Liner Files Reveal 40-Year Bid Behind Trump's Census Obsession." *National Public Radio*, 15 Feb. 2021, www.npr.org/2021/02/15/967783477/immigration-hard-liner-files-reveal-40-year-bid-behind-trumps-census-obsession.

campaign spent $1.3 million.[99] While this money often does not come from the candidate's wealth, it often means a politician has to appeal to monied interests, including either the Republican or Democratic Party, to have political success. Although about 40% of Americans identify as political independents100, there is very little room for citizens who do not want to run in either party to succeed at the national level.

Outside of money spent on a political campaign, other factors determine who runs and wins Congress seats. As mentioned in section 11.6, incumbents have typically enjoyed an advantage electorally. Thus *open seats* without an incumbent are much more desirable. Congress elections also often are impacted by presidential elections to be held in the same year. Suppose a Republican wins the presidency by a large margin. In that case, Republicans running for the Senate and House may enjoy the *coattail effect*, which boosts their chances of winning thanks to a solid presidential campaign from the candidate in their party. After two years in office, the President's party quite frequently will be subject to a *midterm loss* and see their seats in Congress diminished.

And how about the representation of the American electorate? Does Congress look like the voters who elect them? Throughout history, Congress and the American government have had shallow *descriptive representation* levels, how much the legislature looks like the population. While this representation has increased since the times in which only white land-owning males in government, Congress does not have a high descriptive representation level. The 117th Congress is the most racially and ethnically diverse in history, but it is still 77% white[101], which is a percentage significantly higher than that of the general population (60% white). Furthermore, only a handful of congresspeople are not college graduates, despite only 22.5% of Americans above 25 finishing four years of college.[102] Congress is also significantly wealthier than the general population, and only 3% of congresspeople are immigrants despite the United States having the highest immigrant population in the world at 47 million people.

---

[99] For more information on current spending by campaigns in the United States, see Kim, Soo Rin. "The Price of Winning Just Got Higher, Especially in the Senate." *OpenSecrets*, 9 Nov. 2016, www.opensecrets.org/news/2016/11/the-price-of-winning-just-got-higher-especially-in-the-senate/.

[100] Significantly more U.S. adults continued to identify as political independents (42%) in 2018 than as either Democrats (30%) or Republicans (26%). See Jones, Jeffrey M. "Americans Continue to Embrace Political Independence." *Gallup*, 7 Jan. 2019, news.gallup.com/poll/245801/americans-continue-embrace-political-independence.aspx.

[101] Among today's United States senators and representatives, the overwhelming majority of racial and ethnic minority members are Democrats (83%), while 17% are Republicans. See Schaeffer, Katherine. "Racial, Ethnic Diversity Increases Yet Again with the 117th Congress." Pew Research Center, 28 Jan. 2021, www.pewresearch.org/fact-tank/2021/01/28/racial-ethnic-diversity-increases-yet-again-with-the-117th-congress/. .

[102] See the official release of the US Census for more information Bureau, US Census. "U.S. Census Bureau Releases New Educational Attainment Data." The United States Census Bureau, 30 Mar. 2020, www.census.gov/newsroom/press-releases/2020/educational-attainment.html#:~:text=In%202019%2C%20high%20school%20was,from%2029.9%25%20to%2036.0%25 .

Chapter 8: The Legislative Branch

1) A congressional caucus regularly convenes to discuss common interests and consists of which of the following?

   a. House members

   b. Senate members

   c. both House and Senate members

   d. only House leadership

2) All of the following congressional powers could be found in article 1, section 8, except

   a. legal.

   b. financial.

   c. administrative.

   d. national defense.

3) A president needs congressional cooperation primarily to

   a. advance executive policies.

   b. debate public policy.

   c. use the veto process.

   d. limit executive decision-making.

4) A filibuster is a power unique to the

   a. House.

   b. Senate.

   c. House and Senate.

   d. president.

5) A filibuster can only be stopped by a process called

   a. logrolling.

   b. franking.

   c. cloture.

   d. pork-barreling.

6) Congress went from most powerful to increasingly deferential to the White House in the

   a. middle of the twentieth century

   b. early twentieth century

   c. late twentieth century

   d. twenty-first century

7) Today, diversity is more represented in

   a. the House and Senate.

   b. the House.

   c. the Senate.

   d. none of the above

8) A Congress member who cannot promote significant reform would most likely be referred to as a

   a. bass.

   b. minnow.

   c. darter.

   d. none of the above

9) What crime can the House impeach the president for

   a. theft

   b. perjury

   c. high crimes and misdemeanors

   d. murder

10) After the president is impeached the president the trial is held in the

   a. White House

   b. Senate

   c. Supreme Court

   d. House of Representatives

11) A central function of the Speaker of the House is to

   a. settle all debates.

   b. lead the majority party.

c. compromise on key issues.

d. make sure all proposed legislation goes to the president.

12) The second in command in the House is known as the

a. minority leader.

b. majority leader.

c. majority whip.

d. minority whip.

13) Party discipline would most likely be achieved by

a. the Speaker of the House.

b. the majority leader.

c. the majority party whip.

d. the minority leader.

14) The Senate position with the longest experience is known as

a. the vice president.

b. the president pro tempore.

c. the majority leader.

d. the minority leader.

15) The only person who can break a tie in the Senate is the

a. vice president.

b. president pro tempore.

c. minority leader.

d. whip.

16) The greatest concern about the proposed legislation is that

a. it will pass.

b. it will die in a committee.

c. it will develop into an entirely different piece of legislation.

d. it will not be debated.

17) The _____committee is a permanent committee in Congress.

a. select

b. standing

c. conference

d. social

18) Special committees are often referred to as _____ committees.

a. select

b. standing

c. investigative

d. social

19) True or False: The two most important functions of Congress are representation and lawmaking.

20) True or False: The founders created the congressional decision-making process to be fast.

21) True or False: Congressional oversight refers to a congressional committee's monitoring of the executive branch and government agencies to ensure they are acting as Congress intends.

22) True or False: The Senate checks the executive branch through the approval of appointments to the Supreme Court.

23) True or False: The job of confirming presidential appointments belongs to the judiciary.

24) True or False: The reallocation of congressional seats among the states every ten years, following the census, is known as gerrymandering.

25) True or False: The number of representatives with voting privileges in the House of Representatives is currently set at 435 members.

26) True or False: After the census every ten years, House seats are reapportioned among the states to ensure that districts maintain population equality.

27) True or False: The process of redrawing congressional districts to match population shifts in states with more than one representative is called reapportionment.

28) True or False: Redrawing congressional district boundaries to favor a particular group or party is known as gerrymandering.

Discussion Questions

1) What would James Madison say? Develop a comparative perspective about James Madison and how he would view Congress today.

2) What are the central roles of Congress?

3) How do the terms constituents and incumbents relate to congressional power?

4) Is dividing a government a good or bad thing? How can this problem be fixed? What happens when all three branches are controlled by the same party (think FDR)?

Video Resources

Understanding Government: The Legislative Branch (2004)

Cerebellum Corporation

Ken Burns' America: "The Congress" (2004) PBS

Mr. Smith Goes to Washington (1939) Columbia Pictures

How is Congress Doing? Evaluating the Legislative Branch http://bipartisanpolicy. org/event/how-is-congress-doing-evaluating-the-legislative-branch/

Establishment of the Legislative Branch www.c-span.org/video/?295511-1/establishment-legislative-branch

Role and Responsibilities of Legislative Branch www.c-span.org/video/?170130-2/ role-responsibilities-legislative-branch&event=170130&playEvent

Website Resources

Congress.org http://www.congress.org/congressorg/directory/congdir.tt

Real Clear Politics http://www.realclearpolitics.com/welcomead/?ref=http://www. realclearpolitics.com/

270 to Win http://www.270towin.com/

OpenSecrets.org http://www.opensecrets.org/

Government Resources: Legislative Branch Resources - Morningside University http:// morningside.libguides.com/government/legislative

Federal Government Resources Research Guide: Legislative Branch - Rutgers Law School http://libguides.law.rutgers.edu/federal-government-resources/legislative-branch-resources

The Legislative Branch iCivics www.icivics.org/curriculum/legislative-branch

CHAPTER 9

THE EXECUTIVE BRANCH

9.1 Introduction to the Executive Branch

What is an executive, anyway? By definition, the **Executive** is one who has the power to carry out plans, strategies or laws. In some countries around the world, the chief executive is a prime minister. The United States does not have a prime minister, and instead the United States chief executive is a **president**. The executive branch is led by the President who is the leader of the entire federal bureaucracy system. The **Federal bureaucracy** is the vast network of departments, agencies, boards, and commissions that constitute the Federal government. In the United States, these agencies include the FBI, CIA, EPA, and so forth. The president is only the head of the federal bureaucracy and not the legislative branch of government, unlike a prime minister who typically has more control over legislation. The executive branch in the United States is tasked with carrying out and enforcing the law as stipulated in the Constitution. In addition to the President, the Vice President and the Cabinet are tasked with aiding the President.

9.2 The Job of the American President

The American President has specific job descriptions and powers and authority that are granted to the office. The key elements of the President's job description are codified in the Constitution and have been granted to the office through Congress and the Courts. The United States Constitution originally limited the power of the Executive Branch, but throughout the history of the American presidency, the power of the President has been significantly expanded. Yet still, the Constitution gives the president less power than many other chief executives around the world. One of the president's most important powers is executive privilege. **Executive privilege** allows the president to keep certain documents that concern the executive branch or national security confidential.

According to the Constitution, the president must meet certain requirements and conditions in order to serve. The Constitution also lists several restrictions upon the office. The President of the United States must be:

- At least 35 years old
- A natural-born citizen of the United States
- A United States resident for at least 14 years
- Chosen by the Electoral College to serve a four-year term
- Succeeded in the event of death or incapacity by the vice president, elected at the same time
- Removed from office only for "high crimes and misdemeanors" by the House and the Senate
- Unable to receive "emoluments" (that is, profit beyond their normal salary) from the country or any of the states

The job of the American president has been significantly modified through the years despite the formal powers granted by the Constitution remaining the same. Several amendments have modified presidential power and each of these amendments to the constitution have addressed changes in society.

The different amendments of the constitution have contributed to defining the roles of the Presidency. The most important amendments to the office of the president have been the Twelfth, Twentieth, Twenty-Second, and Twenty-Fifth Amendments.

When the Twelfth Amendment was passed, it limited and changed how the President and Vice President were elected by the Electoral College. During the first years of our nation, the two candidates who received the most votes in the Electoral College would serve as President and Vice-President. The Twelfth Amendment states that the President and Vice President would be voted in distinct ballots rather than the second-place in the Electoral College presidential election being selected as the Vice President. The change was made to limit the chance of a President and Vice President being elected from different parties. Additionally, under this amendment, the President and Vice President are not allowed to be residents in the same state. In 2000, the Twelfth Amendment became a point of contention in the election of President Bush and Vice President Cheney. Bush was the Governor of Texas and Cheney had lived in Texas for five years while maintaining a residence in Wyoming[103].

---

[103] Maravilla, Christopher Scott. "That Dog Don't Hunt: The Twelfth Amendment after Jones v. Bush." *Pace Law Review*, vol. 23, no. 1, 2002, pp. 214–270.

The Twentieth Amendment set the official start and end date for a term in office for the President, Vice President, Senate, and House of Representatives. After the amendment, the President and Vice President's term begins and ends on January 20 at noon. Newly elected Senators and Representatives begin their term on January 3, which gives the incoming Congress the power to break a deadlock in the event of a tie in the Electoral College, rather than the outgoing Congress. This section of the amendment served to limit the "lame duck" session, or the time in between presidential terms. It also set out that the vice president takes over if the president dies before taking the oath.

In an effort to limit the power of a popular politician, Congress approved the Twenty-Second Amendment to create term-limits for the President. The amendment was a direct response to President Franklin Delano Roosevelt who served four terms and enjoyed high levels of popularity leading the country out of the Great Depression and through World War II. The Twenty-Second Amendment implemented a two-term limit for any president. Roosevelt is the only American president to serve more than two terms after President George Washington established a two-term norm as the first President of the country.

The impeachment process to remove the President or Vice President from office is mostly laid out in Articles I and II of the Constitution. But, the Twenty-Fifth Amendment created a mechanism for the president to be removed without impeachment. The vice president and a majority of the cabinet or the Congress can remove a president if they determine the president is unable to perform their job. Near the tail end of President Donald Trump's first term in office, several Democratic Representatives called on Vice President Mike Pence to invoke the Twenty-Fifth Amendment to remove Trump from office[104]. The amendment also outlines presidential succession stating "In case of the removal of the President from office or of his death or resignation, the Vice President shall become President."

9.3 The Presidential Job.

The Presidential Succession Act of 1947 delineates additional detail on who does the president's job when he cannot, and it fundamentally changed the Presidential Succession Act of 1886. In the wake of President Roosevelt's death in office in 1945, his successor President Harry Truman sought to change the line of presidential succession. Under this act, the Speaker of the House and the president pro tempore of the Senate

---

[104] Cicilline, David N. *Cicilline, Lieu Lead Judiciary Committee Dems Urging Pence to Invoke 25th Amendment.* cicilline.house.gov/press-release/cicilline-lieu-lead-judiciary-committee-dems-urging-pence-invoke-25th-amendment.

were made third and fourth in line for the Presidency, respectively, after the Vice President. The new act changed succession and moved members of the President's cabinet further down the line of succession, thus not allowing a President to appoint their own line of succession.

In order to govern and lead the country, the president relies on their **cabinet,** an advisory group to the President composed primarily of the heads of the major departments of the federal bureaucracy and the vice president. Each cabinet member carries out elements of the President's agenda. The President's cabinet has 23 members including the vice president, 15 department heads including the Attorney General, Secretaries of State, Treasury, and Defense, and seven other cabinet level members. The Cabinet does not possess any collective executive power, and they have to be submitted to the Senate for approval by a simple majority. While the Cabinet-level positions need to be approved by the Senate, the president can remove Cabinet members at their discretion.

So as no single entity or branch gets too much power, the executive branch exists in a system of checks and balances, and the role of the executive is to make sure that Congress and the Judicial Branch do not usurp more power over other branches of government. In theory, the president has been given just enough legislative and judicial power to hold the other branches in check. While the system is built on checks and balances, the president is the leader of the county and serves as both the head of state and head of government.

In countries with two separate heads of state and government, the **head of state** is a largely ceremonial, apolitical role that rallies the country together. This can be done through the moral or historical influence of the office. The **head of government** is a partisan role, as in the United States, the President serves as the head of the president's political party. Each president utilizes this role differently. A president's talents might suit them better for one or the other of these tasks, for example President George Washington is considered by many to be a great statesman. America, unlike some other countries, has one person, the President, do both jobs.

The Constitution gives the president a limited number of powers, and they are all in Article II, but it grants the president three main executive powers. The president is the chief executive, the commander in chief, and the chief foreign policy maker. As the **Chief executive**, the president is head bureaucrat, making sure the laws are enforced. One of the president's most important powers in this role is **appointment power**. The President has the power to nominate ambassadors to foreign countries, public Ministers, Supreme Court Judges, and various other bureaucrats. As a check on the President's power, some of these nominations have to be approved by the Senate, for example Supreme Court Justices.

The president also serves in the position of commander in chief. In the United States, the **commander in chief** is the civilian head of the armed forces of the United States. The President's exact powers within this role have been hotly contested throughout American history. The President is the commander in chief, but they are not legally allowed to declare war on another country without the approval of Congress. So, the President cannot unilaterally declare war, but if Congress approves a war resolution, the President is considered the head of the operation.

The president is also the **chief foreign policy maker**. As the chief foreign policy maker, the president negotiates treaties with the approval of two-thirds of the Senate. The president also receives ambassadors and represents the United States on the global stage. While Article II of the Constitution grants the president only the limited power to receive foreign ambassadors, this clause is cited to justify the president's powerful and much broader role in foreign affairs.

The president also has a unique power afforded to the office to issue executive agreements. An **executive agreement** is an agreement issued by the president with other countries that enter the countries into binding international obligations. These executive agreements describe how the president will abide by an agreement and can terminate with a new president. An executive agreement is not a treaty, and it is often implemented to circumvent other country's laws regarding the signing of a treaty.

While the president's main responsibilities are related to the office's executive power, the president also has powers of legislative authority. These legislative powers are part of the checks and balances built into the American system. Every year, the president offers **the State of the Union address**. The Constitution says that the president will regularly inform Congress of the state of the union and recommend the measures he considers useful or necessary. While it is not constitutionally required to be a speech, President Woodrow Wilson began the tradition in 193 of addressing Congress and the American people in an annual address.

One of the President's most well-known powers over legislation is the veto. The **Presidential veto** in the Constitution gives the president the option of refusing to sign a bill that Congress has passed. This is a power given to the executive branch in line with the model of checks and balances. There are two types of veto, a direct veto when the President formally sends back the bill with objections, and a pocket veto where the President simply allows the 10-day review period to elapse, leaving the space for the President's signature blank. While the presidential veto is powerful, it can be overridden by Congress. Two-thirds of the Senate and House are required to overturn a presidential veto. Only 4% of all presidential vetoes have been overturned.

Congress has the legislative power to write and pass laws, but when a president wants to create policy that is not passed as law, the president can issue an executive order. An **executive order** is what presidents can issue to fill in details and enforce the laws passed by Congress. These powers direct the federal bureaucracy to act in a particular way. Executive orders can be overturned by the Judicial branch if they are found to be unconstitutional. Executive orders can also be cancelled or revoked by the President, so when a new President is elected, they often review the executive orders of their predecessor. While executive orders are not mentioned in the Constitution, they have become an integral part of a president's power. Before 1900, executive orders were informal and often not made public, nonetheless nearly every president has made some kind of declaration that can be considered an executive order. Modern presidents have issued many more executive orders than their predecessors. Three presidents, Theodore Roosevelt, Calvin Coolidge, and Franklin Delano Roosevelt, issued over 1,000 executive orders during their time in office. More recent presidents have often issued several hundred executive orders.

The president has strong powers of judicial appointment. With **appointment power**, the president can appoint judges, with the advice and consent of the Senate, to the entire federal judiciary. Some of the judicial posts that the president can appoint include the solicitor general, Supreme Court justices, courts of appeals judges, and district court judges. **The solicitor general** is the legal officer who argues cases before the Supreme Court when the United States is a party to that case, as it often is. The president also has removal power. While not in the Constitution, the Supreme Court has ruled in several cases that the president has the sole power to remove some federal appointees. The most important case was *Myers v. United States* in 1926 in which the Supreme Court ruled the president has sole removal authority of federal appointees, except for federal judge appointments.[105]

The president also has the power of the pardon. **The pardon power** of the president means the president can pardon those accused or convicted of federal crimes. The Constitution grants the president the power to pardon. In recent years, many presidents have issued pardons near the end of their terms, and these pardons have caused a great deal of controversy.

9.4 How the American Presidency has changed

The job of the president has become more involved as America itself has become larger and more complex. Citizens' expectations of the presidency have grown over time,

---

[105] Supreme Court of the United States. *Myers v. United States*. Oyez, www.oyez.org/cases/1900-1940/272us52.

but the job's formal powers outlined in Article II of the Constitution have not. The Twenty-Second Amendment is the only constitutional change to affect presidential powers, and it limited them by imposing term limits. The founders envisioned a presidency with limited powers; however, many Presidents have expanded the office's informal powers and the formal powers have been broadly interpreted to increase presidential power. And through this process, the presidency has shifted from a traditional presidency to a modern presidency. The **traditional presidency** was a presidency consistent with the founders' intentions of a president with the limited powers set out by the constitution as the groundwork for the powers of the president. There are 19 powers given to the national government from the constitution, and these powers are known as **delegated powers**. The delegated powers are the explicit forms of power given by the constitution to the federal government. In Article I, Section 8, the itemization of powers to the United States Congress includes functions such as commerce, taxation, and declaration of war. In Article II, Section II, the president is delegated powers including those noted previously (Commander in Chief powers, pardon powers, treaty-making powers, etc.).

The presidency also has inherent powers that have built up over time. **Inherent powers** are powers that were not explicitly laid out but rather were implied in their constitutional duty to take care that the laws be faithfully executed. The inherent powers are given to the federal government so that they can operate the federal bureaucracy systems and government according to new laws that have been passed. Examples of inherent powers given to the federal government include the federal government's oversight of food production and the environment in the form of the FDA and the EPA. The government can use their powers to revise warnings and lists to the American citizens regarding food poisoning health matters and environmental impact issues. There are other certain powers not given to the federal government that were thus reserved for the states by the Tenth Amendment.

These powers not explicitly given to the presidency in the constitution are therefore retained for the individual states. These **reserved Powers** are powers listed in the Tenth amendment to the constitution, and it says that the states retained government authority not explicitly granted to the national government. Some of these reserved state powers include public education, public health, commerce within the state, organizing state elections, prisons and police, other issues regarding arrests and incarcerations, highway and road maintenance, and many more. When the constitution allows for powers to be shared between the national and state governments, these powers are known as **concurrent powers.** A concurrent power is known as the power shared by the national government and the state government such as taxation, and the minimum wage.

The executive branch changed significantly and became much more powerful with President Franklin Delano Roosevelt's New Deal. The limited vision of the executive changed with the stock market crash of 1929 and subsequent economic collapse known as the Great Depression. President Roosevelt's New Deal created a variety of jobs programs and turned the government into a much larger employer to help people out of the Great Depression and build the country's infrastructure. The **wide-reaching** social program built infrastructure, public works, and art, created social insurance programs like Social Security to ensure that a safety net existed for the elderly, disabled, and orphaned, and it reformed the financial system to prevent another repeat depression in the future. The New Deal also signaled the birth of the **modern presidency**, and with this the modern presidency grew the role of the president as compared to the traditional presidency.

After the growth of the modern presidency with FDR, the government grew at all levels. Though presidential candidates started promising to do more and more, the formal powers of the office as outlined in the Constitution stayed the same. The presidency had to find ways to expand its power and influence through more informal channels. It did this through the **power to persuade** and convince Congress to support the executive office plans. This could be done by going directly to the people, known as **going public.** The president's increasing capacity to talk to citizens through the media made this method particularly successful. FDR began having "fireside chats" to talk to the American people informally and discuss the state of the nation.

9.5 Presidents, Popularity, and Congress

To be effective, presidents need to have some level of popularity with the public. This is a minimum requirement to be elected; but it may not be sufficient to make a successful presidency. What factors make a president popular? The president often suffers from steadily declining popularity after an initial peak when they take office. Almost all presidents go through a period called the Honeymoon period. This **Honeymoon period** is the first 100 days of a presidency, when the press is likely to be most kind and the majority of the public is giving the new president the benefit of the doubt. Not all presidents do enjoy a honeymoon. Factors like the state of the economy and external events like wars and natural disasters can influence how popular a president is.

A president's popularity is often split between political parties, with the president enjoying the most popularity within their own party. Due to the **polarization** within American politics, the president's approval is often tied in with how popular their political party is at the moment. This limits how the president can cooperate effectively with Congress, and it can help or hinder how real legislative change occurs because these changes require congressional cooperation. If there is a majority in at least one house that is different from the president's party, then the current government is known as a **divided government** and the power of the president can be significantly hindered. In many divided governments, Congress chooses not to work with the president or the president's legislative liaison. The **congressional liaison** is a presidential appointee whose chief job is to coordinate with Congress on behalf of the president to find points of potential agreement and create a legislative agenda.

Chapter 9: The Executive Branch

1) The branch of the federal government that has changed the most is the

   a. Executive

   b. Legislative

   c. Judicial

   d. all are about the same

2) Presidential power is vaguely defined in

   a. Article 1 of the Constitution

   b. Article 2 of the Constitution

   c. Article 3 of the Constitution

   d. Article 4 of the Constitution

3) Originally, the president would serve a four-year term, which could be renewed

   a. indefinitely.

   b. two times.

   c. three times.

   d. four times.

4) The only president who has served more than two terms was

   a. Ronald Reagan.

   b. James Madison.

   c. Franklin Roosevelt.

   d. Thomas Jefferson.

5) Which amendment bars a president from serving a third term?

   a. the Twenty-second

   b. the Twenty-third

   c. the Twenty-fourth

   d. the Nineteenth

6) The agreed-on way to elect the president is

   a. by Congress.

   b. through the Electoral College.

   c. by the courts.

   d. by the political parties.

7) In the Electoral College, each state's number of votes is _____ its congressional delegation.

   a. greater than

   b. less than

   c. equal to

   d. significantly less than

8) Who determines how electors to the Electoral College are chosen?

   a. states

   b. Congress

   c. President

   d. Political Parties

9) In order to win the presidency, one must win

   a. the Electoral College and popular vote.

   b. the popular vote.

   c. the Electoral College.

   d. a simple plurality in the Electoral College.

10) Executive expressed powers include all of the following except

   a. commander in chief.

   b. power to declare war.

   c. power to make treaties.

   d. power to grant pardons.

11) Treaty ratification can only occur with

   a. House approval.

   b. judicial approval.

   c. Senate approval.

   d. bureaucratic approval.

12) Senatorial approval of a treaty requires

    a. one-third support

    b. two-thirds support

    c. three-quarters support

    d. unanimous support

13) The idea that the executive branch can issue a rule on congressional legislation is known as

    a. proscribed powers.

    b. legislative power.

    c. delegated powers.

    d. enumerated powers.

14) The three forms of presidential powers are

    a. expressed, reserved, and formal.

    b. expressed, delegated, and reserved.

    c. expressed, delegated, and inherent.

    d. inherent, reserved, and delegated.

15) Powers vaguely reflected in Article 2 of the Constitution are known as

    a. reserved powers.

    b. expressed powers.

    c. inherent powers.

    d. de facto powers.

16) Holding enemy combatants without a hearing can be traced to which executive power?

    a. reserved

    b. inherent

    c. delegated

    d. expressed

17) The _____ can determine whether the president exceeded the scope of inherent powers.

    a. Supreme Court

    b. House

c. Senate

d. Bureaucracy

18) Many parliamentary systems grant their executives which of the following?

a. right to use emergency powers

b. right to use partial line-item vetoes

c. right to introduce budgets

d. all of the above

19) Presidents are elected _____ via the Electoral College.

a. indirectly

b. directly

c. by plurality

d. by national popular vote

20) Executive power generally _____during crises.

a. diminishes

b. expands

c. stays the same

d. completely changes

21) The Alien and Sedition Acts can be traced to which presidency?

a. John Adams

b. George Washington

c. Thomas Jefferson

d. James Madison

22) The Alien and Sedition Acts were considered controversial because they punished false and scandalous speech, but they also could be viewed as an attack on which amendment?

a. First

b. Second

c. Third

d. Fourth

23) The idea that no other branch can check the president is known as the

    a. supremacy theory.

    b. unitary executive theory.

    c. imperial theory.

    d. take care clause.

24) The idea that the president could demand swift and even secretive action is supported by

    a. unitary executive theory.

    b. legislative theory.

    c. inherent theory.

    d. pluralist theory.

25) The unitary executive theory can be viewed as

    a. a threat to the system of checks and balances.

    b. an important way to change governmental roles.

    c. a way for the president to serve more than two terms.

    d. a way for Congress to override the president.

26) The idea that an executive could possibly change a republic into an empire is directly related to which of the following theories?

    a. legislative

    b. imperial

    c. pluralist

    d. majoritarian

27) Presidents are highly vulnerable in relation to

    a. foreign affairs.

    b. domestic issues.

    c. legislative issues.

    d. judicial issues.

28) The president presides over the world's largest fighting force and is otherwise known as the

    a. commander in chief.

    b. chief legislator.

c. chief diplomat.

d. chief executive.

29) Free trade agreements, global warming concerns, and the Middle East concerns all require the use of

a. force.

b. economic sanctions.

c. diplomacy.

d. boycotts.

30) The president can act as a _____and recommend and veto measures from Congress.

a. chief legislator

b. chief diplomat

c. chief custodian

d. commander in chief

31) Prior to World War II, what type of standing army did the United States have?

a. large

b. small

c. strong

d. weak

32) After World War II, what type of standing army did the United States have?

a. small

b. large

c. weak

d. all-male

33) An annual event where the president addresses the nation is called

a. the annual talk.

b. the State of the Union address.

c. the Executive Talk.

d. the State of Affairs Talk.

34) Which of the following can formally propose a law?

   a. President

   b. Congress

   c. the Supreme Court

   d. both a and b

35) _____ is the presidential power to block an act of Congress by refusing to sign it.

   a. Executive power

   b. Legislative power

   c. Veto power

   d. Take care clause power

Discussion Questions

1) What is the difference between a leader and a manager, and how does that relate to the modern presidency?

2) Has presidential power gone too far in the fight against terrorism?

3) Will there be a female president in the next 10–20 years, and why?

4) Should the term natural-born citizen be removed as a requirement to run for the presidency?

Video Resources

American Presidents (2005) History Channel

American Presidents (2012) Cerebellum Corporation

American Presidents (2012) Software Lab

Role and Responsibilities of Executive Branch www.c-span.org/video/?170130-1/role-responsibilities-executive-branch&event=170130&playEvent

Scholar Exchange: The Presidency and the Executive Branch With Holly Frey - Constitution Center http://constitutioncenter.org/interactive-constitution/educational-video/scholar-exchange-the-presidency-and-the-executive-branch-with-holly-frey

H.R. 1: Strengthening Ethics Rules for the Executive Branch http://oversight.house.gov/legislation/hearings/hr-1-strengthening-ethics-rules-for-the-executive-branch

Website Resources

The White House http://whitehouse.gov and http://www.whitehouse.gov/about/presidents

National Archives Executive Orders http://www.archives.gov/federal-register/executive-orders

National Archives Executive Orders Disposition Tables Index http://www.archives.gov/federal-register/executive-orders/disposition.html

Maps of War http://www.mapsofwar.com/

CHAPTER 10

THE JUDICIAL BRANCH

10.1 Introduction to the Judiciary

The judiciary is an integral part of checks and balances between different branches of government. Alexander Hamilton wrote an essay advocating for the ratification of the United States Constitution called the Federalist Paper No. 78. Here, Hamilton described what the newly created judicial branch would look like and that the judiciary would be the weakest and thus the "least dangerous branch" of government. Through time, the power of the judiciary has changed. The **judiciary** is the branch of government that interprets and applies the law and solves disputes involving citizens and other government actors.

The courts have changed in their capacity to influence both branches of government. The judiciary has become an enormously powerful branch through *the power of the pen*. The Constitution does not explicitly state that the Supreme Court may determine the constitutionality of an act of the other branches of government. However, judicial review of other branches of the federal government was established in *Marbury v. Madison* when the Court claimed this power for itself.[106] The Court held that American courts have the power to strike down laws, statutes, and some government actions that they find to violate the Constitution of the United States. *Marbury v. Madison* gave the Supreme Court (itself) the ultimate power of deciding what the Constitution means.

10. 2A Kinds of Laws

The United States is a democracy. In a democracy, laws rule. The **rule of law** is a system in which laws are known in advance, they apply the same way to everyone, and if

---

[106] *Marbury v. Madison*, 5 United States 137 (1803).

we feel they have been applied unjustly we can appeal to a higher authority. The laws we notice most limit our behavior and stop us from acting on impulses that are damaging to other people. Laws make collective life possible and even comfortable.

There are different types of laws in the United States judicial system. There are substantive laws, and these laws govern how members of a society are to behave. **Substantive laws** are a body of rules that define what we can or cannot do. When determining what a person cannot do, thereby limiting their freedom, **criminal laws** are a form of substantive law that prohibit behavior that makes collective living difficult or impossible. Engaging in a prohibited behavior is considered a crime and subject to a legal punishment. A **crime** is an action that breaks criminal law. When regulating interactions between people or organizations, it is a civil law. **Civil laws** are laws that regulate interactions between individuals or other private parties, such as a corporation. When an action between individuals causes harm against another person it is a **tort,** which is an action that violates a civil law.

Substantive laws are contrasted with procedural law, which is the set of procedures for making, administering, and enforcing substantive law. **Procedural laws** define how the laws are used, applied, and enforced. Court procedures were founded from the United States Constitution's Fifth and Fourteenth Amendment's guarantee of due process which both state no one shall be "deprived of life liberty or property without due process of law"[107]. Due process requires the government to abide by fair procedures before depriving a person of life, liberty or property.

10. 2B Forms of Law

What form do laws take? Laws originate from different places and different entities have authority to create them. The form of laws and how they are interpreted are important to the judicial system. **Constitutional laws** are established by federal and state constitutions. This body of laws establishes the legal infrastructure of our governments. Constitutions set the framework for the court systems, determine how the three branches of federal government relate to each other and shape the relationship between the federal and state governments. More notably, constitutional law determines how the game of politics is played. Much of constitutional law has grown from federal and state supreme court rulings interpreting their respective constitutions. Constitutional law, and most other court rulings, create **case law or common law** that can be binding precedent. **Precedents** are a series of court rulings of similar issues and facts. These rulings create an authority for courts to apply the same law to future cases that have similar issues or facts.

---

[107] United States Const. Amend. X and XIV.

Unlike case law that was developed by court rulings, **statutory laws** are laws that are made by legislatures. Statutory law is written law passed by a legislative body of local, state or federal government and codified in statute- which means law that is arranged and numbered into a systematic code. **Administrative law** is the body of law that governs the activities of administrative agencies of government. Executive level governmental agency action can include rule making, adjudication, or the enforcement of a specific regulatory agenda. Administrative law is considered a branch of public law. Examples of federal administrative law is the regulation of civil aviation, planes and pilots to protect public safety through the Federal Aviation Administration.

Finally, **executive orders** are rules that also have the full force and effect of law and are issued by the executive branch, such as the President of the United States or the Governor of a state. They are issued based on authority granted to the President or Governor in their respective constitutions and must be consistent with that authority.

10.3 The American Legal System

Legal systems around the world are different. The American legal systems are heavily influenced by political culture. The United States system in particular can be adversarial and is litigious in nature.

The United States system is adversarial in nature. The **adversarial system** or adversary system is a legal system used in the common law countries where two advocates represent their parties' case or position before an impartial person or group of people, usually a judge or jury, who attempt to determine the truth and pass judgment accordingly. An adversarial system is a system that is primarily concerned that the legal process will be fair, and result in a just judgment. This type of system is different from an inquisitorial system. An **inquisitorial system** is a legal system in which the court, or a part of the court, is actively involved in investigating the facts of the case. This is distinct from an adversarial system, in which the role of the court is primarily that of an impartial referee between the prosecution and the defense. An inquisitorial system is a system in which the truth is the goal and if it requires that the judge leave his or her neutral perch to ask questions and investigate, so be it.

The United States legal system is a **litigious system**. Litigation refers to the process of resolving disputes by filing or answering a complaint through the public court system. A litigious system is a system in which citizens prefer to settle their differences in court.[AM1] As discussed above, if the issue of the case is one of criminal law, the two parties will be the state and the defendant where the state is charging the defendant for violating a criminal law. If the issue of the case is based on civil law, the two parties will be private individuals alleging harm was caused to one or both parties.

10.4 The Criminal Justice System

The criminal justice system focuses on justice. Through the process of **adjudication,** the truth can be discovered, and justice served by providing a formal judgment in a disputed matter. If there has been a mistake in the trial, an **appeal** can be filed**,** which is a process brought by a petitioner if that party believes there has been a procedural error or that the judge has applied the law incorrectly.

A right given in criminal trials in the United States is a right to a jury trial. The right to a jury trial in criminal cases is found in both Article III[108] and the Sixth Amendment[109]of the Constitution. If you are accused of a serious offence that carries a potential sentence of more than six months' imprisonment, you are guaranteed a trial by a jury of your peers[5][110]. Jury duty is a collective action problem—we all want to share in the outcome, but many of us try to get out of providing the effort that makes that outcome possible.

10.5 Equality and the Criminal Justice System

One of the hallmarks of American political culture is that everyone should be treated the same. But the procedural value that everyone be treated the same is often not the way things actually work in America. The equality for all people, regardless of race, gender and class has not always existed. Even though the Constitution established the **equal protection clause** which provided in part that "[no state shall] deny any person within its jurisdiction the equal protection of the laws,"[111] the judiciary did not originally interpret this to mean equal protection for black Americans. From its beginnings, the United States has had what amounts to separate criminal justice systems for black and white Americans. America has had stronger punishments for those of color. An example of this was the case of Emmett Till. Till, a 14-year-old boy, was caught and lynched in Mississippi in 1955 for allegedly offending a white woman who later admitted she lied. The white men who killed Till were acquitted by a white jury.

The role that justice has served white and African Americans has developed inconsistently since the inception of the nation. There are dual narratives about who are the "good guys." African Americans and whites have developed very different narratives about the role the criminal justice system plays in their lives.

---

[108] United States Const. Art. III, § 2 provides "The trial of all Crimes, except in Cases of Impeachment, shall be by Jury".

[109] United States Const. Amend. XI provides "In all criminal prosecutions, the accused shall enjoy the right to a speedy and public trial, by an impartial jury."

[110] *United States v. Nachtigal*, 507 United States 1 (1993).

[111] United States Const. Amend. XIV, § 1

Racial profiling has prevented African Americans from receiving equal access to justice. **Racial profiling** is a violation of civil rights in which police target people because they fit the mental image of what a criminal looks like. Obviously, it is not possible to have a stereotype based on race, gender, or class of a person and profile them as a police target. This difference in application of the law is racism. Racism isn't just what you say, it is also an acceptance of different rules of treatment according to race built into the norms of the system. In the criminal justice system, the issue is *equal treatment*. In the civil justice system, the issue is *equal access*.

10.6 The Constitution, Congress, and the Dual Court System

The founders wanted to avoid having a national court system and chose to root the court system under the foundation of Federalism. Because the question of whether there would be a national court system with jurisdiction over the states was such a hot-button issue, the authors of the Constitution tended to gloss over it.

Article I Courts

Only the actions of Article III courts are the subject of this chapter, but it is important to note there are two types of federal courts. Article I courts are created by Congress in order to implement its various legislative powers. For example, the United States Tax Court has jurisdiction over federal income tax subject matters. Judges of such Article I courts do not have a life tenure or protection from salary decreases. Article I courts are sometimes vested with administrative as well as judicial functions, and the congressional power to create such "hybrid" courts has been sustained by the Supreme Court.[112]

Article III Courts

Article III of the United States Constitution states that the "judicial Power of the United States, shall be vested in one supreme Court, and in such inferior Courts as the Congress may from time to time ordain and establish."[113] What this means is that the Constitution provides for one Supreme Court and lower courts established by Congress as necessary. Although Congress has the complete power to set the jurisdictional limits of the federal courts, it is still bound by the standards of judicial power set forth in Article III as to subject matter, parties, and the requirement of "case or controversy" (discussed later). Therefore, Congress cannot require the federal courts to perform nonjudicial functions.

---

[112] *Glidden v. Zdanok*, 370 United States 530 (1962).
[113] United States Const. Art. III, § 1.

What are lower courts? Most court systems have an entry-level court to which you first bring your case or in which you are first tried before a jury. If you lose this entry level court case, you have a **right to appeal,** which is to ask a higher or appeals court to ensure that everything was handled properly and to review the process.

Federal Judges

The Article III constitutional section also authorizes Congress to appoint Judges of federal courts for life terms. This means these judges can only be removed through a vote of impeachment, so they hold their jobs as long as they behave themselves. In order to be a judge in the federal court system, the Constitution requires judges to be appointed according to certain procedures but sets forth no specific required qualifications to serve as a judge. There are no age, citizenship or other requirements. The Constitution specifies only that the judges shall be appointed by the president, with the advice and consent of the Senate. The judiciary is the only unelected branch of the government.

In order to protect federal judges from political interference or pressures, they receive a salary that cannot be reduced during their lifetime terms. The Constitution gives federal judges this protection so that they can make fair and trustworthy decisions on cases without worrying their decision will be publicly or politically unpopular. Judges can, however, be removed from office only if impeached and convicted by the House of Representatives and the Senate, a process that has resulted in only 15 impeachments and eight convictions in more than 200 years.

Federal Court System

The federal court system is three-tiered. First, the lowest level of the federal judiciary hierarchy consists of 94 federal district courts. Each state has at least one **federal district court** located within its borders while the largest states have four. Federal district courts will hear the case first because district courts have **original jurisdiction**. At this level, the court will consider and rule on all the facts of the case during a trial. Each federal district court has a United States attorney that are government attorneys that represent the United States in criminal and civil cases. United States attorneys are appointed by the president and approved or affirmed by the Senate for four-year terms.

Next, once a case is decided by the federal district courts, it can be appealed and heard by the federal **Courts of Appeals**. These courts are arranged into 12 circuits. These circuits are large super districts that encompass several of the district court territories. Each circuit has its own Court of Appeals. The 12th circuit covers just Washington, D.C., and hears all appeals involving government agencies. Cases are heard in the circuit that includes the district court where the case was heard originally. The sole function of these courts is to hear appeals from the lower federal district courts if the losing party believes the law was applied incorrectly and to review the legal reasoning behind the decisions reached there. This is referred to as **appellate jurisdiction**. These courts do not hold trials and generally do not consider the facts of the case. The decisions in the courts of appeals are made by a rotating panel of three judges who sit to hear the case. The judges rotate in order to provide a decision-making body that is as unbiased as possible. Having all the judges present (*en banc*) gives a decision more legitimacy and sends a message that the decision was made carefully.

The third and highest tier of the federal court system is the United States Supreme Court and is discussed below.

The judicial ideology is important for the courts because it can sway important legal concepts in the public policy of the United States, such as abortion rights. Judicial ideology varies by the president that nominates a justice. These days an increasingly important qualification for the job of federal judge is the ideological or policy positions of the appointee. The Senate confirmation process has become more rancorous. The nomination process has been more important to conservatives than to liberals.

State Court System

State court systems are different from federal court systems. Each state establishes their own state courts through state law or their constitution. Therefore, the structures of state court systems vary from state to state. Each state has a tiered system that has a highest court for appeals, which is often, but not always, called a state supreme court. State courts have jurisdiction over state law subject matter and interpret their respective state law and constitutions.

State courts judges are chosen differently than the federal court judges and, again, the procedures are established by state laws. State judges are chosen through three different methods: Appointment by the governor, election by the state legislature, and election by the state population as a whole. The state election of judges can be controversial. Critics argue that judicial elections can create a conflict of interest because few people are able to cast educated votes in judicial elections. There is a further problem that the political nature of elections and campaigning may influence judges' rulings.

10.7 The Supreme Court

The Supreme Court is the highest court of the land. In the United States Judiciary, the top player is the Supreme Court. The founders wanted the Supreme Court to be above politics. The President is not seen going to the Supreme Court and the Supreme Court Justices are not seen visiting the president in order to keep a perceived bias from occurring. The Supreme Court is still a POLITICAL institution. The very reasons that the founders could not be frank about their plans for the Court in the Constitution shows just how politically volatile the whole institution was. As discussed above, the primary job is to determine if laws are permitted under the United States Constitution and provide judicial review of those laws.

The political nature of the Supreme Court can influence laws, freedoms, and civil rights for all Americans for generations. The Supreme Court is political in three respects: (1) How justices are chosen, (2) How the justices make decisions, and (3) The impact of those decisions on all the rest of us.

It is very difficult to get on the Supreme Court. The president appoints Supreme Court justices, and the Senate approves or affirms the nomination of the president. The president and the Senate consider the merit and demographics of the nominee, but mostly the appointing entities are fixated on ideology. Supreme Court justices have always been attorneys, had extensive careers in the legal field and have over-whelmingly been white males. In 1967, Justice Thurgood Marshall became the first African American Supreme Court Justice. And shortly thereafter in 1981, Sandra Day O'Connor became the first woman appointed.

The type of justice appointed to the Supreme Court can either be someone who is a judicial interpretivist or a strict constructionist. A **Judicial interpretivist** is one who believes that the founders could not have anticipated all the changes that make the world today different from theirs and, therefore, that judges should read the Con-stitution as the founders would write it in light of modern-day experience. A **strict constructionist** is a scholar and judge who believes that the Constitution should be read just as it was written. This is a political hot-button issue now because, until Justice Antonin Scalia's death in 2016, there was a 5-4 majority who were sufficiently com-mitted to interpretivism that they supported the right to privacy and the case that was based on *Griswold, Roe v. Wade* (1973).

10.8 Federal Court Jurisdiction

Jurisdiction is the authority of the court to hear the case. The federal courts have jurisdiction over all cases involving a federal question, or **subject matter jurisdiction**, that seeks to answer a question based on federal law or the United States Constitution. Any subject matter involving the federal government or foreign governments would also be within the jurisdiction of federal courts. Federal courts also have **diversity jurisdiction** where the disputes are between two parties that are from different states.

Additionally, courts have diversity jurisdiction to resolve disputes between two different state governments. If Tennessee and Arkansas are disputing rights to Mississippi, the case would be heard in federal court.

Even if a federal court has subject matter or diversity jurisdiction, it still might refuse to hear a case. Whether the court will hear the case (*i.e.,* whether the case is justiciable) depends on whether a **case or controversy** is involved, and whether the other elements of jurisdiction are met. Article III, Section 2 of the United States Constitution also requires federal courts to decide questions that arise out of actual disputes or real cases and controversies.[114] Therefore, federal courts cannot issue advisory opinions in cases involving challenges to governmental legislation or policy whose enforcement is neither actual nor threatened. Although, some state supreme courts do have the judicial power to issue advisory opinions.

A party to a case is generally not entitled to review of a law before it is enforced. Therefore, a federal court will not hear a case that is not **ripe** (case is brought too early). This means the party must have been harmed or there is an immediate threat of harm. A federal court will also not hear a case that has become **moot** (case is brought too late). A "real, live controversy" must exist "at all stages of review", not merely when the complaint is filed.[115]

A person who brings a case to federal court must also have **standing** and show he or she has a concrete stake in the outcome of the controversy. This means the party bringing the action must show an actual injury or harm done and a causal connection between the injury and the conduct complained of (*i.e.,* the injury is traceable to the challenged conduct of the defendant and not another third party). Generally, people do not have standing to challenge the way the government spends tax dollars simply because the person bringing the action is a taxpayer, because their interest is too remote, and the person has not suffered an injury-in-fact.

10.9 The politics of making a decision

Getting a case to the Supreme Court may seem very political and, because the decisions of the Supreme Court affect every American and the Court hears a small majority of the applications it receives, it can be difficult to get your case before the Court. In fact, the Court accepts 100-150 of the 7,000 cases that it is asked to review each year.[116] If four of the nine justices agree to hear the case, then the case will be heard. The court

---

[114] United States Const. Art. III, § 2.
[115] *De Funis v. Odegaard*, 416 United States 312 (1974).
[116] https://www.uscourts.gov/about-federal-courts.

can decide to hear a case or not and is generally under no obligation to approve or deny an application to hear the case.

There are a couple ways that the parties can get their cases heard before the Supreme Court. If a party is not satisfied with a lower court decision and wants to get before the Supreme Court, the party can ask the court for review or certiorari. In law, certiorari is a court process to seek judicial review of a decision of a lower court or government agency. Certiorari comes from the name of an English prerogative writ, issued by a superior court to direct that the record of the lower court be sent to the superior court for review. **Writs of certiorari** are pleas from a party who lost in a lower court who believes there is a procedural or legal problem with the previous verdict. Most cases come before the Supreme Court through writs of certiorari.

When a party who is not a party to a lawsuit would like to influence the court to hear a case, the party may write an amicus curiae brief, **Amicus curiae briefs,** also known as "friend of the court" briefs, are submitted by concerned groups. They are someone who is not a party to a case who assists a court by offering information, expertise, or insight that has a bearing on the issues in the case. The decision on whether to consider an amicus brief lies within the discretion of the court. The phrase amicus curiae is legal Latin.

When a case goes before the Supreme Court that involves the United States and not two private parties, it is led under the **solicitor general,** who is a lawyer of the federal government and supervises the litigation.

Once the Court decides to hear the case, the parties submit written arguments with a **brief**, which is a summary of the argument and states the reasons the Court should rule in their favor. Next, the lawyers for each party will present **oral arguments** before the Court where the justices are able to ask questions. Often, the justices have already reviewed the briefs before the oral arguments and can express how he or she is leaning when asking questions. The justices then meet in private **conference** to discuss the case and make their decisions.

If a case is to be won by any party, it must receive **majority opinion** of the court, which is the opinion of at least five Supreme Court justices. Usually, one justice is tasked with drafting the majority opinion that represents the views of the other justices. The opinion will state the decision, the reasoning for the decision and sets a precedent for lower courts to follow. Sometimes the Supreme Court will issue **concurring opinions,** which are written by justices who agree with the majority opinion but for different or extra reasons. A **dissenting opinion** is written by justices who disagree with the opinion and want to be on the record even though the dissenting opinion is not considered binding precedent that lower courts are required to follow.

10.10 Important Supreme Court Decisions

Some important Supreme Court decisions over the past 200+ years have provided integral interpretations of the rights guaranteed, although not always explicitly, under the United States Constitution. The judiciary is tasked with interpreting exactly what this means and providing judicial review of laws that may violate these rights. Therefore, whenever the government seeks to regulate these rights or freedoms, the Court will weigh the importance of the right against the interest or policies sought to be served by the governmental regulation.

As discussed above, an important issue decided by the Court was that the Court should be the ultimate decider of what is constitutional in the United States federal government and the states. ***Marbury v. Madison***[117] was a landmark United States Supreme Court case that established the principle of judicial review in the United States, meaning that American courts have the power to strike down laws, statutes, and some government actions that they find to violate the Constitution of the United States.

While the Constitution separates governmental powers among the branches of government, the United States Supreme Court interpreted and specified that the separation of powers doctrine specifically prohibits the legislature from interfering with the courts' final judgments in ***Plaut v. Spendthrift Farm, Inc.***[118] In this case, the legislature, through Congress, passed a law to provide a special motion for reinstating the cases dismissed as time-barred by Supreme Court rulings. The Court held the law providing for the reinstatement of dismissed cases violated the separation of powers doctrine- the legislature can't tell the judiciary what to do.

The Constitution also established the **equal protection clause** which provided in part that "[no state shall] deny any person within its jurisdiction the equal protection of the laws."[119] In 1896, the Supreme Court first dissected the meaning of the equal protection clause in ***Plessy v. Ferguson***.[120] The Court reviewed a Louisiana law . railroads in the state to provide separate cars for white and African American passengers and upheld the constitutionality of the state-mandated racial segregation law for all public facilities as long as the segregated facilities were equal in quality, a doctrine that came to be known as "separate but equal". It took the United States sixty more years to reverse this decision and undo the damage done with the "separate but equal

---

[117] *Marbury v. Madison*, 5 United States 137 (1803).
[118] *Plaut v. Spendthrift Farm, Inc.*, 514 United States 211 (1995).
[119] United States Const. Amend. XIV, § 1.
[120] *Plessy v. Ferguson*, 163 United States 537 (1896).

doctrine". ***Brown v. Board of Education***[121] was a landmark decision of the United States Supreme Court in which the Court ruled that state laws establishing racial segregation in public schools are unconstitutional, even if the segregated schools are otherwise equal in quality.

The Court also declared that the Constitution required equal protection for women when it held that a state law that discriminated against women was unconstitutional in ***Reed v. Reed.***[122]

Certain fundamental rights are protected under the Constitution. Various **privacy rights,** including marriage, sexual relations, abortion and childrearing, are fundamental rights. Modern rights to privacy guaranteed under the Constitution have been clarified by the Supreme Court. In ***Griswold v. Connecticut***, the Supreme Court established a "marital zone of privacy" and the fundamental right of a marital relationship protects couples right to buy and use contraceptives without government restrictions.[123] The Supreme Court has also held in ***Roe v. Wade*** that the right of privacy includes the right of a woman to have an abortion under certain circumstances without undue influence from the state.[124]

Another fundamental right is the **freedom of speech** which provides that "Congress shall make no law …abridging the freedom of speech."[125] The freedom of speech protects the free flow of ideas, a most important function in a democratic society. A regulation or law that tries to forbid speech of specific ideas (**content regulation**) is more likely to violate the free speech doctrine. It is usually unconstitutional for the government to prohibit speech based on its content. In ***Brandenburg v. Ohio***, the Court held that the government could not prohibit political speech, or speech with political content, unless it is linked to immediate lawless behavior.[126] However, **conduct regulation**, which is content-neutral and regulates how the speech is conducted, is more likely permitted (*i.e.,* law prohibiting billboards for purposes of traffic safety).

While the Constitution remains largely unchanged and is the most important consideration when deciding a case and applying the facts to the law, the Court has recognized the law needs to be flexible and adapt to changing times. The Court has, and will continue to, overrule outdated precedents.

---

[121] *Brown v. Board of Education*, 347 United States 483 (1954).

[122] *Reed v. Reed*, 404 United States 71 (1971).

[123] *Griswold v. Connecticut*, 381 United States 479 (1965).

[124] *Roe v. Wade*, 410 United States 113 (1973).

[125] United States Const. Amend. I.

[126] *Brandenburg v. Ohio*, 395 United States 444 (1969).

Chapter 10: The Judicial Branch

1) Appellate courts hear cases from the

    a. Supreme Court.

    b. lower courts.

    c. courts of dual jurisdiction.

    d. courts of upper jurisdiction.

2) According to Alexander Hamilton, the weakest of the three branches of government was

    a. Congress.

    b. the presidency.

    c. the judiciary

    d. the bureaucracy.

3) The use of a third party to solve a legal dispute most likely refers to the process called

    a. litigation.

    b. mediation.

    c. civic relations.

    d. adjudication.

4) One of the unusual things about the courts is that

    a. there have always been nine Supreme Court justices.

    b. the Constitution never specified the number of Supreme Court justices.

    c. Congress has an insignificant role in shaping the courts.

    d. the president has a minimal role in influencing who is on the courts.

5) The concept of judicial federalism means

    a. that the US has one main court system.

    b. that the courts should be judicious in making relevant decisions.

    c. that there is both a federal and a state court system in the United States.

    d. that state courts are stronger than federal courts.

6) The ultimate arbiter of all cases is the

    a. trial court.

    b. superior court.

c. US Supreme Court.

d. federal court.

7) In what year was the Supreme Court set at nine justices?

a. 1797

b. 1812

c. 1869

d. 1962

8) Most state judges

a. are appointed for life.

b. are selected by state legislatures.

c. are elected by the public.

d. have terms that are not renewable.

9) The main ways to select a judge are

a. by public vote.

b. by governor's appointment.

c. by merit committees.

d. all of the above

10) Acts of terror, insider trading, and immigration would be heard by

a. state trial courts.

b. federal trial courts.

c. state appeals court.

d. state supreme court.

11) A district court is a

a. state appellate court.

b. state trial court.

c. federal trial court.

d. state supreme court.

12) Texas and California have _____than other states.

a. fewer district courts

b. more district courts

    c. more powerful district courts

    d. weaker district courts

13) District court judges are appointed by the

    a. people.

    b. governor.

    c. president.

    d. state legislature.

14) The role of the circuit courts is to

    a. review the trial record of cases decided in district court.

    b. review the trial record of cases decided in state trial courts.

    c. review the trial record of cases decided in state appellate courts.

    d. review the record of cases decided in mediation.

15) There are _____ federal appellate courts.

    a. 94

    b. 10

    c. 13

    d. 75

16) The main difference between the federal appellate court and the federal district court is that

    a. there are more federal appellate courts.

    b. federal appellate courts use juries.

    c. federal appellate courts do not use juries or cross-examination.

    d. federal district courts do not allow cross-examination.

17) Circuit courts review cases decided in

    a. Supreme Court

    b. District Courts

    c. Bankruptcy Courts

    d. Military Courts

18) Specialized courts hear cases on

    a. immigration.

    b. tax disputes.

    c. treason.

    d. civil rights.

19) Specialized court judges differ from regular federal judges in that

    a. They are older than federal judges.

    b. they are not appointed for life.

    c. they do not require Senate confirmation.

    d. they must be appointed by the governor.

20) If there were a breach of justice by a military member, that case would be heard by

    a. a district court judge.

    b. a military judge.

    c. an appellate court.

    d. a state judge.

21) The principle that enables the courts to check the other two branches of government is known as

    a. legal authority.

    b. judicial autonomy.

    c. judicial review.

    d. statutory relief.

22) The principle of judicial review is traced back to the case of

    a. McCullough v. Maryland.

    b. Gibbons v. Ogden.

    c. Marbury v. Madison.

    d. Plessy v. Ferguson.

23) Judicial review allows the courts to

    a. check only Congress if it has exceeded constitutional authority.

    b. check the executive and legislative branches if they have exceeded constitutional authority.

c. check only the executive branch if it has exceeded constitutional authority.

d. check the military.

24) Judicial review is _____ in the Constitution.

a. clearly mentioned

b. vaguely mentioned

c. not mentioned

d. reflected through the Judiciary Act of 1789

25) The statement "When there is doubt about what the Constitution holds or implies, the Supreme Court makes the call" refers to the principle of

a. stare decisis.

b. judicial review.

c. certiorari.

d. senatorial courtesy.

26) The fact that the Supreme Court has struck down statutes that supported segregation policy is a form of

a. judicial activism.

b. legal rationalism.

c. judicial restraint.

d. strict constructionism.

27) The idea that the Supreme Court can take a vigorous or active approach when reviewing the other governmental branches is a form of

a. judicial activism.

b. judicial restraint.

c. legal activism.

d. common law practice.

28) The idea that the Court should overturn the elected branches of government reluctantly is called

a. judicial reproach.

b. judicial restraint.

c. judicial activism.

d. loose constructionism.

29) The early English legal system was known as

a. majority rule.

b. the Magna Carte.

c. common law.

d. common precedent.

30) Judicial cases today may be important tomorrow because they establish the concept of

a. judicial review.

b. precedent.

c. legal formation.

d. civil law.

31) A judge that makes a legal decision on a case today may look at past case law and follow the concept of

a. precedent.

b. civil law.

c. criminal law.

d. home rule.

32) A person charged with theft will face the rules and consequences under

a. criminal law.

b. civil law.

c. humanitarian law.

d. common law.

33) The person bringing the suit in a civil case is called the

a. prosecutor.

b. litigator.

c. defendant.

d. plaintiff.

34) The person being sued in a civil case is known as the

a. respondent.

b. plaintiff.

c. defendant.

d. petitioner.

35) Federal courts differ from the executive and legislative branches of government because they

a. are above politics.

b. serve more extended periods.

c. are all from one political party.

d. do not have an electoral base.

36) Supreme Court justices are in session

a. all year round.

b. for nine months.

c. for six months.

d. for eleven months.

37) A brief submitted by a person or group that is not a direct party to the case is called

a. amicus curiae.

b. third-party brief.

c. legal extension.

d. case law.

38) The Supreme Court process of selecting a case is known as

a. a gang of four.

b. rule of four.

c. the process of advice and consent.

d. rule of twelve.

39) Which of the following is essential for having a case heard by the Supreme Court?

a. standing

b. legitimate controversy

c. no moot cases

d. all of the above

40) Someone adversely affected or suffering imminent harm would be able to satisfy the concept of

   a. due process.

   b. standing.

   c. amicus curiae.

   d. justiciability.

41) The official statement of the Court is known as

   a. the dissent.

   b. the majority opinion.

   c. the concurring opinion.

   d. the remand.

42) A justice that agrees with the majority opinion but for different reasons is known as

   a. an opposite opinion.

   b. a concurring opinion.

   c. a dissenting opinion.

   d. a circulatory opinion.

43) A statement on behalf of the justices voting in the minority is called the

   a. dissent.

   b. concurring opinion.

   c. differing opinion.

   d. legal treatise.

44) Justices are guided by the concept of _____ in making legal decisions.

   a. common law.

   b. stare decisis.

   c. devolution.

   d. rule of four.

45) "Stand by the things decided" is the definition for which Latin term?

   a. writ of certiorari

   b. writ of mandamus

   c. writ of habeas corpus

   d. stare decisis

46) A judge who observes a living and changing Constitution is known as a

    a. theorist.

    b. pragmatist.

    c. rationalist.

    d. legalist.

47) A judge who literally interprets the Constitution literally is known as a(n)

    a. legalist.

    b. loose constructionist.

    c. originalist.

    d. pragmatist.

48) The case of Marbury v. Madison and the judicial review principle was set forth by which Supreme Court justice?

    a. Robert Taney

    b. John Marshall

    c. Hugo Black

    d. John Marshall Harlan

49) McCulloch v. Maryland was essential to court development because

    a. it allowed the federal government to tax a state.

    b. it evoked the principle of the good faith and credit clause.

    c. it evoked the necessary and proper clause to block Maryland's state from taxing the bank of the United States.

    d. it allowed states to create complex interstate compacts.

50) The outcome of McCulloch v. Maryland affirmed the principle that

    a. the federal government is superior to state governments.

    b. states are superior to the federal government in most instances.

    c. state and federal power are equal.

    d. states can use state mandates to trump federal power.

51) The famous case that denied civil rights to former slaves was known as

    a. Plessy v. Ferguson.

    b. Dred Scott v. Sandford.

c. Marbury v. Madison.

d. Guinn v. United States.

52) A fundamental principle in the Dred Scott case was that slaves could not sue because

a. they did not have enough money.

b. they lacked standing to sue.

c. their cases were only common law concerns.

d. their cases were not federal.

53) The idea that a corporation was viewed as a legal person meant

a. that corporations did not have to pay federal taxes.

b. that corporations were protected under the equal protection clause of the Thirteenth Amendment.

c. that corporations were protected under the equal protection clause of the Fourteenth Amendment.

d. that corporations could use their own lawyers during the trial.

54) Black equality was promoted through which amendments?

a. Seven, Eight, and Nine

b. Thirteen, Fourteen, and Fifteen

c. One, Two, and Three

d. Five, Eight, and Nine

55) The outcome of Plessy v. Ferguson was

a. fair and equal treatment for all people.

b. the promotion of desegregation with all deliberate speed.

c. the separate but equal policy.

d. the development of a color-blind society.

56) The outcome of Schenck v. United States was

a. the equal protection clause.

b. the clear and present danger test.

c. the due process clause.

d. the grave and probable danger test.

57) The case that forced Japanese Americans into internment camps during World War II was

   a. Korematsu v. US.

   b. Schenck v. US.

   c. Gitlow v. New York.

   d. Plessy v. Ferguson.

58) The Korematsu case was significant because it was

   a. one of the first cases to use the strict scrutiny test.

   b. one of the first cases to use the clear and present danger test.

   c. one of the first cases to use the grave and probable danger test.

   d. one of the first cases to use the adverse tendency rule.

59) The case that overturned Plessy v. Ferguson was

   a. Gitlow v. New York.

   b. Guinn v. United States.

   c. Korematsu v. United States.

   d. Brown v. Board

60) The court in Brown v. Board stated that

   a. separate schools are inherently unequal.

   b. separate facilities are inherently unequal.

   c. separate movie theaters are inherently unequal.

   d. separate restrooms are inherently unequal.

61) Mapp v. Ohio addressed concerns over the

   a. Eighth Amendment.

   b. Fourth Amendment.

   c. Third Amendment.

   d. Sixth Amendment.

62) Gideon v. Wainwright was one of the first in a series of landmark judicial decisions addressing

   a. the right to bear arms.

   b. the right of free speech.

    c. the rights of defendants in criminal proceedings.

    d. the rights of immigrant workers.

63) The case that struck down a Texas law outlawing abortion was

    a. Roe v. Wade.

    b. Mapp v. Ohio.

    c. Gideon v. Wainwright.

    d. Miranda v. Arizona.

64) The case that addressed the president's right to use executive privilege was

    a. Roe v. Wade.

    b. US v. Nixon.

    c. US v. Ford.

    d. Bush v. Gore.

65) The idea that the president can withhold sensitive national security information from Congress or the courts is known as an

    a. executive order.

    b. executive pardon.

    c. executive privilege.

    d. executive agreement.

66) Obergefell v. Hodges brought _____ to the Supreme Court.

    a. tax evasion

    b. same-sex marriage

    c. health benefits

    d. death rights

67) The Court used the _____ amendment in deciding Obergefell v. Hodges.

    a. 1st

    b. 11th

    c. 14th

    d. 22nd

Discussion Questions

1) What makes a good judge?

2) Evaluate whether the courts were too influential in Bush v. Gore.

3) Should the US government have a mandated health plan?

4) Should justices have term limits? How long should the term be? Should every president be allowed to nominate a Supreme Court justice? How would that work?

Video Resources

Noah Feldman and Jeffrey Toobin: The Supreme Court Then and Now (2010) 92nd Street Y

The Supreme Court DVD Series (2007) Ambrose Video Publishing

Stare decisis and precedent in the Supreme Court https://www.khanacademy.org/humanities/ap-us-government-and-politics/interactions-among-branches-of-government/legitimacy-of-the-judicial-branch/v/stare-decisis-and-precedent-in-the-supreme-court

Ruth Bader Ginsburg, Brooklyn's Own Supreme Court Justice https://www.youtube.com/watch?v=AsbjuX0YxzY

Court Role and Structure www.uscourts.gov/about-federal-courts/court-role-and-structure

Abbout the Supreme Court https://www.courts.state.wy.us/supreme-court/about-the-supreme-court/

Website Resources

The Supreme Court of the United States http://www.supremecourt.gov/ and

http://www.supremecourt.gov/about/biographies.aspx

United States Courts http://www.uscourts.gov

The Supreme Court Historical Society http://www.supremecourthistory.org

Supreme Court www.oyez.org

CHAPTER 11

PUBLIC OPINION, CAMPAIGNS, AND ELECTIONS

Chapter Summary

The media can influence the governmental implementation of public policies and the development of public opinion. Policymakers pay attention to both preferences and trends among the public. Preferences are not static and may not remain the same over time. Political involvement relies on how strongly people feel about current political issues. Public opinion polls track and affect election campaigns, the Electoral College and strategic campaign considerations, and the ultimate poll—choosing a president at the ballot box.

Opinions start to develop during childhood, and beliefs subjects acquire early in life are unlikely to change much as they age. The socialization process leaves citizens with attitudes and beliefs that create a personal ideology depending on attitudes and beliefs and prioritizing each belief over the others. To run a successful campaign requires understanding the nature of public opinion and its effects during elections. Campaign managers want to know how citizens will vote and persuade them. Candidates and elected public officials use polls' results to decide their future legislative votes, campaign messages, or propaganda.

11.1 Introduction to public opinion, campaigns, and elections

Why does it matter what the American public thinks about political issues? In a federal constitutional democratic republic such as the United States, the national government, headed by the president, shares powers with the Congress and the judiciary as mandated by the Constitution. The federal government also shares some powers with state and local governments, again as prescribed in the Constitution. The American people elect their governmental representatives to serve their interests and influence the policymaking process.

Political office-seekers often use *public opinion polls* to determine voters' preferences on various issues, so they can tailor their campaign messages to secure the possible votes hopefully ascend to public office. They seek to persuade citizens during the *campaign*.

Public opinion is what the people may think on any given topic, especially on political issues for our purposes. In our representative democracy, there are two ways of determining what people may be thinking; first, by taking a headcount through polling, second, by asking them to vote in elections.

Polling public opinion is very different from "going to the polls" in actual elections. First, in a public opinion poll, for the sake of accuracy, those taking the poll sample respondents to create a group as representative of the voting public as possible during periods leading up to the actual casting of ballots. In elections, however, the voters take the lead and select whom they wish to lead their country, states, and localities.

Second, timing is a crucial element in polling. Researchers can conduct polls whenever an educational institution, marketing company, or media outlet has the time, money, and inclination to conduct them. Elections are different, as they are held on scheduled dates.

Third, polls are not binding on anyone, and one can pay them attention or choose to ignore them while elections are final. Still, public opinion polling and elections are essentially two ways of doing the same thing, finding out what people think at a specific point in time.

11.2 The quality of public opinion

Opinions start to develop during childhood, and beliefs subjects acquire early in life are unlikely to change much as they age.[127] The socialization process leaves citizens with attitudes and beliefs that create a personal ideology depending on attitudes and beliefs and prioritizing each belief over the others. To run a successful campaign requires understanding the nature of public opinion and its effects during elections.[128] Ideally, all citizens would be well informed about government, rules, and relevant political

---

[127] See Krutz, Glen S. *American Government 2e.*, 2019. Internet resource. Accessed 9 Mar. 2021. Lau, Tim. Brennan Center for Justice, https://www.brennancenter.org/our-work/research-reports/citizens-united-explained, *Citizens United Explained*, accessed 19 March 2021.

[128] On the manufacturing of public opinion, see McNair.

actors. They would also be tolerant of ideas other than their own and willing to compromise to further the collective interest, and happy to participate at various political levels and engage in civic activities. Subjects should receive their news from diverse sources to get in touch with different viewpoints and perspectives.

Most Americans do not always receive their news from high-quality sources, and while they may be theoretically tolerant, they are often less so in practice. Increasingly, some groups have come to view political compromise as a fundamental betrayal of their values. Additionally, United States elections tend to have meager voter turnout rates compared with other democratic countries. All of which leads people to a fundamental question about their government: Whose views should count?

One of the ideals of democracy is *tolerance*, which means that some people who vote in elections may not necessarily be the ones one would prefer. Some voters may even be pursuing a path of *rational ignorance*, that is, choosing not to be informed about politics because the payoff from participating feels too remote or the difference they make seems to be insignificant.

Still, the country may be delivered from an ill-informed populace by specific shortcuts that can lead people toward rationality. Many citizens suffer from a phenomenon known as *online processing*, which is about ending the day with one's head full of opinions picked up on the fly with no clear idea of how one arrived at them. While people often have good reasons for holding their views, sometimes they process them too quickly and with insufficient information. People probably are not as ignorant as they sound. Moreover, they may find that others around can offer them clues as to the nature of things.

The *two-step flow of information* is a psychological process by which *opinion followers* look to opinion leaders for understanding and cues on how to vote[129]. Opinion followers are the vast majority of citizens. In contrast, *opinion leaders* usually prepare themselves through study and research to be well informed and subsequently get involved in civic activities. Journalists often interview them on TV news and talk shows. Some subjects who receive some higher education may become opinion leaders themselves, providing cues and guidance to family members, friends, and members of groups to which one belongs.

Political parties and interest groups may provide subjects with a form of comprehension similar to the two-step flow, except that the opinion leader is not an individual but a group. Still, one should bear in mind that these shortcuts are not foolproof. There is no guarantee that these shortcuts will lead to decision-making that is, in fact, informed and smart.

---

[129] See Zaller, especially chapter 9, to better understand two-sided and two-step information flows. Zaller, John. *The Nature and Origins of Mass Opinion*. Cambridge University Press, 2011.

11.3 How to know what Americans think?

The science of public opinion polling has come a long way. According to The Gallup Organization, a Washington, D.C.-based analytics company founded in 1935, polls can accurately "tell what proportion of a population has a specific viewpoint."[130]

The modern science of public opinion polling is quite complex. Although statisticians have determined that a random sample of only 1,000 to 2,000 people can be very representative of a state or the country as a whole, modern polling consists of numerous methodologies, techniques, and considerations. For example:

A *random sample* is a representative subset of a larger population in which everyone has an equal chance of being chosen, and no one group is over-represented. *Sample bias*, however, is when one part of the population has been accorded disproportionate weight. One of the most challenging parts of polling these days is persuading people who may be busy or distracted to offer their responses to questions. A *nonresponse bias* may occur in polls if a particular group is less likely to respond than another. To compensate for any sampling bias, polling companies may use a statistical process called *weighting*. Some groups are given more weight to make the results more accurately reflect what the wider public is thinking. Still, in the end, it is an inexact science, and no poll will be perfect.

One way of narrowing the sample is by taking *likely voter polls*, that is, by questioning people who are the most likely to vote in a forthcoming election. In this effort, pollsters may use *likely voter screens*, which are methods that attempt to weed out nonvoters. Furthermore, no matter what techniques pollsters use, polls' accuracy will always be problems, generally called *sampling errors*. Polls may also be skewed by house effects or how a pollster's results favor Democrats or Republicans. Thus, in light of all this, one finds that all polls will vary at least slightly. Sometimes, in an attempt by media outlets to arrive at more accurate results, methods may be used that pull together the results of several polls in what one calls *polling aggregators*.

Polling came into its own when enough Americans owned telephones to make spot digit dialing an effective way to draw a random sample. *Random digit dialing* was how pollsters could randomly sample Americans by calling them on their landlines. Different kinds of national polls measure where Americans stand on particular issues that are released periodically by major media organizations. *Tracking polls* show data movements over periods to detect changes in support for people or issues. They can be

---

[130] Even if polls tell one what proportion of the population has specific viewpoints and shares certain ideas, their purpose is not to change one's mindset. Social researchers are the ones who explain why people believe as they do and what to do about that. For more information, see Nielsen, Eric. What Is Public Opinion Polling and Why Is It Important?, *Gallup World Poll*, http://media.gallup.com/muslimwestfacts/pdf/pollingandhowtouseitr1dreveng.pdf, accessed 15 March 2021.

particularly helpful to those running for political office, enabling them to see how they are doing than their opponents.

Researchers take *exit polls* as people leave their places of voting immediately after casting their ballots. The raw data are sometimes leaked early, before the polls close, creating false expectations of who might win or even influence the eventual results. *Fake polls* are sometimes released to manipulate results, but they tell nothing about the real world. The upshot is that polls, in general, are notably informative if researchers conduct them scientifically, but any individual poll can suffer from sampling errors.

11.4 How do subjects form their opinions?

What elements may combine to shape one's political views when gathering and processing information? For one, a transfer of political attitudes, narratives, and beliefs from one generation to another, called *political socialization*, probably contributes to one's outlook. It helps create a stable, loyal citizenry who buys into the system's foundational values by bringing people together around shared values. Some of the socialization agents are families, schools, religious institutions, peer groups, and the media. *Patriotism*, or shared loyalty to one's country and its institutions, is also a potent socialization agent.

Still, some agents may socialize citizens to break into separate groups. Socialization works through a set of interests and values that tend to divide people according to ideologies. *Party identification*, or which political party one identifies with, is probably the most significant influence on one's opinions and votes. Party identification is not a randomly assigned feature to subjects. Data can reveal to researchers critical information concerning this vital component of political socialization.

Race and ethnicity play significant roles in determining party affiliations. Over time, the Republican Party has become whiter, and one sees that African Americans are far more likely to be Democrats, at about a ten-to-one ratio. So are Latinos and Asian Americans, both at two-to-one. There is also a clear *gender gap* in that women are more likely to be Democrats than are men, who are more likely to be Republicans. This situation is even more evident in the case of millennials than in previous generations. *Religion* may also play a role in party affiliation. White evangelical Protestants are much more likely to be Republicans, while Roman Catholics split along ethnic lines, and religiously unaffiliated people are predominantly Democrats. *Education* factors into party alliances, with more-educated voters moving in recent years toward the Democrats. The *location* has become another determinant factor nowadays, with Democrats tending to cluster in urban and, increasingly, suburban areas. Republicans, on the other hand, tend to live in outer suburban and rural areas.

The generations into which people of varying ages may fall also seem to influence how they vote. All the trends one has discussed here become increasingly more robust as the voter pool gets younger over time. Democrats are what journalist and data analyst Ron Brownstein[131] calls the *coalition of the ascendant*—that is, of the racial and ethnic groups getting more prominent and more visible. Republicans are becoming smaller and aging out, what Brownstein calls the *coalition of restoration*—a group composed of older, blue-collar, evangelical rural whites who want to "restore" the last century's social order. Brownstein's research suggests that without a change in the current trends, the parties' gulf will only widen when post-millennials begin to come of age in the next few years.

People may identify with a party initially because it takes policy positions that they agree with, but eventually, the party can become a kind of information shorthand for them. As Americans become more polarized, adopting "*Us vs. Them*" attitudes, voters are becoming less likely to leave their party's comfort zone to vote with the other.

If partisanship is remarkably important in shaping voters' opinions, do natural and practical concerns even matter? Well, some voters will not consider voting for a candidate who does not share their views on one issue that they consider to be fundamental, regardless of party. One refers to them as *single-issue voters*. A growing segment of voters, perhaps as much as thirty percent, eschew any party affiliations. Researchers call them *independent voters* or swing voters. The upshot is that whether one chooses to act on party cues or other socialization influences may depend on whether a particular candidate can motivate people to vote.

11.5 The ultimate poll is voting in elections

The United States has one of the lowest voter participation rates among industrialized democratic nations. *Voter turnout* is the percentage of eligible voters who cast ballots, and efforts to legally limit who can vote are known as *regulating the electorate*. These efforts to determine who is allowed to vote, which reached a peak in the decades following the United States Civil War, are still alive and well, even resurging in recent years.

The voters who reliably tend to vote are older, whiter, wealthier, and more educated Americans. Younger voters, newer voters, people of color, single moms, and people lower on the socioeconomic scale are less likely to vote, and if they do, they are more likely to vote for the Democrats.

---

[131] *See* Brownstein, Ronald and National Journal. "The Clinton Conundrum." *The Atlantic*, 17 April 2015, www.theatlantic.com/politics/archive/2015/04/the-clinton-conundrum/431949.

The voters who reliably tend to vote are older, whiter, wealthier, and more educated Americans. Younger voters, newer voters, people of color, single moms, and people lower on the socioeconomic scale are less likely to vote, and if they do, they are more likely to vote for the Democrats. Republicans reportedly want to make voting less open, and Democrats want to make it simpler for everyone. Republicans have expressed their concerns about voter fraud, specifically people who are not legal voters casting votes, so they want to tighten regulations.

The political stakes in regulating the electorate are high. The continuing battles about regulating the electorate are a political struggle over which party will have the advantage. Since about 2010, Republicans have found it easier to regulate folks out of the electorate than to reach out to groups that tend to vote against them.

The political stakes in regulating the electorate are high. The continuing battles about regulating the electorate are a political struggle over which party will have the advantage. Since about 2010, Republicans have found it easier to regulate folks out of the electorate than to reach out to groups that tend to vote against them.

So, if Americans stopped regulating the electorate, would the United States voter turnout rates increase? Studies show that voter turnout rates would probably increase if Americans decided to reduce the legal barriers to voting. Studies also show that voter fraud is not the problem that Republicans claim it is. Still, one would not achieve 100 percent turnout rates in the United States, as some potential voters have many personal reasons for not voting. They do not have time in their busy schedules to inform themselves enough to care about their voting issues. According to their mindset, their votes will not make a difference, and thus, they do not feel engaged or connected with American society. These citizens perceive there are no meaningful offers to choose from, or it may seem to them that all the available choices are corrupt.

Sometimes their parties do not engage in *voter mobilization*; they fail to make an effort to get out the votes of people who would support them. Encouraging party members to go to the polls can also be referred to as *get-out-the-vote (GOTV)* efforts. As one has seen above, this is a burden that tends to weigh more heavily on Democrats.

What difference does it make if people do not vote? People's decisions not to vote or their failure to exercise their rights affect the Democrats more than the Republicans, and not voting can reduce an elected government's legitimacy. An endorsement from the voters to govern is called an *electoral mandate*. The upshot is that voting is of great importance so that policymakers, politicians, and researchers account for everyone's policy preferences, and people can feel invested in their government's actions.

11.6 Presidential elections

The ones that usually attract the most attention are the *general elections* held every four years. On the ballot are the president, every member of the House of Representatives, one-third of the Senate, various state and local offices, and any petition initiatives that may make the ballot in some states.

What are the requirements to run for president? Which are the steps to follow? There are three critical steps in the election process:

The first step usually takes place behind the scenes. The *invisible primary* is when candidates test the waters to see if they can obtain support and promises of big money without launching a viable campaign.

The second step is about *getting the nomination*. *Party primaries* are held, statewide elections among members of the same party, or in some states, *party caucuses*, which are meetings where party members may debate the merits of the various candidates, and delegates can then decide for whom they wish to stand. The earlier state contests attract many candidates and media attention, so naturally, everyone wants to be among them. However, New Hampshire and Iowa have made it their business to remain first in line. *Frontloading* is a process by which states try to move their primaries or caucuses to earlier dates, which may not be suitable for democracy. Only the most fervent party activists are paying attention to politics that early in the season. During the primary season, the goal is to be the front runner and hold on to that position through the final contest. The *front runner* is the leader of the pack, as seen in the polls.

Candidates attempt to grab and keep the *momentum* by winning debates and maintaining an advantage in the early contests. If, for some reason, one does not perform as well as one has set up the media to expect, one may look like a loser, which can diminish the momentum during the campaign.

The third step is about rallying the party in the *national nominating conventions*, which are party conventions held near the end of summer or early in the autumn before the election, offering a chance to bring the party together behind a political candidacy. Conventions are party mending, strengthening, and rallying events that the media does not have serious interest in covering. The upshot is that most voters will not be paying close attention until the summer ends in the election year.

11.7 The general election and the Electoral College

The general election campaigns open on Labor Day, even though it may feel like they have been going on forever by then. The campaigns keep their eyes on the ultimate prize--more valuable even than the popular vote! When it comes to presidential elections, the final prize is the *Electoral College*, a body of electors from each state who votes for the president. When a citizen votes for a presidential candidate, one is doing it for a delegate (or an elector) to the Electoral College. He will ultimately go on to vote for one's candidate on behalf of the state.

The Electoral College's inner workings may appear mysterious to the average citizen, established in the United States Constitution in 1787 as a compromise between electing a president by a vote in Congress or a popular vote in an election. State distribution indicates electoral votes. Each state has a certain number of electors equal to their total number of Congress members, including two senators. Except for two, Maine and Nebraska, all states cast all their votes to their state's plurality winner. Any state can change its method of how to allocate its votes. The critical point is that different allocation methods may produce different winners and losers.

The Electoral College has a significant impact on candidates' campaign strategies. Some states have much higher elector payoffs than others, and some states are not really in contention. The political coloring book with which candidates concern themselves is red, blue, and purple. While these colors do not have any significance in and of themselves, they are a media convention that has become a tradition. Those states that are not reliably Democratic blue or Republican red, even though they may trend one way or the other in a given election, are called swing states.

These "purple" political entities have become the battlegrounds in which elections are ultimately contested. There are also swing voters who do not reliably vote for either party and must be vigorously courted by aspiring officeholders' campaigns because they often display a resistance toward traditional candidates. Independents become independents because one is repelled by the current political system--by the self-dealing and arrogance of politicians and political parties.

Winning campaigns are usually notable for having competent teams behind them. These days, campaigns are professional organizations. Generally, the campaign with the most money, expertise, and best data-gathering operation will be able to out-strategize and out-perform those that may be less adept. Also increasingly necessary to gain access to the winner's circle is a solid and memorable message. Most swing voters will want to know what a candidate stands for before casting ballots for them. Thus, citizens expect candidates to clearly explain why they are running for office and towards which goals and objectives. They may also search for *wedge issues*, political disputes that they can use as levers to divide an opponent's voting coalition.

Furthermore, because paid advertising is incredibly costly for any campaign, one of the campaign's first goals is to maximize free coverage by staging events and making appearances that the media will cover. Still, for candidates, a good commercial that goes viral and is seen multiple times on cable news and the internet without paying for it is a great thing. *Negative advertising*, or criticizing the opponent, even without mentioning the advertising candidate's name, runs the risk of turning people off and restraining them from coming out to vote. Still, if the issue over which a candidate goes negative connects with the voters, it may prove to be an effective strategy. *Issue advocacy ads* help a candidate by promoting his or her issues or criticizing the opponent's stances.

One absolute certainty is that advertising requires money, and money is a resource to which candidates devote a great deal of their time chasing. Campaign finance law limits how much hard money an individual can donate (currently $2,900 per election).[132] *Hard money* is those funds donated directly to a candidate, *while soft money* is that they give to parties and other groups that can spend it on a candidate's behalf. Wealthy individuals spend *dark money* without having to identify themselves. *Citizens United v. Federal Election Commission* (2010) was a Supreme Court decision that tilted the financial playing field of elections toward corporations, outside groups, and wealthy donors by allowing them to spend without limit and without identifying themselves.[133]

The court's 5-4 majority opinion held that limiting "independent political spending" violated the right to free speech. In doing so, it overturned election spending restrictions that dated back more than a century. The court ruled that there was no threat of corruption if the spending was not coordinated with a candidate's campaign. The upshot of all this is that elections are big business, and all of the citizens are stakeholders in them and in their results, which will significantly affect our lives.

---

[132] The Federal Election Commission clearly states the contribution limits, *see* Contribution limits, https://www.fec.gov/help-candidates-and-committees/candidate-taking-receipts/contribution-limits/, Federal Election Commission, accessed 19 March 2021.

[133] Dark money is usually election-related spending where the source is disclosed or secret. Citizens United contributed to a major jump in this type of spending, which often comes from nonprofits that are not required to reveal their donors. See Tim Lau and Brennan Center for Justice for more details.

Chapter 11: Public opinion, campaigns, and elections

1) The first presidential caucus of the season is held in
   a. New Hampshire
   b. Massachusetts
   c. Iowa
   d. California

2) What would be a reason for a special election?
   a. officeholder dies
   b. President does not like office holder
   c. voters ask for one
   d. governor asks for one

3) What percentage of the House is elected every two years?
   a. 33%
   b. 50%
   c. 75%
   d. 100%

4) How often is the president elected?
   a. every four years
   b. every six years
   c. every eight years
   d. when he calls an election

5) The state governs the ___and ___ of elections.
   a. "place"… "manner"
   b. "time"… "day"
   c. "practice"… "application"
   d. none of the above

6) The state governs the ___and ___ of elections.
   a. "time"… "manner"
   b. "time"… "day"

    c. "practice"... "application"

    d. none of the above

7) The date of the primary is set by the

    a. state

    b. political party

    c. president

    d. Congress

8) When was the date of elections set?

    a. 1845

    b. 1951

    c. 1917

    d. 1983

9) In parliamentary democracies, what is the usual time in which an election must be held?

    a. three years

    b. four years

    c. five years

    d. six years

10) What month are Senate elections held?

    a. March

    b. November

    c. January

    d. September

11) What day of the week do Americans vote for House members?

    a. Saturday

    b. Friday

    c. Wednesday

    d. Tuesday

12) In what year are House elections held?

    a. even-numbered years

b. years divisible by three

c. years divisible by five

d. odd-numbered years

13) When is election day for House members?

a. first Tuesday after first Monday in November of every even-numbered year

b. first Wednesday after first Monday in November of every even-numbered year

c. first Tuesday after first Thursday in November of every even-numbered year

d. first Tuesday after first Monday in November of every odd-numbered year

14) How much of the Senate is elected every two years?

a. 100%

b. half

c. one-fourth

d. one-third

15) United States senators' term is ___ years; that's one of the ___ elected terms in the world.

a. two… shortest

b. four… quickest

c. six… longest

d. none of the above

16) All American national elections are on a fixed cycle (except when an officeholder resigns or dies). Which of the following dire situations would affect this schedule?

a. war

b. economic collapse

c. terrorist attacks

d. none of the above

17) A prime minister once remarked: "In your system, you guys campaign for 24 hours a day, every day for two years. You know, politics is one thing, but we have to run a government." Which was the origin country of this politician?

a. Belgium

b. France

c. Canada

d. Great Britain

18) The United States was the ___ nation to choose its chief executive by popular election.

a. first

b. second

c. twentieth

d. fourth

19) Today, how many states elect judges?

a. 20

b. 39

c. 50

d. 10

20) The US system sets strict limits on individual donations: no one may contribute more than ___ to any individual candidate.

a. $2,700

b. $3.5 million

c. $45,000

d. $500

21) Parties generally nominate candidates from which office for president?

a. attorney general

b. secretary of state

c. governor

d. House

22) ___ is the date on the primary calendar when most states hold primaries and caucuses on the same day.

a. Super Tuesday

b. Super Election Day

c. Super Primaries and Caucuses Day

d. none of the above

23) Which event typically has the effect of creating an increase in the poll numbers for a presidential candidate?

a. political party convention

b. rock concert

c. graduation ceremony

d. none of the above

24) ___ refers to a system under which the winning candidate receives all the delegates for that state.

a. Winner-take-all system

b. Proportional representation

c. Demographic system

d. none of the above

25) A system of ___ allocates delegates based on the proportion of the vote a candidate wins.

a. winner-take-all

b. demographics

c. proportional representation

d. none of the above

26) Traditionally, which party has adhered to the winner-take-all system?

a. Republicans

b. Democrats

c. Green Party

d. none of the above

27) Traditionally, which party has adhered to the proportional representation system?

a. Republicans

b. Social Party

c. Democrats

d. all of the above

28) During the primary season, candidates must

a. raise as much money as possible

b. visit as many states as possible

c. make a solid first impression

d. avoid television commercials

29) When members of a political party get together before a general election to choose delegates to the convention, they are attending a

   a. primary

   b. general election meeting

   c. caucus

   d. convention planning meeting

30) When only party members can cast a vote in the primary, it is known as a(n)

   a. caucus

   b. open primary

   c. closed primary

   d. private vote

31) When any eligible voter can vote in a primary, it is known as a(n)

   a. caucus

   b. closed primary

   c. public vote

   d. open primary

32) Party officials hope to have a candidate by

   a. Labor Day

   b. Super Tuesday

   c. Fourth of July

   d. Memorial Day

33) Candidates running in the primary are talking to more _____ voters and then to more _____ voters in the general election.

   a. centrist; ideologically driven

   b. ideologically driven; centrist

   c. liberal; conservative

   d. conservative; liberal

34) ____ refers to the tendency for members of Congress to win reelection in overwhelming numbers.

   a. Nepotism advantage

   b. Incumbency advantage

  c. Insider advantage

  d. none of the above

35) What are midterm elections?

  a. Elections held in the middle of the year.

  b. Elections held in the middle of each term.

  c. Elections held in a nonpresidential election year.

  d. none of the above

Discussion Questions

1) Explain the concept of groupthink.

2) What conditions must be met for public opinion to guide the government?

3) Discuss the difference between a push poll and a scientific survey.

4) Why is it essential for survey research to be random?

5) Compare the boomerang and bandwagon effects.

6) Discuss factors affecting how one thinks politically.

7) Why are those better educated more likely to be involved? Should the government work to teach all citizens about civic duty? How would they do so?

8) How do friends and family influence voting behavior? How about the neighborhood? Civic organizations?

Video Resources

Media Education Foundation http://www.mediaed.org/

"Poll Bearers," from The Daily Show http://www.cc.com/video-clips/xd8n18/the-daily-show-with-jon-stewart-poll-bearers

Icount https://icount.com/

PBS Frontline http://www.pbs.org/wgbh/pages/frontline/view/

Firing Line Debates https://www.hoover.org/library-archives/collections/firing-line

Art as Propaganda: The Nazi Degenerate Art Exhibit www.facinghistory.org/resource-library/video/art-propaganda-nazi-degenerate-art-exhibit

Whymediashouldthinktwiceaboutpublic-opinionpolls:Paneldiscussionhttp://journalistsresource.org/politics-and-government/criticism-media-use-public-opinion-polls/

Why policy decisions may not reflect perceived public opinion - Khan Academy www.khanacademy.org/humanities/ap-us-government-and-politics/american-political-ideologies-and-beliefs/evaluating-public-opinion-data/v/why-policy-decisions-may-not-reflect-perceived-public-opinion

Bot or not? How fake social media accounts could influence voting www.pbs.org/newshour/extra/lessons-plans/lesson-plan-how-to-use-social-media-for-social-good/

The Nature of Public Opinion https://courses.lumenlearning.com/os-government2e/chapter/the-nature-of-public-opinion/

Does Public Opinion Matter? World Attitudes on Global Governance www.cfr.org/event/does-public-opinion-matter-world-attitudes-global-governance-0

Website Resources

Public Agenda Online http://www.publicagenda.org/

Center for Civic Engagement http://www.engage.northwestern.edu

Political Resources Online http://politicalresources.com/

Roper Center for Public Opinion Research https://ropercenter.cornell.edu/

Online Library of Liberty http://oll.libertyfund.org/

Polling Report http://pollingreport.com/

Gallup www.gallup.com

Pew Research Center for the People and the Press http://www.people-press.org/

CNN Politics Polling Center http://www.cnn.com/POLITICS/pollingcenter/index.html

CHAPTER 12

BUREAUCRACY

12.1 What Is Bureaucracy and Why Do We Need It?

Bureaucracy comes from the French *bureaucratie* – from *bureau* (office) and *cratie* (power) – and it originally indicated the group of officials who, divided into various hierarchical levels, carry out the functions of the public administration in the state. In this broad sense, bureaucracy is a hierarchical structure that operates following precise rules. At the same time, bureaucracy has been widely considered as being the most efficient form of organization achieved so far - at least at the level of the ideal model - since it is a functional structure for the management of large quantities of work. Hence, this term does not only define political management, but any set of officials of a body, who in some way conduct the management of this organization (Albrow 1970; 16-30).[134]

Drawing from these features, there have been several definitions of bureaucracy in the literature, of which the most famous is Max Weber's definition of **bureaucracy** as: "an organization where tasks are divided among technical specialists who devote their full working capacity to the organization and whose activities are coordinated by rational rules, hierarchy and written documents".[135] According to Weber, bureaucracy was an improvement compared to previous societal forms of political management and it was necessary to resolve many political issues in current societies. Whereas in ancient democracies, such as the Athenian one, small dimensions of the republic and a conception of political involvement based on liberty as self-government required the whole citizenry to take part in the political management of the community, current

---

[134] Albrow M. (1970), *Bureaucracy*, Macmillan International Higher Education, New York.
[135] Weber, M. (1978). Bureaucracy. In Economy and society: An outline of interpretive sociology. Trans. and ed. G. Roth and C. Wittich. Berkeley: University of California Press.

societies are too complex and large to grant equal direct political participation to each citizen. For this reason, current political systems have shifted towards representative forms of government, which means that citizens elect ruling elites which are afterwards in charge of the political decisions of the country (Manin 1997; 67-80).[136]

Representative systems yet encompass certain problematic features from a democratic point of view, since elections are simultaneously aristocratic and democratic. On the one hand, elections are aristocratic because they do not produce similarity between rulers and ruled, rather the opposite. Elections tend to create aristocracies, since they select candidates that prove to have the politically relevant qualities and that are deemed superior by the dominant values in the culture. Yet, on the other hand, elections are also democratic: even if there is inequality regarding who can be selected, citizens possess an equal power in deciding who is worth assuming a certain position (Manin 1997; 156-160).

This dual character is reflected by bureaucracy, since this mechanism can be good at some things - making decisions quickly and consistently and maximizing expertise - but at the same time it can also be easily corrupted because of the lack of transparency and democratic accountability. For this reason, bureaucracy has been a central topic of study in political science over the last centuries. That is, political literature has tried to explain why certain public policy decisions are preferred over others and how relevant officials in the government use these policies to protect or promote their own agency's special interests against other bodies. To understand this debate better, it is first essential to consider how bureaucratic theory has developed over time and how it has been connected to the development of modern society.

12.2 The Framework and History

Bureaucracy is a result of both an economic and political development of our societies. On the one side, the development and enlargement of capitalist industries required economic companies not only to employ more employees, but also more technical and managerial personnel within the industry to deal with the increased managerial requirements of these businesses. On the other side, the expansion of the State into new areas of welfare provision and economic regulation, and the emergence of a mass political party required the expansion of a bureaucratic administration. In this regard, bureaucratization has become a universal feature of modern society and because of its indispensability, any modern organization must rely on some form of bureaucratic management to carry out its tasks. In Weber's words

---

[136] Manin B. (1997), *The Principles of Representative Government*, Cambridge University Press, Cambridge.

(1968; 223)[137]: "the choice is only between bureaucracy and dilettantism in the field of administration".

Bureaucratization was thus the management response to the development of the territorial state and the capitalist economy, whose administrative needs could not be met by traditional means employed by previous societies. In this regard, the wave of democratization that has occurred in western societies over the last centuries has played a significant part in fostering bureaucracy's importance. Democracy has levelled traditional status differences by requiring a system operating on the basis of impartiality between citizens and by offering opportunities for bureaucratic careers that are linked to education and merit rather than family status only.

However, democracy did not foster bureaucratic development by itself, since this latter has always been intertwined with another process typical of modern societies, namely the process of **rationalization**. This latter can be defined as the historical drive towards a world in which "one can, in principle, master all things by calculation" (Weber 1946 [1919]; 139).[138] As for bureaucracy, rationalization processes can be found in many different spheres of society. In the economy, modern capitalism depends on a calculable process of production structured on division of labor, centralization of production control and other processes that enhance the calculability of the production process. For what concerns the legislative and administrative sphere, precise rules, an autonomous judiciary and a professional bureaucracy enhance the predictability in the sociopolitical environment, thus making it easy to govern a large mass society.

This process of rationalization has become so intertwined with modern society that it has influenced the people's values and identity. It is in this regard that Weber maintained that modern organizations require a "person of vocation", namely a rational personality type connected to the protestant ethic (Weber 1946; 140-141). Hence, according to Weber, the interplay between rationalization and bureaucracy structured modern rational western civilization in three main regards.[139]

First, rational action presupposes *knowledge* of the ideational and material circumstances structuring the action. To act rationally is to act conscious of the consequences of the action and it thus requires a means-ends relationships in order to maximize the outcome of the action with the least expenditure of resources. Weber called this process 'intellectualization', whereby modern knowledge replaces old metaphysics based on superstitions and irrational thoughts. Second, rational processes must be *impersonal*

---

[137] Weber M. (1968), *Economy and Society. An Outline of Interpretative Sociology*, Bedminister Press, New York.
[138] Weber M. (1919), "Science as a Vocation", in Gerth. H.H., and Wright Mills C. (1946), *From Max Weber: Essays in Sociology*, Oxford: Oxford University Press.
[139] Brubaker R. (1992), *The Limits of Rationality*, London: Routledge.

and objective. For example, workers in industrial capitalism are reduced to sheer numbers and non-economic considerations are not relevant to their judgment. In the same way, rules obey formal codes and apply equally to all the citizenry. Third, *control* is essential, since technological and scientific development have offered societies the chance to impose their mastery not only over nature, but also over human beings' social life. It is in this regard then that a rational and disciplinary ethos has increasingly penetrated into every aspect of social life.

Finally, bureaucracy and rationalization are also connected because the latter is essential in giving bureaucracy a different source of legitimacy than traditional powers. That is, while traditional societies relied on societal custom and habit to legitimize their power, modern societies achieved this legitimation simply by adhering to precisely defined rules, such as following the conduct of office, governing the criteria for appointment and the scope of authority (Albrow 1970; 84.91). In a nutshell, bureaucracy imposed itself as an indispensable system of administration rooted in the requirements of the modern world, since it allowed governments to coordinate action over a large area, to ensure continuity of operation, to acquire a monopoly of expertise and to guarantee an internal social cohesion and morale.

However, the development of bureaucracy did not lead to positive consequences only, since it also paved the way to political debates concerning its efficiency and negative consequences. One of the first debates arose regarding the **patronage system,** namely the political system where the appointment or hiring of a person to a government post is decided on the basis of partisan loyalty. By means of this system, elected officials had the opportunity to use their power to reward the people who helped them win and maintain office. Originally, proponents of patronage sustained that it promoted direct accountability of those who were selected and it also diminished elitism in politics by allowing commoners to occupy important roles.[140]

Political patronage has a long history in the United States, since it was already included in the Article 2 of the constitution. In this article, it is specified that the President has powers of appointment to choose a large number of U.S. officials, such as ambassadors, agency heads, military office and other high-ranking members of government. This power is yet not absolute, since the Senate has confirmation powers to check this selection. Nonetheless, this practice has often been a powerful political tool for the President. For this reason, appointments became so widespread that they formed a '**spoils system**', namely a political organization where the political party which won the elections gives high-ranking civil service jobs to its supporters, both as a

---

[140] Pollock, J.K. (1937), "The cost of the patronage system.", *The Annals of the American Academy of Political and Social Science*, 189 (1), 29-34.

reward for working toward victory and a way to make sure that they continue working for the party after the victory.[141]

This process is different from a merit system in which offices are assigned independently of political affiliation and according to impartial procedures meant to award candidates on the basis of some measure of merit. This difference created problems at the end of the 19th century, when 'spoils system' became too widespread, especially at local level, thus giving political leaders the opportunity to dominate local government and politics by building a community of supporters whose main aim was to maintain power from one election to another. Hence, patronage encompasses also several deficiencies that may erode public confidence in this system, since it can favor corruption and it can create a system where those appointed are unlikely to speak freely and to criticize their bosses on whom their job depends.[142]

For this reason, at the end of the 19th century, the Pendleton Act of 1883 shifted the appointment process to a merit-based system, in which recruitment was made by means of competitive exams meant to assess competence rather than partisan affiliation. In this way, **neutral competence** became the primary selection method and rulers used it to deliver the message that in an ideal bureaucratic structure power is hierarchical and rule based. That is, a well-functioning bureaucratic system must appoint individuals according to their expertise and it must promote bureaucrats on the basis of merit, not personal affiliations. In this way, a neutral bureaucratic organization can make decisions better and more quickly than a patronage system and even than a democracy based on a self-government ideal.

The percentage of civil service employees recruited according to a neutral competence principle has steadily increased over the years in any society, and in the United State it reached more than 90% after both the Civil Service Reform Act signed by President Jimmy Carter in 1978 and the amendments enacted by the Supreme Court over the years to limit the externalities of partisan patronage (Ingraham & Ban 1984).[143] Nowadays, political patronage is less prevalent than in the past, since presidents now appoint less than 1% of all federal positions. Yet, this does not mean that patronage has lost all its relevance, since strategic appointments are still an important political means used by presidents to reward their supporters and to create a working relationship with members of congress.

[141] Folke, O., Hirano S., and Snyder Jr J.M. (2011), "Patronage and elections in US states.", *American Political Science Review*, 105 (3), 567-585.

[142] Friedrich C.J. (1937), "The rise and decline of the spoils tradition.", *The Annals of the American Academy of Political and Social Science*, 189 (1), 10-16.

[143] Ingraham, P. W. and Ban C. (1984), *Legislating Bureaucratic Change: Civil Service Reform Act of 1978*, SUNY Press, New York.

In sum, the historical development of bureaucracy describes that this form of organization has become an essential feature for the management of complex modern societies. However, at the same time, bureaucracy transfers political power from the citizenry to technical officers, so the former may question the latter's power and they could request increased accountability and transparency in return for the transfer of power. That is, citizens want to have some form of control over the elites ruling government and other institutions and corporations. Above all, citizens want to know how governments are using the people's money, especially concerning taxpayer funds.

One way of posing such control is to make bureaucrats accountable by requiring them to follow rules designed to treat people fairly, to refrain from politics on the job, and to fill out paperwork. However, these requests may also lead to unforeseen externalities, such as **the Red Tape issue**, which defines an excessive regulation or conformity to formal rules that is considered redundant and hinders action or other decision-making processes. This issue draws its name from the case in the 16th century when Henry VIII besieged Pope Clement VII with a significant amount of petitions for the annulment of his marriage to Catherine of Aragon. The pile of documents was rolled and stacked in original condition, each one sealed and bound with the obligatory red tape, as was the custom. Hence, the name red tape issue to describe an excessive amount of procedures to follow.[144]

The problem is thus that in order to respond to the people's request for accountability, civic service employees may be asked to fill out unnecessary paperwork, to obtain unnecessary licenses, to have multiple people or committees approve a decision and finally, to follow various minor rules that unavoidably slow down the whole bureaucratic process. In short, "red tape" indicates the governmental problem for which any official routine or procedure marked by excessive complexity results in delay or inaction. Therefore, governments must find a way to balance their need to get things done and to satisfy the people's need for transparency and accountability. To resolve this problem, the US government divided the federal bureaucracy in three branches: legislative, executive and judiciary.

12.3 Bureaucracy in the United States

The legislative branch drafts proposed laws, confirms or rejects presidential nominations for heads of federal agencies, federal judges and the Supreme Court, it has the authority to declare war and finally, it also disposes of substantial investigative powers.

---

[144] Bozeman, B. (1993), "A theory of government "Red tape", *Journal of public administration research and theory*, 3.3, 273-304.

American citizens have the right to vote for Senators and Representatives through free, confidential ballots. This branch includes a *Congress* composed of two parts: The Senate and the House of Representatives. In order to pass legislation and send it to the President for the signature, both these bodies must pass the same bill by majority vote (Little & Ogle 2006; 25-31).[145]

The Senate includes two elected senators per state for a total of 100 Senators, with the Vice-President serving as President of the Senate. These latter are in charge for a period of six years and their terms are staggered so that about 1/3 of the Senate is up for reelection every two years, even though there is no limit to the number of terms an individual can serve. Overall, the Senate is meant to confirm President's appointments that require consent, to provide advice on treaties' ratification, to impeach cases for federal officials and it has also to approve appointments to the Vice Presidency and any treaty that involves foreign trade.[146]

The House of Representatives has several powers, such as initiating revenue bills, impeaching federal officials, and electing the President in the case of an Electoral College tie. This institution includes 435 elected Representatives, which are divided among the 50 states in proportion to their total population. There are additional 6 non-voting delegates who represent the District of Columbia, Puerto Rico and the territories. The presiding officer of the chamber is the speaker of the House and it is elected by other representatives. These elected officials serve a two-year term, and there is no limit to the number of terms an individual can serve.

The legislative branch encompasses also special agencies and offices that provide support services to Congress, the list of which includes agencies such as the Architect of the Capitol, the Congressional Budget Office, the Congressional Research Service, the Copyright Office, the Government Accountability Office, the Government Publishing Office, the House Office of Inspector General, the House Office of the Clerk, the Joint Congressional Committee on Inaugural Ceremonies, the Library of Congress, the Medicaid and CHIP Payment and Access Commission, the Medicare Payment Advisory Commission, the Office of Compliance, the Open World Leadership Center, the Stennis Center for Public Service, the U.S. Botanic Garden, the U.S. Capitol Police and the U.S. Capitol Visitor Center.

Second, the **executive branch** carries out and enforces laws. Executive power is vested in the President of the United States, namely the individual in charge of leading

---

[145] Little, T. H., Ogle D. B. (2006), *The legislative branch of state government: people, process, and politics*, ABC-CLIO, California.

[146] The White House Government, "The Legislative Branch", retrieved at: https://www.whitehouse.gov/about-the-white-house/our-government/the-legislative-branch/

the country. He or she is the head of state, leader of the federal government, and Commander in Chief of the United States armed forces. The president serves a four-year term and can be elected no more than two times. During his or her mandate, the president is responsible for implementing the laws written by Congress, while it is responsibility of the Cabinet and of independent federal agencies to take care of the day-to-day enforcement and administration of federal laws. These bureaucracies do so by providing regulations and restrictions on businesses and individuals, like limitations on allowable air pollution from factories, or the requirements that cars have airbags, or making sure that people do not have unfettered access to certain classes of drugs or overstay their visas.[147]

The president is supported by the Vice-president and when the former is unable to serve, the latter becomes president. The vice president can be elected and can serve an unlimited number of four-year terms as vice president, even under a different president. Vice-President is part of The Cabinet together with other advisors such as the heads of executive departments and other high ranking government officials. These advisors are nominated by the President and must be approved by a simple majority of the Senate.

Much of the work in the executive branch is thus done by executive departments, independent agencies and other boards, commissions, and committees. The most important executive department is 'The Executive Office of the Presidency' which was born in the New Deal expansion of federal power and that is aimed at coordinating the bureaucracy. The Executive Office of the Presidency (EOP) is home to agencies that the president appoints to help him manage the large range of issues that the White House has to deal with on a daily basis. This office – composed by different bodies such as the office of the President, the National Security Council, the Office of the United States Trade Representatives, etc. - is in charge of communicating the president's message and deals with the federal budget, security, and other high priorities.[148]

The office of the president cooperates with the **Executive Departments**, namely the 15 main agencies of the federal government that cover essential government functions or policy areas where clientele groups have been effective at lobbying for representation at the executive level, such as the U.S. department of Defense, Commerce, Justice, Labor and so on. The heads of these 15 agencies – also called "secretaries", except for the head of the Justice Department, who is called the "attorney general" are also members of the president's cabinet. These 15 main agencies are divided in

---

[147] The White House Government, "The Executive Branch", retrieved at: https://www.whitehouse.gov/about-the-white-house/our-government/the-executive-branch/.

[148] Branches of the U.S. Government, USA Government, retrieved at: https://www.usa.gov/branches-of-government.

Executive Sub-agencies and Bureaus, namely smaller sub-agencies aimed at supporting specialized work within their parent executive department agencies.

Finally, there are also independent agencies that are not represented in the cabinet and are not part of the Executive Office of the president, but which are structured similarly to other executive bodies with a presidential appointee at the top (some of whom can be fired by the president, and some of whom cannot). These bodies deal with government operations and issues concerning the economy and regulatory oversight. In case there are areas that do not fall under these agencies (historic preservations, endangered species, Nuclear waste, etc.), Congress or the President can establish Boards, Commissions and Committees to manage these specific tasks. Even though they are not officially part of the executive branch, these bodies are also quasi-official agencies, namely organizations that are required by federal statute to release certain information about their programs and activities in the Federal Register, the daily journal of government activities.[149]

Overall then, the executive branch consists of several agencies as the president's cabinet, the departments under the responsibility of the cabinet members and all the agencies, boards, and commissions that put the laws of Congress into action. Moreover, these bodies also include everyone serving in the U.S. military and public corporations like the U.S. Post Office. Overall then, the Federal bureaucracy performs different central functions like diplomacy, defense, and internal affairs. Yet, these branches also perform 'minor' tasks such as responding to clientele groups of veterans, farmers, teachers, or other groups who feel that they have particular concerns.

Third, **the Judicial Branch** interprets the meaning of laws, applies laws to individual cases, and decides if laws violate the Constitution. It is composed of the Supreme Court and other federal courts. The former is the highest court in the United States, whose nine Justices – a Chief Justice and eight Associate Justices - are nominated by the president and must be approved by the Senate. To decide a case. there must be a minimum or quorum of six Justices, while if there is an even number of Justices and a case results in a tie, the lower court's decision stands. These Justices' service is not fixed term, since they serve until their death, retirement, or removal in exceptional circumstances.[150]

Together with the Supreme Court, the Constitution gives Congress the authority to establish other federal courts to handle cases that involve federal laws including

---

[149] Cohen, J. E. (1988), *The politics of the US cabinet: Representation in the executive branch, 1789-1984.* University of Pittsburgh Press, Pennsylvania.
[150] The White House. "The Judiciary Branch", retrieved at: https://www.whitehouse.gov/about-the-white-house/our-government/the-judicial-branch/

tax and bankruptcy, lawsuits involving U.S. and state governments or the Constitution, and more. Other federal judicial agencies and programs support the courts and research judicial policy. The appointments for these federal judgeships follow the same basic process as the one for the appointment of Supreme Court Justices.

First, the President nominates a person to fill a vacant judgeship, then the Senate Judiciary Committee holds a hearing on the nominee and votes on whether to forward the nomination to the full Senate. If the nomination moves forward, the Senate can debate the nomination. Debate must end before the Senate can vote on whether to confirm the nominee. A Senator will request unanimous consent to end the debate, but any Senator can refuse. Without unanimous consent, the Senate must pass a cloture motion to end the debate. It takes a simple majority of votes - 51 if all 100 Senators vote - to pass cloture and end debate about a federal judicial nominee. Once the debate ends, the Senate votes on confirmation. The nominee for Supreme Court or any other federal judgeship needs a simple majority of votes - 51 if all 100 Senators vote - to be confirmed.

Therefore, these three sides of government are bureaucracies that perform essential tasks for the management of the United States, since they provide administration, rule-making which is filling in all the technical details in the laws Congress passes so that they can be enforced, and bureaucratic discretion when the bureaucracy exercises legislative power delegated to it by congressional law through judgment.

Chapter 12: Bureaucracy

1) The bureaucracy, compared to Congress,

   a. is older.

   b. is younger.

   c. is much more diverse.

   d. is more educated.

2) The practice, by which political winners reward their supporters with government jobs and contracts, is known as

   a. the spoils system.

   b. pandering.

   c. pay-for-play.

   d. the nepotism system.

3) The act of Congress requiring the federal government to hire well-qualified public servants in 1883 was

   a. the Hatch.

   b. the Hire Qualified Government Workers Act of 1883.

   c. the McCain-Feingold Act.

   d. the Pendleton Civil Service Act.

4) A transparent chain of command, where all employees know who their supervisors are and who reports to them, is an example of a

   a. hierarchy.

   b. merit-based system.

   c. spoils system.

   d. patronage.

5) The ultimate purpose of creating a professional merit-based civil service system is to

   a. give jobs to friends

   b. hire well-qualified individuals

   c. win elections

   d. hire party members

6) The effort to outlaw all liquor under Prohibition created a new law enforcement agency in the

   a. Church of Jesus Christ of Latter-day Saints.

   b. Department of the Interior.

   c. Federal Bureau of Investigation.

   d. Department of the Treasury.

7) The Federal Reserve was created

   a. to stabilize banking.

   b. to save money.

   c. to prepare for World War I.

   d. to build Fort Knox.

8) Laws written by Congress are typically

   a. very precise.

   b. consensual.

   c. detailed.

   d. vague.

9) After an agency has devised a rule, it sends the rule to the _____ for approval.

   a. Office of Rule Enforcement

   b. General Accounting Office

   c. Federal Register

   d. Office of Management and Budget

10) The daily journal of the federal government is

   a. The Federal Register.

   b. The New York Times.

   c. The Journal of Rules.

   d. The Hill.

11) Because bureaucracies are so rule-based, they

   a. make decisions that usually only serve public employees.

   b. make poor decisions.

    c. make conflicting and confusing decisions.

    d. make decisions with accountability and equality, but also with much bureaucratic red tape.

12) Bureaucracies exist

    a. in both the private and public sectors.

    b. only in government.

    c. at the federal level.

    d. in Europe, for the most part.

13) The final rule is published in the

    a. Federal Rule Book

    b. Federal Guidelines

    c. Federal Bureaucracy Guidelines

    d. Federal Register

14) Bureaucracies touch

    a. every aspect of our lives.

    b. very little of our day-to-day existence.

    c. the economy, mainly.

    d. social issues, mainly.

15) Which of the following is an example of a federal agency designed to serve a clientele group?

    a. State Department

    b. Department of Justice

    c. Homeland Security

    d. Agriculture

16) President George Washington's administration had all of the following cabinet departments except

    a. Interior.

    b. War.

    c. State.

    d. Treasury.

17) All of the following are events that led to growth in the federal bureaucracy except

    a. 9/11.

    b. The Emancipation Proclamation.

    c. WWII.

    d. The Great Depression.

18) The cabinet secretary who sits farthest away from the president at cabinet meetings is

    a. Secretary of Defense.

    b. Secretary of Treasury.

    c. Secretary of Homeland Security.

    d. Secretary of State.

19) Who defined bureaucracy as "an organization where tasks are divided among technical specialists who devote their full working capacity to the organization and whose activities are coordinated by rational rules, hierarchy and written documents"

    a. Douglas North

    b. Karl Marx

    c. Max Weber

    d. None of the above.

20) True or False: According to Weber, bureaucracy was a decline compared to previous societal forms of political management and it was necessary to resolve many political issues in current societies

21) True or False: Bureaucracy has not been a central topic of study in political science over the last centuries.

22) According to Bernard Manin, elections tend to create

    a. democracies

    b. monarchies

    c. aristocracies

    d. None of the above

23) True or False: According to Bernard Manin, elections tend to create aristocracies, since they select candidates that prove to have the politically relevant qualities and that are deemed superior by the dominant values in the culture.

24) Which article of the United States Constitution included political patronage?

a. Article 1

b. Article 2

c. Article 4

d. Article 5

25) True or False: U.S. citizens want to know how governments are using the people's money, especially concerning taxpayer funds

Discussion Questions

1) How many bureaucracies do you think you deal with in a day?

2) Who controls the bureaucracy?

3) Should bureaucrats be elected?

4) Bureaucrats have a negative perception. Is this deserved or exaggerated?

5) Do bureaucrats do good or is it all bad?

Video Resources

PBS Frontline

Judicial Branch and the Federal Bureaucracy - Bill of Rights Institute http://billofrightsinstitute.org/videos/judicial-branch-and-the-federal-bureaucracy-apgov-prep-webinar

Bureaucracy - A documentary by Dr Richard Cole www.youtube.com/watch?v=B_nsZlcC12g

Too Big to Fail (2011) HBO Films

Apollo 13 (1995)

Brazil (1985)

Yes, Minister (1980–1984) BBC

Yes, Prime Minister (1986–1988) BBC

The Trial (1962)

Catch-22 (1970)

Dr. Strangelove or: How I Learned to Stop Worrying and Love the Bomb (1964)

Website Resources

Federal Register https://www.federalregister.gov/

USA.gov http://www.usa.gov/

Who are the bureaucrats? http://www.ushistory.org/gov/8c.asp

What is the Federal Bureaucracy? https://www.youtube.com/watch?v=PZg1gp2VZDo

Bureaucracy Basics: Crash Course Government and Politics #15 https://www.youtube.com/watch?v=I8EQAnKntLs

POLITICAL PARTIES AND INTEREST GROUPS

Both political parties and interest groups are social bodies bound together by shared interests. Political parties are modern forms of factions in the sense that they seek goals particular to their interests. Interest groups have a shared vision to use the political system to attain their goals. Parties can develop higher degrees of cohesion in fragmented political systems. Interest groups use lobbying as a tool. Lobbying can be both direct and indirect; it is trying to persuade government officials to do something.

In countries with more than two parties, partisanship likely bows to practicalities and compromise. In the United States, it is challenging for third parties to get any relevant traction at the national level. There may be structural reasons that justify the maintenance of the two-party system in the United States. The Democrats and the Republicans dominate the national political spectrum today, which will likely remain so for the following years.

13.1 Parties and Interest Groups

Both political parties and interest groups are social bodies bound together by shared interests. They do their best to take advantage of the political system to accomplish their political goals. These are the factions James Madison feared would be so destructive of democracy. The way they go about working the system to get political goals realized is very different.

Political parties are modern forms of factions in the sense that they seek goals particular to their interests. *Political parties* are groups bound by common interests which seek to use the political system to attain their goals from inside the system by control-ling government. Different factors may affect and influence parties and interest groups' internal processes, such as choosing a favorite candidate and getting him elected. This form of *electioneering* is nominating and electing candidates to office. Once they are in office, they are *governing public officials* and run the political show.

Interest groups have a shared vision to use the political system to accomplish their goals. *Interest groups*, including corporations, are societies bound by common interests which endeavor to use the political system to achieve their policy goals by persuad-ing inside people in power that will give them what they want. This form of action is known as lobbying. The act of persuading officials is a type of lobbying. It is typical for party representatives in government and interest group lobbyists outside the gov-ernment to develop close working relationships where their interests overlap. These actions magnify their power.

13.2 The Role of Parties in a Democracy[151],[152]

What is involved with the duties of a political party? A political party must repre-sent the interests of its members by gaining control of the government. Parties have vital advantages and tools to strengthen and facilitate democracy in some crucial ways. Parties act as democracy-strengthening agents by providing a bridge and connection between voters and their elected officials.

Political parties also practice partisan politics. *Partisanship* is about identifying one's interests with a party's platform. Elected officials can be held accountable to the people who vote for them through re-election. *Accountability* is about ensuring our elected officials do what they say they are going to do. When a political party is helping to create accountability, they provide cohesion. Parties can develop higher degrees of cohesion in fragmented political systems. Parties also provide a voice to those in power, and they provide the opposition voice to those who are not in government.

13.3 Political Parties Create the Normality

Political parties create the normality that people countenance since they politically shape the social and cultural environment. The *responsible party model* is when political

---

[151] For information on the role of political parties in socialist countries, see Corwin 11-24. Generally, in Cuba, as in China, only members of the Communist Party are allowed to vote or hold public office, and the party's most relevant members make all government decisions. Some exceptions to this rule may apply in China since the Asian country has a multiparty system, in which the Communist Party has authority over the rest.

[152] Under certain conditions, The Chinese political system allows for the participation of some non-CCP members (independents) and members of minor parties in the National People's Congress (NPC). The CCP is the only party that effectively holds power at the national level.

parties conform to paragons about how parties should ideally operate. One of these tools is the party platform. A *party platform* is a distinct set of policies based on a party's ideology, whose candidates align. People expect them to follow the party's platform and promises. If elected, citizens expect candidates to enact the values and policies of the party.

Voters make their choices based on the public policies political parties promote through their platforms; they are willing to vote against the party's candidates if they fail to keep their campaign promises successfully. Voters will likely reject party officials at the polls if party officials poorly carry out their partisan platforms' commitments. In the United States, the responsible party model is nothing but a yardstick against which actual parties can be measured.

United States parties can create unique party platforms different from each other in the political system. With several levels and branches, the national system offers many places where people and groups can engage the government. Candidates, in general, promise to support their party's platform if elected. People choose the political party they want to support through a process called partisan sorting. *Partisan sorting* identifies with the party because it most closely stands for their views and values and not for regional or other non-ideological reasons. Partisan sorting has historically been enforced by voters rather than by tight political party regulations. Increasingly, party members are not only partisan (that is, they identify with the political team); they are hyperpartisan.

Hyper-partisanship is when people are loyal to the party at all costs. Hyper-partisanship is an ideology that suggests that someone would choose their team over the other every time, even if it may require that they change their minds on policy priorities or values to do so. When voters are unwilling to vote against their party, even when it lets them down because the priority is to deny their opponents a win, they send a message to their party that it is acceptable not to keep promises.

To follow the dictates of the political party leaders to which they belong, House members and senators in the United States Congress may sometimes ignore the voters in their home states and the groups that represent them. For example, a member of the United States Congress from a state with a sizable elderly population may be inclined to vote in favor of legislation that will likely increase the benefits for retired people. However, their political party leaders, who disapprove of government spending on social programs, may ask for a vote against the legislation. The opposite can also occur, especially in the case of a legislator soon facing re-election. With two-year terms of office, it is more likely to see House members buck their party in favor of their constituents. (Corwin, 21)

13.4 Party Organization and Decision-Making

In liberal democratic countries, political parties no longer choose leaders in smoke-filled rooms behind the scenes. There is a formal and transparent process. Historically, *party machines* were organizations in which party leaders or "bosses" made the decisions and kept their voters' loyalty by providing them with services and support. Reforms included bringing party decisions, like whom to nominate, out of the proverbial "smoke-filled rooms." The way we are choosing political candidates today is in the smoke-free air of democratic transparency.

Political parties choose candidates through primaries and caucuses. *Primary elections*, often abbreviated to *primaries*, are processes by which voters can indicate their political preference for their party's candidate, or a general candidate, in an upcoming general election, local election, or by-election. *Primaries* are usually party-held preliminary elections.

A *caucus* is a meeting of political supporters or members (usually active) of a specific political party or movement. The definition of this term varies between countries and political cultures. *Caucuses* are the party gatherings where partisans debate candidate choices openly. While party officials still have a great deal of clout and resources, they are no longer "the boss."

Generally, political parties in the United States do not like nominating methods that allow non-party members to participate in selecting party nominees. In 2000, the United States Supreme Court heard a case brought by the California Democratic Party, the California Republican Party, and the California Libertarian Party. At the time, the parties argued that they had the right to determine who associated with the party and who participated in choosing the party nominee. The Supreme Court ultimately agreed to limit the states' choices for nomination methods to closed and open primaries.

13.5 A four-part party structure

The party structure rests in, more or less, four essential elements that make the party structure. The people in the electorate who identify with the party are people who vote party lines. These citizens are known as the *party followers* (1). On the other hand, *party activists* (2) are the party base, the most ideologically extreme of the party's voters. These activists are the ones that are the core group of people within the political party. *Party leaders* (3) are those who act as the official representatives of the political party.

The *party organization* is the official group, whose career party officials are part of it, that runs the party. This party organization is the functioning of the party within the state. Those who win an election are known as the *party-in-government members* (4) because they represent the people. *Party identification* is when people think of themselves as partisans (team members) and generally vote for the party. Identity politics are crucial to understanding national politics since political representation is, for some experts, rooted in the representatives' racial, ethnic, socioeconomic, gender, and sexual identity.

13.6 Why does the United States have a two-party political system?

In countries with more than two parties, partisanship likely bows to practicalities and compromise. If not, a party typically gets left out in the cold. In the United States, it is challenging for third parties to get any traction at the national level. There are structural reasons for the two-party system in the United States. The primary structural reason is that the United States does not have a proportional representation system, often found in parliamentary governments. The United States follows a *single member, first past the post district* model. These congressional districts in the United States have only one person elected—the person who gets the most votes.

The United States has made legal barriers to third parties to access federal funds. This situation implies that candidates are no longer dependent on the parties for their infrastructure. Third parties are vulnerable to the ability of social media to be manipulated and weaponized against them.

Third parties are cutting into fundraising against the major two parties. The parties are struggling to keep financial control in the age of the Internet. There is now much more opportunity for those not blessed by a major party's nomination to stage a campaign. Unlimited corporate and interest group funds are available to parties. A third-party candidate must get a certain number of signatures on a petition to get on the ballot in most states. Usually, when a third party begins to get traction, one of the parties will co-opt the winning issues.

13.7 The Parties Today

The Democrats and the Republicans dominate the United States political spectrum today. Democrats seek an activist government that believed it could and should solve economic and social problems at the national level. Republicans seek a hands-off, antiregulatory business party. By the 1960s, Democrats had a solid hold on the United States Congress. *Richard Nixon's "southern strategy"* took advantage of race as a wedge issue to break conservative southern Democrats away from the Democrats and give the Republicans a majority.

Republicans seek a government that attends to its inherent responsibilities of maintaining a stable monetary and fiscal climate, encouraging a free and competitive economy, and enforcing law and order. Republicans seek a balance between the branches of government and every level. The Republican Party perceives that communism is the principal significant disturber of peace in the world today. Thus, they are reluctant to have relations with countries run by communist leaders and parties.[153]

The "new" Republican coalition began with the rise of evangelical Christian politics. Generally, traditional southerners were far more hierarchical, authoritarian, and evangelical-Christian than the average economic conservative Republican. The relationship between these two Republican groups ultimately led to considerable political friction because of broken promises and misunderstandings. For a time, economic conservatives paid lip service to social conservatives' concerns to keep the peace.

As one understands them today, national political parties did not exist in the United States during the republic's early years. At various points in the past 170 years in the United States history, national elites and voters have sought to create and foster alternatives to the existing party system. Political parties formed as alternatives to the Republican and Democratic parties are known as third parties or minor parties. Third parties, often born of frustration with the current political system, attract supporters from one or both of the existing and leading parties during an election but fail to attract enough votes to win. No third-party candidate has ever won the presidency, and historians still discuss why.

The Republican Party and the Democratic Party still have their economic and social left-right divisions. Trump's coalition's conservative social dimension is an interesting one, as critics argue that social conservatives seem to have set aside the traditional values that so motivated them in years past.

In the United States, two political movements formed fifteen years following John Kennedy's election: the American New Left and the American New Right. The New Left supports the call for social, economic, and political justice based on the equality of class, gender, and race rather than by the traditional leftist-Marxist dogma that socialism would replace the decadent capitalist system. On the other hand, the New Right focuses on downsizing the federal government, supporting state's rights, resisting communism, and reducing government regulations. Even if experts often describe both tendencies as radical movements, they are less orthodox than the traditional Left and the traditional Right.

---

[153] For an in-depth analysis of the values of the two leading parties of the United States, see Donaldson, Robert. *Modern America: a Documentary History of the Nation Since 1945: A Documentary History of the Nation Since 1945*, 2014. London: Routledge. Internet resource.

13.8 Interest Groups' Basics

Madison's definition of factions can apply to both interest groups and political parties. Political parties and interest groups both work together and compete for social influence, although in different ways. Even though its writers did not mention the term interest group in the United States Constitution, the text's framers were aware that individuals would eventually band together in an attempt to use the governmental structure in their favor. One should especially consider that, while interest group activity often transcends political party lines, one can perceive many interests as more supportive of one party than the other. Thus, interest groups and political parties are related and may even closely work together as long as they support similar causes. For example, The American Conservative Union, Citizens United, the National Rifle Association, and National Right to Life will likely have relationships with Republican lawmakers than with Democratic ones.[154]

Interest groups do not need to be moderate—in fact, it is quite the opposite. The more stalwart and uncompromising interest groups stand on their positions, the better situated they are to draw a membership who shares their particular views. Individual citizens can join interest groups that promote and support the causes they favor.

Interest groups help provide representation to the people. The United States Constitution bases political representation almost entirely on geography. Interest groups give people a chance to get other interests they care about represented in government policy pursuing. Interest groups also help with political participation. *Political efficacy* is when people's sense of their ability to have a higher degree of control of their lives. Interest groups give people political participation opportunities that they would not typically have. Interest groups amplify the power of one. What one voice may not achieve, a chorus of multitudes may do much more quickly.

The role the interest groups provide in educating the public is essential. Interest groups usually provide information on their cause to policymakers by testifying in front of congressional committees, working with bureaucrats, or communicating directly with their members. Interest groups provide agenda building. By publicizing the values and interests they care about to the public and policymakers, interest groups can get onto their radar screens. This focus provides program alternatives and program monitoring.

---

[154] Corwin, Edward. "The Basic Doctrine of American Constitutional Law." *Michigan Law Review*, vol. 12, no. 4, 1914, pp. 247–276. JSTOR, www.jstor.org/stable/1276027. Accessed 8 Mar. 2021.

13.9 Understanding Interest Groups

Interest groups can benefit society. Interest groups provide collective goods. *Collective goods* are benefits that, if the group is successful in obtaining them, can be enjoyed by everyone, whether they were members of the group and contributed to the purpose or not. There may be a problem with people who do not contribute to the interest group and only profit from it. *The free-rider problem is* a quandary with getting people to join an interest group if they enjoy the benefit? Does a member get *material benefits* provided of actual monetary worth, like insurance discounts or professional paybacks? Are there *solidary benefits t*hat appeal to one's desire to associate with other people who care about the same things one does? Are there *expressive benefits* which are the opportunity to do work for something that matters deeply to one? Does the interest group provide *selective incentives* which benefit offered to induce people to join up?

We can understand interest groups' politics best if we think about the kinds of interests that bind their members together into different groups. *Economic interest groups* are those which seek to influence policy for the pocketbook issues of their members. On the other hand, *equal opportunity interest groups* pretend to influence the policymaking process by politically targeting citizens who feel unrepresented. These are different from public interest groups which aspire to change policy according to values that they consider are good for every citizen. *Government interest groups* are groups hired by governments to lobby other governments.

13.10 Interest Group Politics

What does one mean by "interest group politics"—are lobbyists politicians? Interest groups and their lobbyists are political actors in that they can bring considerable power to bear on elected officials. Power is relative amongst interest groups. Power can come from strength in numbers and resources.

Interest groups use lobbying as a tool. Lobbying can be direct and indirect. *Lobbying* is trying to persuade government officials to do something. *Lobbyists* are professionals who promote agendas and persuade public officials. *Direct lobbying* impacts public officials directly, while *indirect lobbying* focuses on the public to get the public to put pressure on public officials.

Professional lobbyists come from the ranks of professional politicians. There is a *revolving door* between lobbyists and politicians. The revolving door theory explains how people move from the public to the private sector and then sometimes back to the public sector. With direct lobbying of Congress, the Congress member's lobbyists focus on the committees and subcommittees that deal with the policies they mind.

Interest groups research and investigate policy options and bring their findings to Congress members who cannot become experts on every topic they pass a law on.

Interest groups give money. *Political action committees (PACs)* can raise money but are limited in their contributions to candidates. One practical way for interest groups to increase their power is to form coalitions with other groups conveniently. Interest groups are as interested in influencing the people who implement the laws as they are interested in determining who makes them. The result is the public being shut out of the policymaking process, known as the Iron Triangle. Often, lobbyists, bureaucrats, and Congress members end up working together closely on laws affecting a particular sector that they finally come to identify with each other's interests. *Iron triangles* are the close policymaking relationships between legislators, regulators, and state-regulated groups.

Interest groups provide direct and indirect lobbying. Direct lobbying of the courts happens at the state level. State judges are frequently elected and willing to take campaign contributions. Lobbyists also operate in the Supreme Court and carry out their political mission by writing and submitting amicus curiae briefs on behalf of groups with interest in a particular case. Challenging a law in court is one way of lobbying the court to change the law. Indirect lobbying occurs when groups find it more beneficial to stay concealed behind an ostensible social movement. In these cases, they attempt to persuade the public to put pressure on our representatives.

People outside the political culture can lobby as well. When citizens become lobbyists, they are known as grassroots. Groups that orchestrate *grassroots lobbying* are usually those that arise from spontaneous popular movements and revolts. Fake grassroots movements are known as *Astroturf lobbying*. This lobbying type occurs through an orchestrated effort by an established interest group dressed up to look like a genuine popular movement. Astroturf lobbying is made more convenient by the Supreme Court rulings that say that spending money by individuals, groups, or corporations is a form of *protected free speech*.

Chapter 13: Political Parties and Interest Group

1) James Madison warned against interest groups in Federalist no. ____
   a. 5.
   b. 7.
   c. 10.
   d. 25.

2) Madison refers to interest groups in the Federalist no. 10 as
   a. lobbyists.
   b. factions.
   c. special interests.
   d. political parties.

3) Which of the following terms does not refer to a group primarily interested in gaining government support to pursue its specific policy goals?
   a. allied group
   b. special interest group
   c. faction
   d. interest group

4) An interest group is defined as
   a. an organization whose goal is to influence citizens.
   b. an organization whose goal is to get members elected to office.
   c. an organization whose goal is to disrupt the lawmaking process.
   d. an organization whose goal is to influence the government.

5) The two crucial elements in the definition of an interest group are
   a. membership and money.
   b. organization and influence.
   c. bribery and blackmail.
   d. persuasion and information.

6) A _____ is an individual who contacts government officials on behalf of a particular cause or issue.
   a. lobbyist

  b. constituent

  c. member of Congress

  d. specialist

7) One of the threats of strict or intense partisanship is that it could lead to

  a. increased participation.

  b. effective conflict.

  c. a decrease in ideological thinking.

  d. increased apathy.

8) Which of the following is an example of a membership group?

  a. AARP

  b. Lockheed-Martin

  c. American Israel Public Affairs Committee

  d. US Chamber of Commerce

9) Which of the following is not a primary function of interest groups?

  a. Informing members about political developments.

  b. Buying the votes of members of Congress.

  c. Communicating members' views to government officials.

  d. Mobilizing the public.

10) Which branch of government do lobbyists contact to convey their opinions and push their policy priorities?

  a. executive branch

  b. legislative branch

  c. judicial branch

  d. all of the above

11) For an interest group to be successful, it must

  a. inform members about political developments.

  b. communicate members' views to government officials.

  c. mobilize the public.

  d. all of the above.

12) When an issue arises in Washington that is of interest to a group, the group tends to

  a. Gain more members.

b. Boost its spending.

c. Get ignored by legislators.

d. both a and c

13) On high-profile issues like climate change, lobbying

a. Has little effect on the views of members of Congress.

b. Has great potential to change the views of members of Congress.

c. Has an effect on some members and no effect on other members of Congress, regardless of party.

d. Has little effect on members of Congress who are Democrats, but great effect on members of Congress who are Republicans.

14) Beginning in the mid-1960s, the number of lobbyists

a. increased dramatically.

b. decreased dramatically.

c. stayed the same as pre-1960s.

d. decreased only slightly.

15) In Federalist no. 10, Madison suggests how to prevent factions from killing off the popular government is to

a. outlaw them.

b. increase the number of them.

c. ignore them.

d. limit how many there can be.

16) Interest groups today represent

a. virtually every political or social topic and concern.

b. a limited number of political or social groups.

c. a tiny number of wealthy individuals.

d. none of the above

17) "An interest group primarily organized with voluntary members, often with a non-profit or public advocacy focus" is a good definition for a

a. membership group.

b. lobbying coalition.

c. special interest.

d. faction.

18) A _____ is a group of lobbyists working on related topics or a specific legislative proposal.

  a. special interest

  b. faction

  c. membership group

  d. lobbying coalition

19) When interest groups mobilize the public to do something on their behalf, this includes actions such as

  a. letter writing.

  b. protesting.

  c. contributing funds.

  d. all of the above

20) When interest groups mobilize the public, they typically reach out through

  a. TV ads.

  b. Facebook posts.

  c. mailgram alerts.

  d. all of the above

21) Pluralism is defined as

  a. an open, participatory style of government in which many different interests are represented.

  b. a closed system of government in which only a handful of individuals may participate.

  c. a system that can only benefit the wealthy.

  d. an open style of government in which only a few individuals are represented.

22) Which of the following theories best explains the bank bailouts of 2008–2009?

  a. demosclerosis

  b. power elite theory

  c. hyperpluralism

  d. both a and c

23) The interest group lobbying reform of 2007 worked to

  a. close loopholes in previous lobbying reform laws.

  b. decrease the number of interest groups in Washington, DC.

    c. allow underrepresented segments of the public to form interest groups.

    d. all of the above

24) What is an issue network?

    a. A shifting alliance of public and private interest groups, lawmakers, and other stakeholders focused on the same policy area.

    b. The cozy relationship in one issue area between interest group lobbyist, congressional staffer, and executive branch agency.

    c. An organization run by the White House staff.

    d. The relationship between the president and the cabinet.

25) What are public officials' attempts in one part of the government to influence their counterparts elsewhere—in another branch or at a different (state or local) government level?

    a. judicial precedent

    b. reverse lobbying

    c. intergovernmental lobbying

    d. bureaucratic rule-making

26) Which term refers to attempts by government officials to influence interest groups on behalf of their preferred policies?

    a. reverse lobbying

    b. bureaucratic rule-making

    c. judicial precedent

    d. intergovernmental lobbying

Discussion Questions

1) Discuss how sometimes disparate interest groups come together on the same side of an issue. For example, the Christian Coalition and the American Civil Liberties Union both lobby against campaign finance reform.

2) What are coalition lobbying and reverse lobbying?

3) Compare and contrast pluralism with power elite theory. Which has broader explanatory capacity?

4) Discuss the pros and cons of two-party dominance, noting the value of automatic majorities and the lack of representation that occurs.

5) Discuss the emotional attachment many people feel toward their preferred political party. Ask them to think critically about the possible irrationality of solid partisan positions.

6) Discuss the different electoral preferences of members of the "party in the electorate" and members of "party organizations."

Video Resources

AP US Gov - Political Parties and Their Platforms www.youtube.com/watch?v=LA8aIwEwiP4

Political Parties | Crash Course Government and Politics www.pbslearningmedia.org/resource/political-parties-crashcourse-video-1040/political-parties-crash-course-government-and-politics-40/

WatchKnowLearn.org on third parties (and the lack thereof) in the United States http://www.watchknowlearn.org/Video.aspx?VideoID=14226&CategoryID=3450

The Difference between Political Parties and Interest Groups https://www.youtube.com/watch?v=MOOF8p3Q11E

Website Resources

The Association for Education in Journalism and Mass Communications http://www.aejmc.org/home/about/groups/interest-groups/

The North Carolina Central University James E. Shepard Memorial Library http://shepard.libguides.nccu.edu/content.php?pid=156096&sid=1330246

The Library of Congress http://www.loc.gov/rr/main/alcove9/usgov/intgroups.html

About.com, "US Government Info" http://usgovinfo.about.com/blorgs.htm

Shmoop.com http://www.shmoop.com/political-parties/websites.html

Ron Gunzburger's Politics http://www.politics1.com/parties.htm

Democratic National Committee http://www.democrats.org/

Republican National Committee http://www.gop.com

Libertarian Party http://www.lp.org/

Green Party http://www.gp.org/index.php

CHAPTER 14

MEDIA AND POLITICAL COMMUNICATION

People make decisions throughout their lives according to their perceptions and biases, eventually shaped by the information they receive from the media. News agencies influence our actions, judgments, and beliefs. Depending on how critical citizens are, media corporations will alter their perception of the world more or less. In countries like the United States, the government controls the media by the use of licensing. Reporting is not only about accurately reporting facts but also about increasing advertiser revenues and audience shares. Media outlets are looking to make a profit. Real reporting means digging out nuggets of truth and stitching them together into a coherent story that accurately informs the public of what is happening in their world. Ideally, in the entertainment and media industry, stories, pieces, and narratives are both fact-based and fact-checked. Respectable journalists do not write or spread fake news. Journalists can lose sight of what is necessary and still ethically acceptable for the sake of media sales and revenues.

14.1 Introduction to Media and Political Communication

How politicians and governments communicate with people occurs in all types of forms, such as the internet, books, television, and advertisements in mass media. The media can influence the governmental implementation of public policies and the development of public opinion. The media uses established communication channels for transmitting news, as well as influencing human behavior. The powerful complex of media technology not only carries information to us, but it also collects information about us.

The way media companies monitor and collect data about us creates a narrative and empowers companies. A significant component of power-building is control of the information or how one assembles data into narratives that influence public opinion. The rise of both cable and satellite television audiences translates into more options for media dissemination.

The phenomenal increase in channels through which information can flow for the informed citizen has made understanding the relationships among power, narratives, and political communication all the more central. The media are all-encompassing, enormously powerful and invasive, and yet, at the same time, more porous and open to our influence than ever before. The past decades have witnessed dramatic changes in the media environment, which have deepened during the social media revolution.

By intending to democratize political participation, social media has changed the way politicians, journalists, and public figures interact with the citizens. In real-time, social media users can respond to each other and influence public opinion. Citizens deliberate about policy-making in social media networks such as Facebook, Twitter, Instagram, Reddit, and more. Social media have these days the potential to both shape political campaigns and influence power relations in political parties as they allow candidates to campaign with a higher degree of independence than before.

14.2 Media Sourcing

The origin of media and the stories reported is a relevant aspect to verify. The roots of our thoughts and beliefs can be very blurry. Some media channels create their own stories through scientific reporting methods, while other sources merely report other news stories. A *media aggregator* is a channel that only picks and chooses from the reporting of others. Media aggregators do not always verify facts. They disseminate stories, even if the narrative is false.

Competent media reporting rests on reporting up to standards. *Reporting* in the media is the process by which professional journalists track down facts, check them, and ask hard questions, not settling for easy answers and pushing until they have found the truth. When looking for truth, the truth is not relative—it is verifiable with empirical (real-world) evidence. More and more news sites rely on using others' work, including the wire services like the Associated Press. Without the reporting of skilled, assiduous, and persistent journalists, our system would be in serious trouble.

Even though traditional forms of international diplomacy persist, one can see that modern hybrid wars also take place in the media. In this context, global public opinion is the prize. Governments, business organizations, religious-related entities, terrorist groups, and large-scale international NGOs pursue their political objectives by using the media. Throughout the world, public opinion is essential to the welfare of every government. Publicists do their best to create powerful narratives that are convincing enough for people all around the globe.

14.3 How we get and consume our news

A hallmark of authoritarian political systems is the state's effort to control the narrative by managing the press[155]. When the government controls the story, then truth can be relative to the media producer. He who controls the narrative-setting process also regulates what people think and feel about something. Our media channels that seek out truth include word of mouth, print media, broadcast media, or electronic media sources.

Print media is in decline and it is struggling to figure out its role in the electronic world. The use of magazines and newspapers has evolved to appease today's audiences and advertisers. TV news, especially local news, still draws older generations, and its audience is dwindling. The internet is rapidly becoming the go-to place for people, predominantly the youth, to seek information.[156]

In today's busy world, we get in touch with the media from numerous sources and places. *Media convergence* is the process by which most of us get our news from many different sources. You may receive information from a multiplicity of news sources every day—paper, the internet, and television. People are becoming acclimatized to the media narrative in their life. A *mediated citizen*[157] is a citizen whose media dictate his lines of communication and thought. People live within a media bubble; however, it is possible to pop that bubble.

When people are comfortable in their information bubble, they are less likely to make changes. An *information bubble* is a person's media comfort zone, in which they listen to the news, curate social media, and meet new people, all of which reinforce the ideas they already have. Popping the bubble should be a fundamental goal of an educated person. We are vulnerable to manipulation tactics. Public opinion-influencing tactics leave us especially vulnerable to be controlled by those who guide the information we get. We live our lives according to the information we receive from the media.

---

[155] On media biases and political repression, see Davenport, Christian. *Media Bias, Perspective, and State Repression: The Black Panther Party*. Cambridge University Press, 2010.

[156] Newspaper revenues declined considerably between the years 2008 and 2018. Advertising revenue fell from $37.8 billion in 2008 to $14.3 billion in 2018, which evidences a 62% decline. For more information on this, see Grieco, Elizabeth. "Fast Facts about the Newspaper Industry's Financial Struggles as McClatchy Files for Bankruptcy." *Pew Research Center*, 14 Feb. 2020.

[157] On mass media depictions of citizens and the influence of those depictions, see Shumow, Moses. *Mediated Communities: Civic Voices, Empowerment and Media Literacy in the Digital Era*. Peter Lang, 2015.

News agencies influence our actions, decisions, and beliefs. Depending on how critical we are, the media will more or less be able to alter our perception of the world. They have the adequate tools to do so.

14.4 Media Ownership and Government Regulations

In the United States, the government does not own the media and news sources. Who owns media agencies if the government does not own them? And how does the government regulate the media? The government controls the media by the use of licensing. The government sells licenses to radio and TV stations and is now questioning the role social media plays in national security-related issues. Because of that, policymakers carefully examine which threats the media represent and boost. News agencies are big businesses all around the world.

Only in the United States, six corporations own most of the major media outlets. What difference does that fact make? How important is media ownership for us? How having little to no diversity in media ownership can affect us? Those who control the media are known as gatekeepers. *Gatekeepers* are the people in charge of what information gets to us, and most importantly, how it does. Today, most news comes from—or at least through—massive, corporate-owned sources. One can these days see a *commercial bias* in the media toward what will increase advertiser revenues and audience shares. When taking news stories and information from the media in a context that could be considered reliable, one should adequately contextualize and understand the media bias nature and the outlets' ideological and political views.

Having money, however, does not necessarily help when building effective political communication. Innovation and creativity play a crucial role in political communication, as in other forms of cultural integration, and are not only a thing of the wealthy. Money certainly gives an advantage over the rest, but there are other factors that one should consider. Small and medium-sized news outlets can adjust to their budget and still create engaging and convincing narratives.

There is a continuous effort to get large audiences and keep them engaged. The media does that while also making way for increased advertising, which results in a reduced emphasis on political news, particularly for local television. Journalists lighten and dramatize the content of the information we get through the media. News is turned into *infotainment or soft news* to keep audiences tuned in and engaged.

Similarly, on the internet, infotainment is used to generate more news leads and story reads. *Clickbait* is the sensational headlines that tease you into clicking a link to find some intriguing-sounding information. By appealing to emotions and feelings, journalists aim to obtain more clicks from you. Today's media's corporate ownership means that the media outlets frequently face conflicts of interest in deciding what news to cover and how to cover it.

When doing their best to avoid getting "scooped" by another station or newspaper, reporters and editors alike sometimes jump the gun. Today, anyone can start a blog, a website, a podcast, or a YouTube Channel and start publishing his/her independent views. Social media networking has given voice to many new actors that influence public opinion.

If small media outlets and new-coming influencers look like they will be profitable, enterprising corporations likely have an incentive to scoop them up. Today, some outlets look like alternative media but have the funding of giants behind them. They are not independent at all. By appearing to be alternative or independent can attract new potential audiences that mistrust larger media outlets.

Media in the United States of America functions like a private enterprise system in which large businesses seek profit. The media in this country is almost entirely privately-owned, but they do not operate without some degree of public control. With fewer limitations on how many stations an owner can possess, the potential for media monopoly has become enormous over the years.[158]

The internet is known as a place in which the media can freely operate. However, that is only true as long as there is internet freedom in that country. Should the internet be regulated? Is it time to consider internet connectivity a basic human right? And are we prepared if it turns against us? Supporters of net neutrality believe that the internet should be an open-access forum for innovation. In the aftermath of Russian hacking and social media manipulation during the 2016 election, the internet has been up for scrutiny in Congress.

It is important to note that U.S. Congress members are mostly not among the generations that are internet savvy. It comes as no surprise that they often don't seem to know what they are searching for. Even though there has been significant-tech adoption since 2012 among older generations, Millennials still stand out for their technology use. On the other hand, Gen Z's are tech native.

14.5 What Do Journalists Do?

Both reporters and journalists gather information to later present it as news stories, feature articles, or documentaries. Journalists usually work on the staff of news

[158] On media monopoly and the hilling effects of corporate ownership and mass advertising on the nation's news, see Bagdikian, Ben. *The Media Monopoly*. Beacon Press, 2000.. Since 1983, the number of corporations controlling most of America's daily newspapers, magazines, radio and television stations, book publishers, and movie companies has dwindled from fifty to ten to six.

organizations, but they work freelance as well. Freelance journalism means that they write stories for whoever pays them. General reporters cover all kinds of news stories, while other journalists specialize in specific areas such as politics, business, or fashion.

Journalists play a relevant, far-reaching, and essential role in our political system because they chase the news and deliver information to the rest of society. Valid-reporting means seeking answers. Reporting means digging out nuggets of truth and stitching them together into a coherent story that truly informs the public of what is happening in their world. Self-claiming that one is a journalist is not enough to be an authentic journalist. Citizens have to keep a keen eye on whether they contribute valuable, high-quality, factual, and not-strongly biased information to the public debate.

Journalism falls into four principal journalistic roles. The first role is to be a *gatekeeper* of truth. Editors and high-authority reporters who decide about what should be covered and what should not are the gatekeepers of truth for society. The second role is to be a disseminator. A *disseminator* is a reporter who mainly focuses on getting out facts rather than opinions. The third role of a journalist is to be a *researcher/analyst.* This type of journalist is a person who digs for information and interprets both its transcendence and significance by contextualizing it. The fourth type of reporter is a *public mobilizer.* This journalist usually has an agenda, and it is part of their job to make citizens aware of what is going on around them and encourage them to take action.

Journalists do not only communicate about what is going on in the world but also influence public opinion. In his seminal study of *Public Opinion*, Walter Lippmann observed that political action mostly derived from voting rights and mass media communications rather than from the collectively arrived at the will of rational, enlightened men. Citizens politically decide, more or less, through the exercise of the vote and the influence of public opinion. Lippmann recognized in 1922 that public opinion was a constructed and manufactured thing that could be shaped and manipulated by those with the resources and interests in doing so[159]. Publicists, press agents, and journalists are part of a social class situated between political organizations and media institutions. Their job is often to influence the public opinion-building process according to the needs of their clients.[160]

---

[159] On the role of news in the process of manufacturing public opinion, see Lipmann.

[160] For more information about how the press agents influence public opinion, see McNair, Brian. *An Introduction to Political Communication.* Routledge, Taylor & Francis Group, 2018. Political programs, policy agendas, electoral messages, pressure group campaigns, and acts of domestic and global terrorism have the potential for communicative effectiveness.

14.6 Issues, challenges, and controversies professional journalism faces

Professional journalists are often in a position that does not allow them to earn money from their work. It is too easy to make money off their work without paying them for it. News aggregators pose a threat to journalism because high-quality reporting costs both time and money. If a news source only retells another agency's story, the original story writer loses revenue for their work.

Another problem with professional journalism is that people have equated journalism with print journalism. Nowadays, people do not buy or subscribe to print outlets as they used to in the past. People object to paying for content online. There is a slow appreciation of electronic media. Major outlets are doing their best to maintain old business models based on subscription and print ad revenue while still successfully venturing into the digital world. As citizens distrust the media in general, it becomes more difficult for the public to trust the media. The public distrusts the media, which lacks credibility these days.

Respectable journalists do not write fake news. Fake news is out there, but credible journalists do their best to confront it. What is distinctive about good journalism is the reporters' commitment to accuracy, objectivity, and detail in telling their stories. Journalists have to properly research and verify their facts because they act as communicators who work in service of the truth, even if it is troublesome.

Low-quality journalism may allow disinformation and misinformation to originate in or leak into the news industry, which is likely to mislead public opinion. Strong ethical journalism and professional standards are required as antidotes to both disinformation and misinformation. As long as we do not control the avalanche of disinformation, the public may come to disbelieve all content, including journalism. Citizens are likely to take as credible whatever content their close friends and preferred influencers share in social networks. Disinformation campaigns do not necessarily aspire to convince the public to believe that its content is veracious but rather impact the agenda-setting. Fake news can shape what people think is relevant and what is not.

One should consider that when people use the phrase "fake news," for the most part, what they are trying to do is to control the narrative. Fake news accusations are used as a way of delegitimizing a journalist's work. Because of its popularity, the term has recently been weaponized to leverage attacks against the media. Citizens may use the term "fake news" to satisfy their need for structure in the world. Cognitively speaking, people need to satisfy their need to see the world around them as an orderly, coherent, and structured place rather than solely to express their political, cultural, or personal ideology. One can already see the negative impacts of this situation on public beliefs about health, science, and intercultural affairs.

News organizations in the United States recognize fake news as a sociopolitical problem while acknowledging the challenge in defining it because of its many uses and connotations depending on the context. In general, specialists consider fake news as a social media phenomenon thriving on political polarization driven by mostly ideological and partisan, but sometimes also cultural and financial motivations. It has become common throughout the world to blame for the rise of fake news to the current political environment, to technological platforms Google, Twitter and Facebook, and some particular audiences as well.

14.7 Media Shapes The Political Narrative

The media has historically played an integral role in influencing social trends. The information era, a new history term used to capture the way the world has recently developed to rely on information for most of the actions that people take, remains significantly different from all the other periods in the history of humankind.

More than ever, information and narratives now have significant powers to change and influence the way people think and act. Most importantly, the reasoning they help portray on various relevant topics in society. The media is essential to push for specific narratives and messages in the modern world.

The contemporary media industry has emerged as the most advanced system of communication that humanity has ever experienced. Unlike in the past, when information and narratives could take long periods to reach citizens, the situation is radically different in our times since information travels the world in seconds. Researchers have studied the role of the contemporary media in political driving narratives quite extensively. The media drives our social, economic, and political trends. Communication outlets influence the reasoning that people hold as truths.

The primary purpose of the mass media outlets is to tell convincing yet engaging stories. Ideally, in the media industry, stories and narratives are not only fact-based but also fact-checked. And who exactly are the storytellers? At the pinnacle of political reporting are the Washington press corporations. Some of them have been politicians or at least members of the political world. As politicians move from the political to the private sector, the list of government officials regularly changes. This *revolving door-like process* consists of moving from the political sector to the public or the private ones. Some journalists are ethically stellar, but others' loyalty may lie more toward their political allies than their audiences.

14.8 Media and politicians will try to create a narrative line and spin the facts that fit the narrative

When a politician *spins* a story, they are likely to purposely select pieces of information that fit their political narrative and intentionally interpret data to make things look different by distorting facts and ignoring relevant factors. In political journalism, spins are attempts to control communication to deliver one's preferred message and persuade audiences. The term is commonly used to refer to the sophisticated art of promoting one's agenda by selling and spreading specific messages in favor of one's interests and views. Political spins often imply a certain degree of deception. A person who offers to give their opinion or commentary to mass media outlets on a particular subject area (most typically *political analysis*) is a pundit. A *pundit* is a person who can sometimes fall into the "analyst" category of journalists and sometimes into the bloviator category. The journalist can spin a story through different methods.

Journalists can spin a tale by creating an agenda for their news source and creating an important story that people focus on. *Agenda setting* is what a journalist, editor, or producer decides is important, becomes news and ends up on the political agenda.161 This agenda-setting can frame issues so that one or two topics become relevant in the national discussion for the day. *Framing* the political debate and public opinion is about telling people what matters the most and what to pay attention to when reading the news. There should be a reliance on skilled and professional communicators who stick to engaging, easy, and already existing narratives to shape and influence political debates.

Journalists can lose sight of what is necessary for the sake of media sales and revenues. A *feeding frenzy* is a process by which a scandal turns average journalists into sharks-like beings waiting for the next tidbit of news to drop. This situation can cause trouble when people focus on scandal and clickbait instead of seeking the truth. During election cycles, it is a common problem to only focus on the person winning a race. This *horse race-type of journalism* in election reporting focuses on who is ahead, who is losing support, and who is a surprisingly long shot, but not on the substance of what the election is really about. Much of the time, the end result is the *soundbite* generated, which is a short and snappy memorable line that commentators may repeat over and over. Often, they do so by taking facts out of context.

---

[161] See Zaller, John. *The Nature and Origins of Mass Opinion.* Cambridge University Press, 2011 for more information on the tactics to influence public opinion throughout history.

Chapter 14: Media and Political Communications

1) _____ is all the ways people get information about politics and the wider world.

   a. Twitter

   b. Tumblr

   c. Media

   d. World Wide Web

2) A significant change in media over the past fifty years is

   a. information comes slower

   b. more formats

   c. the public is less active in new media platforms

   d. new media outlets are less popular than the traditional ones

3) Facebook is an example of

   a. newspaper

   b. magazine

   c. old media

   d. new media

4) A role of media in a democratic system is

   a. public watchdog

   b. electing candidates

   c. broadcasting the political agenda

   d. sharing candidate ideology

5) Media can help make informed voters through the role of

   a. public watchdog

   b. providing information

   c. shaping the political agenda

   d. showing candidate mistakes

6) In the 1830s, _____ became the first mass media.

   a. letters

   b. radio

c. telegrams

d. newspapers

7) What is the definition of mass media?

a. Facebook for all.

b. Internet access for all.

c. Media for you and me.

d. Information and entertainment for audiences

8) Which war was known as the first media war?

a. Korean War

b. Spanish-American War

c. World War I

d. Vietnam War

9) People with strong opinions are affected by new information in what way?

a. they change their opinion

b. they look for similar information

c. new information reinforces their existing opinions

d. they ignore it

10) Between 2000 and 2015, American newspapers slashed what percentage of their staff?

a. 40

b. 13

c. 3

d. 47

11) During the 1930s, who delivered a weekly radio address known as the "Fireside Chat"?

a. Theodore Roosevelt

b. Karl Marx

c. Walt Whitman

d. Franklin Roosevelt

12) What is the primary demographic for talk radio?

    a. middle-aged white male and conservative

    b. middle-aged African American and liberal

    c. age forty-five to sixty-four white female and conservative

    d. age forty-five to sixty-four Hispanic male and liberal

13) The corporate setting helps blur the line between news, politics, and entertainment, a phenomenon now described as

    a. minor media.

    b. global information.

    c. infotainment.

    d. entertainment.

14) In new media, who chooses the material to be seen?

    a. Newspaper editor

    b. Director

    c. Producer

    d. Reader

15) How long does it take a reader to respond to a story on digital media?

    a. immediately

    b. 24 hours

    c. 48 hours

    d. 3-4 days

16) Who does the reporting for new media?

    a. Readers

    b. Traditional organization reporters

    c. Web-based reporters

    d. Editors

17) Which of the following is not considered "new media"?

    a. Facebook

    b. Twitter

    c. Internet

    d. cable news

18) What type of story attracts young viewers?

    a. sensational

    b. educational

    c. local interest

    d. Routine

19) One of the ways the Internet could enhance democracy is by

    a. making everyone a potential news reporter.

    b. raising the bar for entry into politics.

    c. exposing fallacious points of view.

    d. allowing more people to stay at home with no need to attend public rallies.

20) Which media form is likely to include a variety of viewpoints?

    a. Facebook page

    b. Newspaper

    c. Personal Twitter

    d. Instagram

21) An example of perceived fake news is

    a. report on the number of injuries in an auto accident

    b. Global Warming is not a scientific fact

    c. Dow Jones went down 40 points

    d. The president is visiting China

22) An example of a citizen turned into a news provider is

    a. Citizen interviewed for the news

    b. Television cameraman catching an auto accident on tape

    c. Passerby filming an accident on a cellphone

    d. President answer questions at a press conference

23) Which type of media bias is most evident to academics?

    a. commercial

    b. liberal

    c. conservative

    d. realism

24) Which group is most likely to claim the media is biased?

    a. liberals

    b. Republicans

    c. Democrats

    d. the public as a whole

25) Which of the following is a media reporter likely to identify as?

    a. Republican

    b. Libertarian

    c. Democrat

    d. Independent

Discussion Questions

1) What are the pros and cons of public ownership of the media?

2) Do partisan newspapers or television stations prompt a more effective or less effective political discourse?

3) How is technology breaking down the ability of authoritarian governments to censor information?

4) What problems are caused by the "Americanization" of media around the world?

5) What possible media biases come about as the result of the profit motive?

6) How can "new media" enhance or hamper the quality of political discourse?

7) How have new technologies altered the nature and quality of news reporting; historically and today?

8) What are the pros and cons of a "Fairness Doctrine" approach to media regulation?

Video Resources

New Media and Political Communication www.youtube.com/watch?v=y6l5QGuHqOY

What's Next for Journalism and Political Communication? www.youtube.com/watch?v=b0kgR1MezGA&t=31s

Do Facts Still Matter? Media and Politics in a Post-Truth Era www.asc.upenn.edu/news-events/annenberg-video/annenberg-lecture-videos-faculty-videos/do-facts-still-matter-media-and

Saving American Journalism (NOW on PBS, 2010).

Jihad TV: Terrorism and Mass Media (2006).

State of the Union: Politics in Red and Blue (2006).

Website Resources

The Association for Education in Journalism and Mass Communications http://www.aejmc.org/home/about/groups/interest-groups/

Fact Check http://www.factcheck.org/

Center for Digital Democracy http://www.democraticmedia.org/

Fairness & Accuracy in Reporting (FAIR) http://www.fair.org/

Politifact.com's Truth-O-Meter® http://www.politifact.com/truth-o-meter/

FAIR: Challenging Media Bias Since 1986 https://fair.org/

Asia-Pacific Institute for Broadcasting Development http://www.aibd.org.my/node/1227

Mashable Social Media http://www.mashable.com/2012/04/18/social-media-and-the-news/

CHAPTER 15

DOMESTIC POLICY

15.1 Introduction to Policy

A **policy** is a prescribed course of action for those who work for the government. It creates a set of operational principles through which to accomplish desired goals.

Setting **domestic policy** creates standard operational procedures by which a government operates. Policies are put in place to guide the bureaucratic agencies that work under the Executive Branch.

When governments create laws and policies, either domestic or foreign, it is called policymaking. **Policymaking** is the process by which the Congress creates public policies. A **public policy** is a government plan of action to solve a problem that people share collectively or that they cannot solve on their own. These public policies are meant to create solutions to problems for the greater good of society. We can understand public policy as a purposeful course of action intended by officials to solve problems of society.

15.2 Making Public Policy

The power to make public policy in the United States begins with Congress. Policies are usually created by legislators in the form of new proposals or bills, which are passed by both the House and Senate and signed into law by the president. The role of influencing and creating public policy also resides in limited form within the Executive Branch.

A president may also create policy through multiple pathways: by placing an issue on the public agenda, including in their budget proposal, vetoing a law passed by Congress, or issuing an **executive order** that establishes a new policy or augments an existing one. Executive orders are directed only to government bureaucracies at the federal, state, or local levels. These agencies can wield enormous control over policy through how they enforce such orders.

The court system also can make public policy. When a court rules on what the government can, should or should not do, it is clearly taking an active policy making role. The courts, especially the **Supreme Court**, can create public policy by hearing cases that change policy adoption, allow for policy to be formulated, or create standards by which we interpret public law.

15.3 Types of domestic public policy

Scholars have come up with a typology of domestic problems that require different kinds of policies to solve them. These categories help determine the types of social and economic policies that the nation adopts.

The method by which a policy is implemented may vary according to the type of economic and political policy. Some policies are considered redistributive in nature. These **redistributive policies** use resources from affluent segments of society to provide benefits for those less likely to participate in the political sector. Redistributive policies are less likely to occur in more capitalistic market systems.

Domestic policies that are equally taxing on all of the population are called distributive in nature. A **distributive policy** is one whose costs are borne by the entire population. An example would be a flat-based tax system that is the same across all income brackets.

Some domestic policies, however, do not deal with the allocation of goods and resources in society. A domestic policy that does not distribute resources but exerts control within society through behaviors it requires is called a regulatory policy. **Regulatory policies** control behavior rather than distributing resources.

15.4 Social Policy

Many domestic policies are designed as social policies. **Social policies** are primarily distributive and redistributive policies that improve Americans' quality of life. If a social policy is distributive or redistributive for social welfare needs, it is a **social welfare policy,** a government program designed to provide for those who cannot, or sometimes will not, provide for themselves. Those programs that care for those who cannot care for themselves are the most redistributive in nature. Often there are rules and requirements, usually based on income potential.

Social policies that filter who is eligible or not for the redistribution of wealth often utilize means-tested programs. **Means-tested programs** require that beneficiaries prove they lack the necessary income or resources to provide for themselves, according to the government's definitions of eligibility. This is usually based on income-earning potential. In the United States, these types of programs often carry a social stigma and are contentious during elections.

Certain types of means-tested social programs are designed to help families in need. One example is the **Temporary Assistance to Needy Families (TANF)** program that replaced AFDC. This program provides block grants to state governments, giving states greater control over how they spend their money. The TANF program caps the amount that the federal government will pay for welfare and requires work in exchange for time-limited benefits. Other requirements may include recipients finding jobs within two years, then removing them from welfare rolls after a total of five years or less, depending on the state.

Another domestic policy program for helping people who make less than a federally legislated income level is the **Supplemental Nutrition Assistance Program (SNAP).** SNAP is the largest United States food assistance program for low-income families, providing vouchers to purchase food. This program helps those without enough resources for food and sustenance.

In modern times, many Americans are unaware that the policy we have referred to for years as "welfare" is mostly gone.

One of the best-known social policies is Social Security Insurance. **Social insurance policies** are longer-term distributive programs that provide benefits to a specific segment of the population. **Social Security** is a program born in the Great Depression to provide retirement funding for the elderly. It works through an economic input, or buy-in, when workers pay into the federally backed program. People contribute to Social Security during their working lives in order to receive benefits after they retire. Current workers pay the Social Security of retirees, with any leftover money going into the Social Security trust fund. Most people, at least those who are older, see Social Security as something they have earned and to which they are entitled, not as a government handout.

Still, there are problems with Social Security. With longer life spans, most people end up getting much more back from Social Security and Medicare than they may have contributed.

Many workers who have paid into the system see Social Security as an entitlement. **Entitlement programs** require benefits to be paid to people who are entitled to receive them. They are not needs-based nor do they follow a means-tested approval system. Even though there is talk of the Social Security system going insolvent, it could be made sustainable. Some potential remedies, however, are politically unpalatable and vigorously opposed by interest groups, including the American Association of Retired People (AARP).

Domestic policies to ensure the health care of people are increasing. The **Patient Protection and Affordable Care Act** established and made access to health insurance more available and affordable for most Americans. The United States stands out among industrialized nations as the only one that doesn't have a universal health-care system guaranteeing minimum basic care to all. Historically, healthcare in America pre-2010 utilized Medicare (covering old people) and Medicaid (covering the poorest people) for health care coverage of those without insurance. The consequences were that many uninsured people fell through the cracks.

Medicare was a social insurance program designed to help the elderly pay their medical costs. This program has been modified since the inception, however, it is still focused on elderly care. Medicare has become an extraordinarily expensive program. **Medicaid** is a means-tested welfare program designed to assist the poor -- especially children -- with their medical costs. This program undergoes adjustments when domestic policies allow for increased coverage and care for different segments of society.

15.4 Economic Policy

Government creates economic policies to keep the economy stable, growing, and functioning smoothly. **Economic policies** include all the different strategies that government officials, elected and appointed, employ to solve economic problems, to protect economic rights, and to provide procedural guarantees to keep the financial markets running smoothly. The government can control and regulate the marketplace or allow it to go mostly unregulated, with each approach depending on the political policy and party in power.

The consequences of a largely unregulated market vary. More regulation of the commerce of food and energy can increase the cost of goods and services for consumers. Traditionally, policymakers have felt that the government should pursue a hands-off economic policy. This allows for consumers to decide how much they are willing to pay for goods and services. Since the Great Depression, the goal of economic policymakers has been to even out the dramatic cycles of inflation and recession without undermining the vitality and productivity of a market-driven economy. America has gone through various series of recessions, depressions, and economic growth, often influenced by the domestic policies set by the government.

Economic policies are complicated, so for the sake of brevity we will provide a short and simple description. The government uses fiscal policy to grow or shrink the economy through taxation. **Fiscal policy** is the government's power to tax and spend with the aim of stabilizing the economy. This is done to create both surpluses and deficits in national spending. A **surplus** is money saved after spending on the government's domestic policy. A **deficit** is money owed after spending beyond what is actually available.

There are many tools available to create a healthy fiscal policy. One power of the government is known as monetary policy. **Monetary policy** is the power to control the money supply by manipulating interest rates. When interest rates are low, people can borrow money at a lower cost, spurring more business activity. The monetary policy of the United States is run by the **Federal Reserve System (the Fed)**. The Federal Reserve System is a group of 12 banks run by a board of governors whose chair is appointed by the president. It sets interest rates for the nation and is autonomous of the Executive Branch or Congress.

The government has the power to take from every citizen and business a share of their revenue for the purpose of ensuring the national interest. Taxation is the power to charge people a percentage of their income for the domestic and foreign policy needs of the government. **Tax policy** is the way in which the government requires that individuals and businesses contribute to collective costs. Taxation levels may be different for people depending on their income levels. A **progressive income tax** is a tax on people with more money at a higher rate than the rate applied to people with less money. This is different from a **regressive tax.,**. A regressive tax may take a higher percentage of a poorer person's gross resources, like sales taxes or value-added taxes (VATs) or some proposals for a flat income tax. There are other types of taxes as well, including **capital gains taxes**, a controversial tax that may be levied on the return from capital investments.

15.5 Environmental Policy

President Richard Nixon in 1970 signed a National Environmental Policy Act that a year later became the **Environmental Protection Agency**, or EPA. During the 1970s, laws were passed regarding clean air and clean water, as well as protections for endangered species. With these, sources of air and water pollutants came under federal regulation. Environmental policy attempts to balance the protection and conservation of natural resources with economic growth and jobs. Industries are required to follow federal and state rules designed to protect the natural environment. The rigor with which these regulations are enforced often depends on the political party in power at any particular time. For example, President Ronald Reagan in 1982 cut EPA funding by 30 percent.

The **Department of the Interior** was established in 1849 to manage natural resources, and oversees energy development on federal lands as well as offshore leases. A division, the **Bureau of Land Management**, was formed in 1946 to manage the federal lands that total almost 250 million acres.

15.6 Energy Policy

U.S **energy policy** is sometimes connected to environmental policy, especially when energy production and consumption involves the exploitation of natural resources and creates pollutants. Legislation, regulations, international treaties, subsidies and taxation are all modes of policy implementation. Coal, oil, natural gas, hydroelectric and nuclear power, and more recently renewables including wind and solar power have powered America through the years and been subjects of energy policies. Fossil fuels still account for most United States energy consumption. Federal tax policies and subsidies can be used as incentives for the development of specific energy sources.

There is concern in the United States and worldwide over greenhouse gas emissions that are related to climate change. China and the United States are the biggest carbon polluters, and many nations and industries are taking steps to reduce such emissions and move toward energy efficiencies and renewable sources, though there has been no firm global agreement on such policies as yet.

15.7 Health Policy

America's massive and complex health-care industry accounts for about 17 percent of all spending, mostly on medical services to diagnose and treat illnesses and injuries, both physical and mental. **Health policy** has therefore become a contentious issue between political parties and is often adjusted, depending on who is in power. The United States system is a third-party payer arrangement in which health insurance companies reimburse medical providers a portion of the cost of services to patients. Almost half of Americans participate in private health insurance plans through their employers. Medicare (15 percent), for people over 65, and Medicaid (16 percent), for low-income people, are public programs touched on earlier under social policies. While the Affordable Care Act, also known as Obamacare, has helped expand coverage since its passage in 2010, there are still about 30 million (13 percent) of Americans who are uninsured, mostly because of the high costs of healthcare. Soaring costs have also driven employers to reduce the reimbursements paid to medical providers and to increase the burden of insurance premium payments on their employees.

15.8 Transportation Policy

The Department of Transportation (DOT) plans and coordinates federal transportation projects to enhance national economic competitiveness, facilitating the movement of people and goods and also setting safety regulations for all major modes of transport, including air, water, and land – both roads and railways. **National Transport Policy** also attempts to reduce negative impacts on the environment. The Federal Aviation Administration, Highway Administration, Railroad Administration, Transit Administration and other agencies are related to the DOT.

Many federal infrastructure programs and policies have failed to modernize in recent decades, according to DOT research, leading to five major challenges, which involve crumbling infrastructure, congestion, climate change, injuries and fatalities as well as unequal economic opportunity.

Transportation is the biggest source of United States greenhouse gas emissions, with more than 100 million people living amid pollution that exceeds health-based air quality standards. Traffic congestion costs the economy more than $165 billion in wasted productivity and fuel each year. Additionally, many infrastructure assets including highways, public transit and rail systems have come to the end of their useful lives and require repair or replacement. New modes of transport will also be necessary to handle the demands of both the economy and the environment in the future.

Chapter 15: Domestic Policy

1) Public policy can be defined as _____.

    a. a government plan of action to solve a social problem

    b. a ruling made by the Supreme Court that addresses a social problem

    c. an agreement among the president, Congress, and the Supreme Court to take a certain course of action

    d. a government plan of action passed only by legislatures

2) Someone who would be in favor of a policy that would provide healthcare for everyone regardless of employment status would MOST likely identify as _____.

    a. a Republican

    b. a Libertarian

    c. a Democrat

    d. a Federalist

3) Redistributive policies are relatively rare because _____.

    a. the United States is not a socialist country

    b. there is little need for them

    c. those who are the beneficiaries do not want them

    d. those who must pay for them are much better equipped to fight political battles than are potential beneficiaries

4) What is the president's role in making public policy?

    a. to create new laws based on constituent and interest group preferences

    b. to put an issue on the public agenda or include it in the budget proposal

    c. to lobby for certain bills to be passed

    d. to rule on what the government can or cannot do

5) Why are distributive policies popular?

    a. The costs are spread across taxpayers, but targeted groups receive them.

    b. The costs are generally low.

    c. The projects supported by such spending are rarely of questionable value.

    d. They often benefit the needy.

6) Which group is most likely to benefit from a distributive policy?

   a. veterans

   b. all Americans

   c. the wealthy

   d. foreign countries

7) Which is an example of a distributive policy?

   a. welfare

   b. emissions regulations

   c. a law restricting the use of the death penalty

   d. farm subsidies

8) Which statement regarding the formation of public policy is accurate?

   a. The role of Congress in making policy is relatively small compared to the role of the president.

   b. The Supreme Court holds most of the power when it comes to proposing and making policy.

   c. Solutions to public problems often generate new problems.

   d. National policies can be best thought of as packages made by Congress alone.

9) Which type of policy limits and controls the actions of individuals or groups?

   a. regulatory

   b. redistributive

   c. foreign

   d. distributive

10) _____ is the second step in making policy.

   a. Policy evaluation

   b. Policy formulation

   c. Policy implementation

   d. Policy adoption

11) Government agencies have their largest role in _____.

   a. agenda setting

   b. policy adoption

    c. policy implementation

    d. policy formulation

12) Policies that are aimed at improving the quality of life for those in need are known generally as _____.

    a. lending-hand policies

    b. group-effort policies

    c. distributive policies

    d. social policies

13) Anita participates in a government program that requires her to submit a pay stub and other documents in order to receive income assistance. This is an example of _____.

    a. a distributive program

    b. a means-tested program

    c. a social insurance program

    d. a public policy

14) Public policy that seeks to meet the basic needs of people who are unable to provide for themselves is _____ policy.

    a. civil rights

    b. social welfare

    c. regulatory

    d. distributive

15) What was the primary purpose of the Aid to Families with Dependent Children program?

    a. to make sure poor families could support their children

    b. to make sure children could eat school lunch

    c. to make sure families with more than one child could afford basic needs

    d. to make sure single mothers could care for their children

16) What are social insurance policies?

    a. programs funded by only one group of taxpayers that are distributed only to noncitizens

    b. programs that protect people from losing their homes during a natural disaster

c. government programs that offer benefits in exchange for contributions

d. programs designed to restrict or change the behavior of certain groups or individuals

17) Most social welfare policies can be categorized as _____.

a. entitlement programs

b. regulatory policies

c. private policies

d. redistributive policies

18) Which is a way the Social Security trust fund could be made sustainable?

a. lowering the retirement age

b. increasing taxes

c. increasing benefit levels

d. eliminating means-testing

19) A federal program that guarantees benefits to all qualified recipients is known as _____.

a. a welfare program

b. a mandate program

c. a means-tested program

d. an entitlement program

20) Financial incentives given by the government to corporations, individuals, or other governments for the purpose of encouraging certain activities or behaviors are _____.

a. entitlements

b. subsidies

c. welfare programs

d. grants

21) How did the Great Depression impact American public policy?

a. The government realized that it had to eliminate environmental restrictions on businesses to help them prosper, which set back efforts to pass stronger environmental policies.

b. It was the first time that education subsidies were provided to the middle class.

c. For the first time, people began to view poverty as a problem requiring government action.

d. The government put more pressure on churches and businesses to help eradicate poverty.

22) Which was a major criticism of the Aid to Families with Dependent Children (AFDC) program?

a. It had no work requirements.

b. Families were able to receive aid only for a short period of time.

c. The aid to most families was not sufficient to meet basic needs.

d. Too many poor people received no aid.

23) _____ is a welfare program of block grants to states that encourages recipients to work in exchange for time-limited benefits

a. Aid to Families with Dependent Children

b. Temporary Assistance to Needy Families

c. Supplemental Nutrition Assistance Program

d. Social Security

24) _____ is an example of a social insurance program.

a. Aid to Families with Dependent Children

b. Temporary Assistance to Needy Families

c. Medicare

d. Supplemental Nutrition Assistance Program

25) Prior to the health care reform that was passed in 2010, the government's role in health care was limited to _____.

a. Medicare and Medicaid

b. Temporary Assistance to Needy Families

c. United State Universal Healthcare

d. the Patient Protection Act

26) The federal government's insurance program for the elderly and disabled is called _____.

a. AFDC

b. Medicaid

c. Medicare

d. AARP

27) Which is likely the strongest ideological argument against a system of universal health care in the United States?

a. Such a system has not been adopted in an industrialized country like the United States.

b. The American public is generally satisfied with the current system.

c. The costs of Medicare and Medicaid would skyrocket under such a system.

d. A universal health care policy runs against the American economic system and gives the government too much control.

28) What type of policy addresses the problem of economic security for society as a whole?

a. social welfare

b. economic

c. private

d. social insurance

29) The basic principles that regulate the economic market and influence the price of a good are known as laws of _____.

a. antitrust policy

b. supply and demand

c. production and consumption

d. monetary policy

30) Fiscal policy refers to _____.

a. the government's use of taxing and spending powers to regulate the economy

b. the use of interest rates to control the money supply in order to regulate the economy

c. policies designed to regulate business, labor, and trade

d. regulations designed to regulate business, labor, and trade

31) The manipulation of interest rates to control the money supply in order to regulate the economy is known as _____ policy.

a. budgetary

b. monetary

c. fiscal

d. regulatory

32) Monetary policy is _____ policy.

a. a distributive

b. a redistributive

c. a regulatory

d. a fiscal

33) A tax levied on returns from capital investments, such as profits from the sale of real estate, is _____ tax.

a. a capital gains

b. an excise

c. a consumption

d. a value-added

34) The policy that says the United States should put its interest first and not interfere in global concerns is known as _____.

a. the Reagan Doctrine

b. manifest destiny

c. "One Hemisphere"

d. isolationism

35) Which is an example of an intergovernmental organization?

a. the United Nations

b. Greenpeace

c. the U.S. State Department

d. General Motors

36) Foreign policy that lays out a country's basic stance toward international actors or issues is _____.

a. foreign economic policy

b. structural defense policy

c. crisis policy

d. strategic policy

37) The Cold War policy of the United States seeking to prevent the spread of communism is an example of _____.

a. isolationism

b. roll-back

c. containment

d. the domino theory

38) The State Department is the executive department responsible for managing _____.

a. military affairs

b. foreign affairs

c. Medicaid and Medicare

d. parks and forests

39) The Department of Defense is responsible for _____.

a. manufacturing expensive and secret weapons

b. managing the country's military personnel, equipment, and operations

c. conducting espionage

d. advising the president on how to execute his powers as commander-in-chief

40) The _____ was Congress's attempt to limit the president's ability to use troops in hostilities without congressional approval

a. War Powers Act

b. Gulf of Tonkin Resolution

c. National Defense Act

d. Helms-Burton Act

41) True or False: Distributive policies are popular because their costs are not noticed as they are spread among all taxpayers, but their benefits go to a specific group who knows they are benefitting.

42) True or False: Government agencies have their largest role in policy evaluation.

43) True or False: Public policy that seeks to meet the basic needs of people who are unable to provide for themselves is social welfare policy.

44) True or False: A federal program that guarantees benefits to qualified recipients is an entitlement program.

45) True or False: Economic policy addresses the problem of economic security for the benefit of the wealthiest members of society.

46) True or False: Tax policy is a regulatory policy.

47) True or False: The system of 12 banks run by a board of governors with a chair who is appointed by the president is known as the Federal Reserve.

48) True or False: U.S. foreign policy is almost always carried out for the good of American citizens or in the interest of national security.

49) True or False: According to the concept of isolationism, in order for the United States to be safe, the country must be actively engaged in shaping the global environment and be willing to intervene.

50) True or False: Nike and Apple are examples of multinational corporations.

Discussion Questions

1) Class brainstorms on events from the past. How did these events change public policy? Did the changes go far enough to assist in future similar events, or is more change needed?

2) How can the United States wean itself from foreign oil?

3) How can the United States improve its trade deficit?

4) How should the United States concern itself with other nations?

Video Resources

A Civil Action (1998)

Hacking Democracy (2006) HBO Films

How Weed Won the West (2012) Sacred Cow Productions

Kansas v. Darwin (2008) Unconditional Films

PBS Frontline: "The Card Game"

Prohibition (2011) Ken Burns and Lynn Novick

Why We Fight (2005)

No End in Sight (2007) Magnolia

The Fog of War (2003) Sony Pictures Classic

Argo (2012) GK Films

United States Domestic Policy - Harvard Kennedy School http://iop.harvard.edu/forum/united-states-domestic-policy

Developing Domestic Policy www.c-span.org/video/?286994-2/developing-domestic-policy

Domestic Policy Issues www.c-span.org/video/?73714-1/domestic-policy-issues

US ELECTIONS AND DOMESTIC POLICY www.sipa.columbia.edu/file/us-elections-and-domestic-policy

Website Resources

Maps of War http://www.mapsofwar.com/

Foreign Policy http://www.foreignpolicy.com/

Foreign Policy Research Institute http://www.fpri.org

The White House http://www.whitehouse.gov/issues/foreign-policy

Foreign Affairs http://www.foreignaffairs.com/

The Brookings Institution www.brookings.edu/

Policy Studies Journal http://onlinelibrary.wiley.com/journal/10.1111/(ISSN)1541-0072

Institute for Women's Policy Research www.iwpr.org/

Rand Corporation http://www.rand.org/

Urban Institute http://www.urban.org/?gclid=CKSe8eCxpLMCFcaDQgod1AUAnw

CHAPTER 16

FOREIGN POLICY

16.1 Foreign policy

Foreign policy determines how the United States reacts and responds to governments and non-governmental groups beyond its borders. **Foreign policy** is the official policy designed to solve problems that occur between the United States and actors from abroad. It is important to have successful policies for national self-preservation. Without a strong and effective foreign policy, America's security as a rich and peaceful country could come under threat. Although the United States has little control over the other actors involved. its foreign policy is generally carried out for the good of American citizens or in the interest of national security.

16.2 Two fundamental perspectives on our relationship with the world

Relationships with other nations can be seen through two distinct perspectives: isolationism and interventionism. **Isolationism** is a foreign policy view holding that Americans should put themselves and their problems first and not interfere in global concerns. The United States pursued an isolationist policy after World War I, but this experiment was seen largely as a failure. The second fundamental perspective is **interventionism**, which holds that to keep the republic safe, the United States must be actively engaged in shaping the global environment and willing to intervene in order to create desired outcomes.

16.3 Foreign policy and external actors

Many organizations are external actors within the current foreign policy environment. Intergovernmental organizations are bodies that have countries as members, including the United Nations, NATO, OPEC, and the EU. These international bodies work together to create agreements among nations regarding international policies. American foreign policy relies on the concept of **American Exceptionalism**, which teaches that the United States is unique, marked by a distinct set of ideas including equality, self-rule, and limited government. The aim of foreign policy is to create a commonly held theory of democratic peace teaching that democratic nations are less likely to engage in wars with one another

The president is the chief negotiator for the United States, and any treaty negotiated must then be ratified by the Senate. The president has ample resources available to fulfill the obligations of the office. The **National Security Council (NSC)** is the president's inner circle that advises on matters of foreign policy and is coordinated by the national security adviser. Foreign policy is negotiated through the **Department of State, which** is charged with managing foreign affairs. The secretary of state is part of the president's cabinet and fulfills a variety of foreign policy roles, including maintaining diplomatic and consular posts around the world, sending delegates and missions (groups of government officials) to a variety of international organization meetings, and negotiating treaties and executive agreements with other countries. The **Department of Defense (DOD)** manages the United States military and its equipment in order to protect the nation. It is headed by the secretary of defense, and under that office are the **Joint Chiefs of Staff**, service chiefs of the Army, Navy, Marine Corps, Air Force, Space Force, and the National Guard Bureau. While the chief of the Coast Guard is not an official member of the Joint Chiefs, a Coast Guard admiral routinely meets with the group.

The Defense Department is the government's biggest agency and accounts for a large portion of the national budget, along with health spending and Social Security. It employs almost 3 million service members and civilians in more than 160 countries and is headquartered in the iconic Pentagon building in Arlington, Virginia, just outside Washington DC.

16.4 Trade policy

United States **trade policy** objectives in recent decades have included reducing protections both at home and abroad, opening foreign markets for American exports, and increasing global economic integration. While there has much success in integrating the world's economies, the United States has seen its share of the gross world product (GWP) plummet since the post-war period, and its position as the world's biggest economy challenged first by Japan in the 1990s and now by China, which is expected to overtake it in the future. America's international trade deficit now routinely exceeds

$600 billion annually, as the United States buys far more foreign goods and services than it sells.

The **Department of Commerce** is charged by the president with helping the economy expand through working to ensure fair trade and providing the data necessary to support commerce. It also helps negotiate bilateral trade agreements, enforces laws and issues sanctions that attempt to ensure a level playing field for United States businesses.

Even more directly concerned with trade policy is the office of the **United States Trade Representative** (USTR), which is responsible for developing and recommending trade policy to the president. It also conducts trade negotiations for the executive branch and participates in the World Trade Organization (WTO).

Tariffs are customs duties levied on imported and exported goods and services. They are typically used to protect domestic industries or as leverage in trade negotiations and disputes. While Congress originally had the power to levy tariffs granted by the Constitution, the president has the power to negotiate international agreements, so Congress has partially delegated to the executive the latitude to negotiate trade agreements and set **tariff policy**. The United States has been a member of the WTO since 1995, and as such makes tariff policies within the regulatory context of the global trading system.

Tariffs are actually a type of tax paid on goods sourced from other countries and usually paid to United States customs authorities by importing companies. While tariffs may offer some protection to domestic industries by raising prices of competing imported goods, they are ultimately paid by United States consumers to whom cost increases are passed by importers.

Chapter 16: Foreign Policy

1) What does United States foreign policy determine?

   a. how the United States government filters who is eligible or not for the redistribution of wealth, often utilizing means-tested programs.

   b. how the United States government coordinates federal transportation projects to enhance national economic competitiveness.

   c. how the United States government reacts and responds to governments and non-governmental groups well beyond its borders.

   d. how the United States government develops longer-term distributive programs that provide benefits to a specific segment of the population.

2) Why is foreign policy one of the most critical to United States' national security?

   a. America's security as a rich, stable and peaceful country may come under threat without an adequate foreign policy.

   b. The current global order is based on the maintenance of alliances.

   c. America cannot act alone to pursue its own interests.

   d. The search of new markets for American companies.

3) What are isolationists' viewpoints regarding to foreign policy?

   a. Interventionism is acceptable but only up to a certain degree.

   b. America should intervene in the affairs of other countries but avoid going to war at any cost.

   c. America should focus on itself and not intervene in the affairs of other countries.

   d. America should indirectly intervene in the affairs of other countries by third-party actors.

4) Why do some experts perceive that isolationism has been a failure in the United States?

   a. Because of the poor experience after World War II. Results were not as satisfactory as expected.

   b. Because interventionism has been more effective than isolationism to benefit the interests of the American people.

   c. Because Latin America is very unstable, and thus, poses a risk to the United States.

   d. Because isolationism means less profit and work for the defence industry.

5) What is interventionists' main viewpoint regarding to foreign policy?

   a. Interventionism is necessary for the liberal global order based on democracy, free-trade, and Western international institutions.

   b. Interventionism is sometimes needed to restore law and order in foreign countries.

   c. Interventionism can help in creating a stable environment for transitioning states.

   d. To keep the republic safe, America should be actively engaged in shaping the global political order and willing to do what it takes to create the desired outcomes.

6) What is American Exceptionalism?

   a. A concept that teaches that the United States is unique because of its notion of equality, self-rule, and limited government.

   b. A concept that teaches that the United States is unique because of its intensely antiliberal character, which is rooted in a sense of its special mission.

   c. A concept that teaches that the United States is a great global power, and uses it sparingly.

   d. None of the above.

7) What is the influence of American exceptionalism in United States foreign policy?

   a. American exceptionalism is the core of imperialist foreign policy.

   b. Policymakers perceive that America has a special mission to spread the benefits of its particular liberal political system globally.

   c. The United States is divinely destined to rule the world.

   d. None of the above.

8. True or False: International bodies, such as the United Nations, NATO, and OPEC, work together to create agreements among nations regarding international policies.

9) True or False: The Department of Defense (DOD) manages the United States military and its equipment to protect the nation.

10) Which of these is defined as the president's inner circle that advises on matters of foreign policy and is coordinated by the national security adviser?

   a. The White House.

b. Department of State.

c. Department of Defense.

d. National Security Council.

11) Which is the biggest government's agency in the United States?

a. Department of Defense.

b. Department of State.

c. CIA.

d. None of the above.

12) Which executive department is charged with managing foreign affairs?

a. Department of State.

b. Department of Interior.

c. Department of Justice.

d. Department of Treasury.

13) Which executive department is charged with helping the economy expand through working to ensure fair trade?

a. Department of State.

b. Department of Interior.

c. Department of Commerce.

d. Department of Treasury.

14) True or False: U.S. foreign policy is related to the country's trade policy objectives since in recent decades they have included reducing protections both at home and abroad.

15) Who is responsible for developing and recommending trade policy to the U.S. president?

a. Secretary of State.

b. United States Trade Representative.

c. Secretary of Commerce.

d. Secretary of Treasury.

16) The United States has been a member of the WTO since

a. 1945

b. 1933

    c. 2001

    d. 1995

17) True or False: Tariffs are actually a type of tax paid on goods sourced from other countries and usually paid to United States customs authorities by importing companies.

18) True or False: the Joint Chiefs of Staff act as service chiefs of the Army, Navy, Marine Corps, Air Force, Space Force, and the National Guard Bureau.

19) How many service members and civilians does the Department of Defense employ?

    a. Almost 2 million

    b. Almost 3 million

    c. 1 million

    d. Almost 5 million

20. True or False: American liberal internationalists argue that America needs the transatlantic relationship because it lends legitimacy to its global leadership

21. True or False: Russia opposes proposals for Ukrainian membership of NATO because Russians fear the spread of United States influence in Eastern Europe.

22. Which of these is a source of contemporary American exceptionalism?

    a. Military primacy

    b. Economic dynamism

    c. Political diversity

    d. All of the above

23. True or False: Cultural homogeneity is a source of contemporary American exceptionalism

24. Why might American exceptionalism likely lead to opposition to a central world government?

    a. Its general anti-statism

    b. Its individualistic core

    c. Its fascist core

    d. All of the above

25. True or False: The U.S. acting president can initiate war without prior express military authorization from Congress.

26. How many times in history have U.S. presidents initiated war without prior express military authorization from Congress?

    a. On at least 100 occasions

    b. On at least 200 occasions

    c. On at least 35 occasions

    d. On at least 125 occasions

Discussion Questions

1) What are the advantages and disadvantages of an isolationist foreign policy?

2) What are the advantages and disadvantages of an interventionist foreign policy?

3) In what ways foreign policy might be more challenging than domestic policy?

4) What do you know about the U.S. Department of State?

5) Why does the United States offer foreign assistance to other countries?

6) What is the Universal Declaration of Human Rights?

7) How does diplomacy help promote trade, commerce, and investment?

8) How did the collapse of the Soviet Union affect U.S. foreign policy? Is it now more complex or simpler?

9) Should the United States maintain the NATO alliance, even if doing so will likely create more conflicts with Russia?

Video resources

The US' Overseas Military Base Strategy www.youtube.com/watch?v=A0qt0hdCQtg

Media Education Foundation http://www.mediaed.org/

Icount https://icount.com/

PBS Frontline http://www.pbs.org/wgbh/pages/frontline/view/

The United States and NATO www.nato.int/cps/en/natohq/declassified_162350.htm

Navigating US-Russia relations in 2020 and beyond www.brookings.edu/blog/order-from-chaos/2020/01/09/highlights-navigating-us-russia-r

A New Vision for American Foreign Policy https://www.youtube.com/watch?v=KsQYkvDB9L4

Early 1800s US Foreign Policy https://billofrightsinstitute.org/videos/early-1800s-us-foreign-policy-homework-help

Iceland and NATO https://www.nato.int/cps/en/natohq/declassified_162083.htm

Website Resources

Real Clear Politics http://www.realclearpolitics.com/welcomead/?ref=http://www.real-clearpolitics.com/

International Affairs http://www.internationalaffairs.com/

United Nations http://www.un.org/

Maps of War http://www.mapsofwar.com/

Foreign Policy http://www.foreignpolicy.com/

Foreign Policy Research Institute http://www.fpri.org

The White House http://www.whitehouse.gov/issues/foreign-policy

Foreign Affairs http://www.foreignaffairs.com/

The Brookings Institution www.brookings.edu/

Policy Studies Journal http://onlinelibrary.wiley.com/journal/10.1111/(ISSN)1541-0072

FirstGov http://www.firstgov.gov/

US Agency For International Development http://www.usaid.gov/

Factbook - CIA World Factbook https://www.cia.gov/library/publications/the-world-factbook/

APPENDIX A

THE DECLARATION OF INDEPENDENCE

When in the Course of human events, it becomes necessary for one people to dissolve the political bands which have connected them with another, and to assume among the powers of the earth, the separate and equal station to which the Laws of Nature and of Nature's God entitle them, a decent respect to the opinions of mankind requires that they should declare the causes which impel them to the separation.

We hold these truths to be self-evident, that all men are created equal, that they are endowed by their Creator with certain unalienable Rights, that among these are Life, Liberty and the pursuit of Happiness. —That to secure these rights, Governments are instituted among Men, deriving their just powers from the consent of the governed, —That whenever any Form of Government becomes destructive of these ends, it is the Right of the People to alter or to abolish it, and to institute new Government, laying its foundation on such principles and organizing its powers in such form, as to them shall seem most likely to effect their Safety and Happiness. Prudence, indeed, will dictate that Governments long established should not be changed for light and transient causes; and accordingly all experience hath shewn, that mankind are more disposed to suffer, while evils are sufferable, than to right themselves by abolishing the forms to which they are accustomed. But when a long train of abuses and usurpations, pursuing invariably the same Object evinces a design to reduce them under absolute Despotism, it is their right, it is their duty, to throw off such Government, and to provide new Guards for their future security. —Such has been the patient sufferance of these Colonies; and such is now the necessity which constrains them to alter their former Systems of Government. The history of the present King of Great Britain is a history of repeated injuries and usurpations, all having in direct object the establishment of an absolute Tyranny over these States. To prove this, let Facts be submitted to a candid world.

He has refused his Assent to Laws, the most wholesome and necessary for the public good.

He has forbidden his Governors to pass Laws of immediate and pressing importance, unless suspended in their operation till his Assent should be obtained; and when so suspended, he has utterly neglected to attend to them.

He has refused to pass other Laws for the accommodation of large districts of people, unless those people would relinquish the right of Representation in the Legislature, a right inestimable to them and formidable to tyrants only.

He has called together legislative bodies at places unusual, uncomfortable, and distant from the depository of their public Records, for the sole purpose of fatiguing them into compliance with his measures.

He has dissolved Representative Houses repeatedly, for opposing with manly firmness his invasions on the rights of the people.

He has refused for a long time, after such dissolutions, to cause others to be elected; whereby the Legislative powers, incapable of Annihilation, have returned to the People at large for their exercise; the State remaining in the mean time exposed to all the dangers of invasion from without, and convulsions within.

He has endeavoured to prevent the population of these States; for that purpose obstructing the Laws for Naturalization of Foreigners; refusing to pass others to encourage their migrations hither, and raising the conditions of new Appropriations of Lands.

He has obstructed the Administration of Justice, by refusing his Assent to Laws for establishing Judiciary powers.

He has made Judges dependent on his Will alone, for the tenure of their offices, and the amount and payment of their salaries.

He has erected a multitude of New Offices, and sent hither swarms of Officers to harrass our people, and eat out their substance.

He has kept among us, in times of peace, Standing Armies without the Consent of our legislatures.

He has affected to render the Military independent of and superior to the Civil power.

He has combined with others to subject us to a jurisdiction foreign to our constitution, and unacknowledged by our laws; giving his Assent to their Acts of pretended Legislation:

For Quartering large bodies of armed troops among us:

For protecting them, by a mock Trial, from punishment for any Murders which they should commit on the Inhabitants of these States:

For cutting off our Trade with all parts of the world:

For imposing Taxes on us without our Consent:

For depriving us in many cases, of the benefits of Trial by Jury:

For transporting us beyond Seas to be tried for pretended offences

For abolishing the free System of English Laws in a neighbouring Province, establishing therein an Arbitrary government, and enlarging its Boundaries so as to render it at once an example and fit instrument for introducing the same absolute rule into these Colonies:

For taking away our Charters, abolishing our most valuable Laws, and altering fundamentally the Forms of our Governments:

For suspending our own Legislatures, and declaring themselves invested with power to legislate for us in all cases whatsoever.

He has abdicated Government here, by declaring us out of his Protection and waging War against us.

He has plundered our seas, ravaged our Coasts, burnt our towns, and destroyed the lives of our people.

He is at this time transporting large Armies of foreign Mercenaries to compleat the works of death, desolation and tyranny, already begun with circumstances of Cruelty & perfidy scarcely paralleled in the most barbarous ages, and totally unworthy the Head of a civilized nation.

He has constrained our fellow Citizens taken Captive on the high Seas to bear Arms against their Country, to become the executioners of their friends and Brethren, or to fall themselves by their Hands.

He has excited domestic insurrections amongst us, and has endeavoured to bring on the inhabitants of our frontiers, the merciless Indian Savages, whose known rule of warfare, is an undistinguished destruction of all ages, sexes and conditions.

In every stage of these Oppressions We have Petitioned for Redress in the most humble terms: Our repeated Petitions have been answered only by repeated injury. A Prince whose character is thus marked by every act which may define a Tyrant, is unfit to be the ruler of a free people.

Nor have We been wanting in attentions to our Brittish brethren. We have warned them from time to time of attempts by their legislature to extend an unwarrantable jurisdiction over us. We have reminded them of the circumstances of our emigration and settlement here. We have appealed to their native justice and magnanimity, and we have conjured them by the ties of our common kindred to disavow these usurpations, which, would inevitably interrupt our connections and correspondence. They too have been deaf to the voice of justice and of consanguinity. We must, therefore, acquiesce in the necessity, which denounces our Separation, and hold them, as we hold the rest of mankind, Enemies in War, in Peace Friends.

We, therefore, the Representatives of the united States of America, in General Congress, Assembled, appealing to the Supreme Judge of the world for the rectitude of our intentions, do, in the Name, and by Authority of the good People of these Colonies, solemnly publish and declare, That these United Colonies are, and of Right ought to be Free and Independent States; that they are Absolved from all Allegiance to the British Crown, and that all political connection between them and the State of Great Britain, is and ought to be totally dissolved; and that as Free and Independent States, they have full Power to levy War, conclude Peace, contract Alliances, establish Commerce, and to do all other Acts and Things which Independent States may of right do. And for the support of this Declaration, with a firm reliance on the protection of divine Providence, we mutually pledge to each other our Lives, our Fortunes and our sacred Honor.

The 56 signatures on the Declaration appear in the positions indicated:

Column 1
Georgia:
Button Gwinnett
Lyman Hall
George Walton

Column 2
North Carolina:
William Hooper
Joseph Hewes
John Penn

South Carolina:
Edward Rutledge
Thomas Heyward, Jr.
Thomas Lynch, Jr.
Arthur Middleton

Column 3
Massachusetts:
John Hancock

Maryland:
Samuel Chase

William Paca
Thomas Stone
Charles Carroll of Carrollton

Virginia:
George Wythe
Richard Henry Lee
Thomas Jefferson
Benjamin Harrison
Thomas Nelson, Jr.
Francis Lightfoot Lee
Carter Braxton

Column 4
Pennsylvania:
Robert Morris
Benjamin Rush
Benjamin Franklin
John Morton
George Clymer
James Smith
George Taylor
James Wilson

George Ross

Delaware:
Caesar Rodney
George Read
Thomas McKean

Column 5
New York:
William Floyd
Philip Livingston
Francis Lewis
Lewis Morris

New Jersey:
Richard Stockton
John Witherspoon
Francis Hopkinson
John Hart
Abraham Clark

Column 6
New Hampshire:
Josiah Bartlett
William Whipple

Massachusetts:
Samuel Adams
John Adams
Robert Treat Paine
Elbridge Gerry

Rhode Island:
Stephen Hopkins
William Ellery

Connecticut:
Roger Sherman
Samuel Huntington
William Williams
Oliver Wolcott

New Hampshire:
Matthew Thornton

THE CONSTITUTION AND AMENDMENTS

We the People of the United States, in Order to form a more perfect Union, establish Justice, insure domestic Tranquility, provide for the common defence, promote the general Welfare, and secure the Blessings of Liberty to ourselves and our Posterity, do ordain and establish this Constitution for the United States of America.

Article. I.

Section. 1.

All legislative Powers herein granted shall be vested in a Congress of the United States, which shall consist of a Senate and House of Representatives.

Section. 2.

The House of Representatives shall be composed of Members chosen every second Year by the People of the several States, and the Electors in each State shall have the Qualifications requisite for Electors of the most numerous Branch of the State Legislature.

No Person shall be a Representative who shall not have attained to the Age of twenty five Years, and been seven Years a Citizen of the United States, and who shall not, when elected, be an Inhabitant of that State in which he shall be chosen.

Representatives and direct Taxes shall be apportioned among the several States which may be included within this Union, according to their respective Numbers, which shall be determined by adding to the whole Number of free Persons, including those bound to Service for a Term of Years, and excluding Indians not taxed, three fifths of all other Persons. The actual Enumeration shall be made within three Years after the first Meeting of the Congress of the United States, and within every subsequent Term of ten Years, in such Manner as they shall by Law direct. The Number of Representatives shall not exceed one for every thirty Thousand, but each State shall have at Least one Representative; and until such enumeration shall be made, the State of New Hampshire shall be entitled to chuse three, Massachusetts eight, Rhode-Island and Providence Plantations one, Connecticut five, New-York six, New Jersey four, Pennsylvania eight, Delaware one, Maryland six, Virginia ten, North Carolina five, South Carolina five, and Georgia three.

When vacancies happen in the Representation from any State, the Executive Authority thereof shall issue Writs of Election to fill such Vacancies.

The House of Representatives shall chuse their Speaker and other Officers; and shall have the sole Power of Impeachment.

Section. 3.

The Senate of the United States shall be composed of two Senators from each State, chosen by the Legislature thereof, for six Years; and each Senator shall have one Vote.

Immediately after they shall be assembled in Consequence of the first Election, they shall be divided as equally as may be into three Classes. The Seats of the Senators of the first Class shall be vacated at the Expiration of the second Year, of the second Class at the Expiration of the fourth Year, and of the third Class at the Expiration of the sixth Year, so that one third may be chosen every second Year; and if Vacancies happen by Resignation, or otherwise, during the Recess of the Legislature of any State, the Executive thereof may make temporary Appointments until the next Meeting of the Legislature, which shall then fill such Vacancies.

No Person shall be a Senator who shall not have attained to the Age of thirty Years, and been nine Years a Citizen of the United States, and who shall not, when elected, be an Inhabitant of that State for which he shall be chosen.

The Vice President of the United States shall be President of the Senate, but shall have no Vote, unless they be equally divided.

The Senate shall chuse their other Officers, and also a President pro tempore, in the Absence of the Vice President, or when he shall exercise the Office of President of the United States.

The Senate shall have the sole Power to try all Impeachments. When sitting for that Purpose, they shall be on Oath or Affirmation. When the President of the United States is tried, the Chief Justice shall preside: And no Person shall be convicted without the Concurrence of two thirds of the Members present.

Judgment in Cases of Impeachment shall not extend further than to removal from Office, and disqualification to hold and enjoy any Office of honor, Trust or Profit under the United States: but the Party convicted shall nevertheless be liable and subject to Indictment, Trial, Judgment and Punishment, according to Law.

Section. 4.

The Times, Places and Manner of holding Elections for Senators and Representatives, shall be prescribed in each State by the Legislature thereof; but the Congress may at any time by Law make or alter such Regulations, except as to the Places of chusing Senators.

The Congress shall assemble at least once in every Year, and such Meeting shall be on the first Monday in December, unless they shall by Law appoint a different Day.

Section. 5.

Each House shall be the Judge of the Elections, Returns and Qualifications of its own Members, and a Majority of each shall constitute a Quorum to do Business; but a smaller Number may adjourn from day to day, and may be authorized to compel the Attendance of absent Members, in such Manner, and under such Penalties as each House may provide.

Each House may determine the Rules of its Proceedings, punish its Members for disorderly Behaviour, and, with the Concurrence of two thirds, expel a Member.

Each House shall keep a Journal of its Proceedings, and from time to time publish the same, excepting such Parts as may in their Judgment require Secrecy; and the Yeas and Nays of the Members of either House on any question shall, at the Desire of one fifth of those Present, be entered on the Journal.

Neither House, during the Session of Congress, shall, without the Consent of the other, adjourn for more than three days, nor to any other Place than that in which the two Houses shall be sitting.

Section. 6.

The Senators and Representatives shall receive a Compensation for their Services, to be ascertained by Law, and paid out of the Treasury of the United States. They shall in all Cases, except Treason, Felony and Breach of the Peace, be privileged from Arrest during their Attendance at the Session of their respective Houses, and in going to and returning from the same; and for any Speech or Debate in either House, they shall not be questioned in any other Place.

No Senator or Representative shall, during the Time for which he was elected, be appointed to any civil Office under the Authority of the United States, which shall have been created, or the Emoluments whereof shall have been encreased during such time; and no Person holding any Office under the United States, shall be a Member of either House during his Continuance in Office.

Section. 7.

All Bills for raising Revenue shall originate in the House of Representatives; but the Senate may propose or concur with Amendments as on other Bills.

Every Bill which shall have passed the House of Representatives and the Senate, shall, before it become a Law, be presented to the President of the United States; If he approve he shall sign it, but if not he shall return it, with his Objections to that House in which it shall have originated, who shall enter the Objections at large on their Journal, and proceed to reconsider it. If after such Reconsideration two thirds of that House shall agree to pass the Bill, it shall be sent, together with the Objections, to the other House, by which it shall likewise be reconsidered, and if approved by two thirds of that House, it shall become a Law. But in all such Cases the Votes of both Houses shall be determined by yeas and Nays, and the Names of the Persons voting for and against the Bill shall be entered on the Journal of each House respectively. If any Bill shall not be returned by the President within ten Days (Sundays excepted) after it shall have been presented to him, the Same shall be a Law, in like Manner as if he had signed it, unless the Congress by their Adjournment prevent its Return, in which Case it shall not be a Law.

Every Order, Resolution, or Vote to which the Concurrence of the Senate and House of Representatives may be necessary (except on a question of Adjournment) shall be presented to the President of the United States; and before the Same shall take Effect, shall be approved by him, or being disapproved by him, shall be repassed by two thirds of the Senate and House of Representatives, according to the Rules and Limitations prescribed in the Case of a Bill.

Section. 8.

The Congress shall have Power To lay and collect Taxes, Duties, Imposts and Excises, to pay the Debts and provide for the common Defence and general Welfare of the United States; but all Duties, Imposts and Excises shall be uniform throughout the United States;

To borrow Money on the credit of the United States;

To regulate Commerce with foreign Nations, and among the several States, and with the Indian Tribes;

To establish an uniform Rule of Naturalization, and uniform Laws on the subject of Bankruptcies throughout the United States;

To coin Money, regulate the Value thereof, and of foreign Coin, and fix the Standard of Weights and Measures;

To provide for the Punishment of counterfeiting the Securities and current Coin of the United States;

To establish Post Offices and post Roads;

To promote the Progress of Science and useful Arts, by securing for limited Times to Authors and Inventors the exclusive Right to their respective Writings and Discoveries;

To constitute Tribunals inferior to the supreme Court;

To define and punish Piracies and Felonies committed on the high Seas, and Offences against the Law of Nations;

To declare War, grant Letters of Marque and Reprisal, and make Rules concerning Captures on Land and Water;

To raise and support Armies, but no Appropriation of Money to that Use shall be for a longer Term than two Years;

To provide and maintain a Navy;

To make Rules for the Government and Regulation of the land and naval Forces;

To provide for calling forth the Militia to execute the Laws of the Union, suppress Insurrections and repel Invasions;

To provide for organizing, arming, and disciplining, the Militia, and for governing such Part of them as may be employed in the Service of the United States, reserving to the States respectively, the Appointment of the Officers, and the Authority of training the Militia according to the discipline prescribed by Congress;

To exercise exclusive Legislation in all Cases whatsoever, over such District (not exceeding ten Miles square) as may, by Cession of particular States, and the Acceptance of Congress, become the Seat of the Government of the United States, and to exercise like Authority over all Places purchased by the Consent of the Legislature of the State in which the Same shall be, for the Erection of Forts, Magazines, Arsenals, dock-Yards, and other needful Buildings;—And

To make all Laws which shall be necessary and proper for carrying into Execution the foregoing Powers, and all other Powers vested by this Constitution in the Government of the United States, or in any Department or Officer thereof.

Section. 9.

The Migration or Importation of such Persons as any of the States now existing shall think proper to admit, shall not be prohibited by the Congress prior to the Year one thousand eight hundred and eight, but a Tax or duty may be imposed on such Importation, not exceeding ten dollars for each Person.

The Privilege of the Writ of Habeas Corpus shall not be suspended, unless when in Cases of Rebellion or Invasion the public Safety may require it.

No Bill of Attainder or ex post facto Law shall be passed.

No Capitation, or other direct, Tax shall be laid, unless in Proportion to the Census or enumeration herein before directed to be taken.

No Tax or Duty shall be laid on Articles exported from any State.

No Preference shall be given by any Regulation of Commerce or Revenue to the Ports of one State over those of another: nor shall Vessels bound to, or from, one State, be obliged to enter, clear, or pay Duties in another.

No Money shall be drawn from the Treasury, but in Consequence of Appropriations made by Law; and a regular Statement and Account of the Receipts and Expenditures of all public Money shall be published from time to time.

No Title of Nobility shall be granted by the United States: And no Person holding any Office of Profit or Trust under them, shall, without the Consent of the Congress, accept of any present, Emolument, Office, or Title, of any kind whatever, from any King, Prince, or foreign State.

Section. 10.

No State shall enter into any Treaty, Alliance, or Confederation; grant Letters of Marque and Reprisal; coin Money; emit Bills of Credit; make any Thing but gold and silver Coin a Tender in Payment of Debts; pass any Bill of Attainder, ex post facto Law, or Law impairing the Obligation of Contracts, or grant any Title of Nobility.

No State shall, without the Consent of the Congress, lay any Imposts or Duties on Imports or Exports, except what may be absolutely necessary for executing it's inspection Laws: and the net Produce of all Duties and Imposts, laid by any State on Imports or Exports, shall be for the Use of the Treasury of the United States; and all such Laws shall be subject to the Revision and Controul of the Congress.

No State shall, without the Consent of Congress, lay any Duty of Tonnage, keep Troops, or Ships of War in time of Peace, enter into any Agreement or Compact with another State, or with a foreign Power, or engage in War, unless actually invaded, or in such imminent Danger as will not admit of delay.

Article. II.

Section. 1.

The executive Power shall be vested in a President of the United States of America. He shall hold his Office during the Term of four Years, and, together with the Vice President, chosen for the same Term, be elected, as follows

Each State shall appoint, in such Manner as the Legislature thereof may direct, a Number of Electors, equal to the whole Number of Senators and Representatives to which the State may be entitled in the Congress: but no Senator or Representative, or Person holding an Office of Trust or Profit under the United States, shall be appointed an Elector.

The Electors shall meet in their respective States, and vote by Ballot for two Persons, of whom one at least shall not be an Inhabitant of the same State with themselves. And they shall make a List of all the Persons voted for, and of the Number of Votes for each; which List they shall sign and certify, and transmit sealed to the Seat of the Government of the United States, directed to the President of the Senate. The President of the Senate shall, in the Presence of the Senate and House of Representatives, open all the Certificates, and the Votes shall then be counted. The Person having the greatest Number of Votes shall be the President, if such Number be a Majority of the whole Number of Electors appointed; and if there be more than one who have such Majority, and have an equal Number of Votes, then the House of Representatives shall immediately chuse by Ballot one of them for President; and if no Person have a Majority, then from the five highest on the List the said House shall in like Manner chuse the President. But in chusing the President, the Votes shall be taken by States, the Representation from each State having one Vote; A quorum for this Purpose shall consist of a Member or Members from two thirds of the States, and a Majority of all the States shall be necessary to a Choice. In every Case, after the Choice of the President, the Person having the greatest Number of Votes of the Electors shall be the Vice President. But if there should remain two or more who have equal Votes, the Senate shall chuse from them by Ballot the Vice President.

The Congress may determine the Time of chusing the Electors, and the Day on which they shall give their Votes; which Day shall be the same throughout the United States.

No Person except a natural born Citizen, or a Citizen of the United States, at the time of the Adoption of this Constitution, shall be eligible to the Office of President; neither shall any Person be eligible to that Office who shall not have attained to the Age of thirty five Years, and been fourteen Years a Resident within the United States.

In Case of the Removal of the President from Office, or of his Death, Resignation, or Inability to discharge the Powers and Duties of the said Office, the Same shall devolve on the Vice President, and the Congress may by Law provide for the Case of Removal, Death, Resignation or Inability, both of the President and Vice President, declaring what Officer shall then act as President, and such Officer shall act accordingly, until the Disability be removed, or a President shall be elected.

The President shall, at stated Times, receive for his Services, a Compensation, which shall neither be encreased nor diminished during the Period for which he shall have been elected, and he shall not receive within that Period any other Emolument from the United States, or any of them.

Before he enter on the Execution of his Office, he shall take the following Oath or Affirmation:—"I do solemnly swear (or affirm) that I will faithfully execute the Office of President of the United States, and will to the best of my Ability, preserve, protect and defend the Constitution of the United States."

Section. 2.

The President shall be Commander in Chief of the Army and Navy of the United States, and of the Militia of the several States, when called into the actual Service of the United States; he may require the Opinion, in writing, of the principal Officer in each of the executive Departments, upon any Subject relating to the Duties of their respective Offices, and he shall have Power to grant Reprieves and Pardons for Offences against the United States, except in Cases of Impeachment.

He shall have Power, by and with the Advice and Consent of the Senate, to make Treaties, provided two thirds of the Senators present concur; and he shall nominate, and by and with the Advice and Consent of the Senate, shall appoint Ambassadors, other public Ministers and Consuls, Judges of the supreme Court, and all other Officers of the United States, whose Appointments are not herein otherwise provided for, and which shall be established by Law: but the Congress may by Law vest the Appointment of such inferior Officers, as they think proper, in the President alone, in the Courts of Law, or in the Heads of Departments.

The President shall have Power to fill up all Vacancies that may happen during the Recess of the Senate, by granting Commissions which shall expire at the End of their next Session.

Section. 3.

He shall from time to time give to the Congress Information of the State of the Union, and recommend to their Consideration such Measures as he shall judge necessary and expedient; he may, on extraordinary Occasions, convene both Houses, or either of them, and in Case of Disagreement between them, with Respect to the Time of Adjournment, he may adjourn them to such Time as he shall think proper; he shall receive Ambassadors and other public Ministers; he shall take Care that the Laws be faithfully executed, and shall Commission all the Officers of the United States.

Section. 4.

The President, Vice President and all civil Officers of the United States, shall be removed from Office on Impeachment for, and Conviction of, Treason, Bribery, or other high Crimes and Misdemeanors.

Article III.

Section. 1.

The judicial Power of the United States, shall be vested in one supreme Court, and in such inferior Courts as the Congress may from time to time ordain and establish. The Judges, both of the supreme and inferior Courts, shall hold their Offices during good Behaviour, and shall, at stated Times, receive for their Services, a Compensation, which shall not be diminished during their Continuance in Office.

Section. 2.

The judicial Power shall extend to all Cases, in Law and Equity, arising under this Constitution, the Laws of the United States, and Treaties made, or which shall be made, under their Authority;—to all Cases affecting Ambassadors, other public Ministers and Consuls;—to all Cases of admiralty and maritime Jurisdiction;—to Controversies to which the United States shall be a Party;—to Controversies between two or more States;—between a State and Citizens of another State,—between Citizens of different States,—between Citizens of the same State claiming Lands under Grants of different States, and between a State, or the Citizens thereof, and foreign States, Citizens or Subjects.

In all Cases affecting Ambassadors, other public Ministers and Consuls, and those in which a State shall be Party, the supreme Court shall have original Jurisdiction. In all the other Cases before mentioned, the supreme Court shall have appellate Jurisdiction, both as to Law and Fact, with such Exceptions, and under such Regulations as the Congress shall make.

The Trial of all Crimes, except in Cases of Impeachment, shall be by Jury; and such Trial shall be held in the State where the said Crimes shall have been committed; but when not committed within any State, the Trial shall be at such Place or Places as the Congress may by Law have directed.

Section. 3.

Treason against the United States, shall consist only in levying War against them, or in adhering to their Enemies, giving them Aid and Comfort. No Person shall be convicted of Treason unless on the Testimony of two Witnesses to the same overt Act, or on Confession in open Court.

The Congress shall have Power to declare the Punishment of Treason, but no Attainder of Treason shall work Corruption of Blood, or Forfeiture except during the Life of the Person attainted.

Article. IV.

Section. 1.

Full Faith and Credit shall be given in each State to the public Acts, Records, and judicial Proceedings of every other State. And the Congress may by general Laws prescribe the Manner in which such Acts, Records and Proceedings shall be proved, and the Effect thereof.

Section. 2.

The Citizens of each State shall be entitled to all Privileges and Immunities of Citizens in the several States.

A Person charged in any State with Treason, Felony, or other Crime, who shall flee from Justice, and be found in another State, shall on Demand of the executive Authority of the State from which he fled, be delivered up, to be removed to the State having Jurisdiction of the Crime.

No Person held to Service or Labour in one State, under the Laws thereof, escaping into another, shall, in Consequence of any Law or Regulation therein, be discharged from such Service or Labour, but shall be delivered up on Claim of the Party to whom such Service or Labour may be due.

Section. 3.

New States may be admitted by the Congress into this Union; but no new State shall be formed or erected within the Jurisdiction of any other State; nor any State be formed by the Junction of two or more States, or Parts of States, without the Consent of the Legislatures of the States concerned as well as of the Congress.

The Congress shall have Power to dispose of and make all needful Rules and Regulations respecting the Territory or other Property belonging to the United States; and nothing in this Constitution shall be so construed as to Prejudice any Claims of the United States, or of any particular State.

Section. 4.

The United States shall guarantee to every State in this Union a Republican Form of Government, and shall protect each of them against Invasion; and on Application of the Legislature, or of the Executive (when the Legislature cannot be convened), against domestic Violence.

Article. V.

The Congress, whenever two thirds of both Houses shall deem it necessary, shall propose Amendments to this Constitution, or, on the Application of the Legislatures of two thirds of the several States, shall call a Convention for proposing Amendments, which, in either Case, shall be valid to all Intents and Purposes, as Part of this Constitution, when ratified by the Legislatures of three fourths of the several States, or by Conventions in three fourths thereof, as the one or the other Mode of Ratification may be proposed by the Congress; Provided that no Amendment which may be made prior to the Year One thousand eight hundred and eight shall in any Manner affect the first and fourth Clauses in the Ninth Section of the first Article; and that no State, without its Consent, shall be deprived of its equal Suffrage in the Senate.

Article. VI.

All Debts contracted and Engagements entered into, before the Adoption of this Constitution, shall be as valid against the United States under this Constitution, as under the Confederation.

This Constitution, and the Laws of the United States which shall be made in Pursuance thereof; and all Treaties made, or which shall be made, under the Authority of the United States, shall be the supreme Law of the Land; and the Judges in every State shall be bound thereby, any Thing in the Constitution or Laws of any State to the Contrary notwithstanding.

The Senators and Representatives before mentioned, and the Members of the several State Legislatures, and all executive and judicial Officers, both of the United States and of the several States, shall be bound by Oath or Affirmation, to support this Constitution; but no religious Test shall ever be required as a Qualification to any Office or public Trust under the United States.

Article. VII.

The Ratification of the Conventions of nine States, shall be sufficient for the Establishment of this Constitution between the States so ratifying the Same.

Done in Convention by the Unanimous Consent of the States present the Seventeenth Day of September in the Year of our Lord one thousand seven hundred and Eighty seven and of the Independance of the United States of America the Twelfth In witness whereof We have hereunto subscribed our Names,

G. Washington
Presidt and deputy from Virginia

Delaware
Geo: Read
Gunning Bedford jun
John Dickinson
Richard Bassett
Jaco: Broom

Maryland
James McHenry
Dan of St Thos. Jenifer
Danl. Carroll

Virginia
John Blair
James Madison Jr.

North Caruolina
Wm. Blountz
Richd. Dobbs Spaight
Hu Williamson

South Carolina
J. Rutledge
Charles Cotesworth Pinckney
Charles Pinckney
Pierce Butler

Georgia
William Few
Abr Baldwin

New Hampshire
John Langdon
Nicholas Gilman

Massachusetts
Nathaniel Gorham
Rufus King

Connecticut
Wm. Saml. Johnson
Roger Sherman

New York
Alexander Hamilton

New Jersey
Wil: Livingston
David Brearley
Wm. Paterson
Jona: Dayton

Pensylvania
B Franklin
Thomas Mifflin
Robt. Morris
Geo. Clymer
Thos. FitzSimons
Jared Ingersoll
James Wilson
Gouv Morris

Constitutional Amendments

The U.S. Bill of Rights (Amendments 1–10)

The Preamble to The Bill of Rights

Congress of the United States begun and held at the City of New-York, on Wednesday the fourth of March, one thousand seven hundred and eighty nine.

The Conventions of a number of the States, having at the time of their adopting the Constitution, expressed a desire, in order to prevent misconstruction or abuse of its powers, that further declaratory and restrictive clauses should be added: And as extending the ground of public confidence in the Government, will best ensure the beneficent ends of its institution.

Resolved by the Senate and House of Representatives of the United States of America, in Congress assembled, two thirds of both Houses concurring, that the following Articles be proposed to the Legislatures of the several States, as amendments to the Constitution of the United States, all, or any of which Articles, when ratified by three fourths of the said Legislatures, to be valid to all intents and purposes, as part of the said Constitution; viz.

Articles in addition to, and Amendment of the Constitution of the United States of America, proposed by Congress, and ratified by the Legislatures of the several States, pursuant to the fifth Article of the original Constitution.

Note: The following text is a transcription of the first ten amendments to the Constitution in their original form. These amendments were ratified December 15, 1791, and form what is known as the "Bill of Rights."

Amendment I

Congress shall make no law respecting an establishment of religion, or prohibiting the free exercise thereof; or abridging the freedom of speech, or of the press; or the right of the people peaceably to assemble, and to petition the Government for a redress of grievances.

Amendment II

A well regulated Militia, being necessary to the security of a free State, the right of the people to keep and bear Arms, shall not be infringed.

Amendment III

No Soldier shall, in time of peace be quartered in any house, without the consent of the Owner, nor in time of war, but in a manner to be prescribed by law.

Amendment IV

The right of the people to be secure in their persons, houses, papers, and effects, against unreasonable searches and seizures, shall not be violated, and no Warrants shall issue, but upon probable cause, supported by Oath or affirmation, and particularly describing the place to be searched, and the persons or things to be seized.

Amendment V

No person shall be held to answer for a capital, or otherwise infamous crime, unless on a presentment or indictment of a Grand Jury, except in cases arising in the land or naval forces, or in the Militia, when in actual service in time of War or public danger; nor shall any person be subject for the same offence to be twice put in jeopardy of life or limb; nor shall be compelled in any criminal case to be a witness against himself, nor be deprived of life, liberty, or property, without due process of law; nor shall private property be taken for public use, without just compensation.

Amendment VI

In all criminal prosecutions, the accused shall enjoy the right to a speedy and public trial, by an impartial jury of the State and district wherein the crime shall have been committed, which district shall have been previously ascertained by law, and to be informed of the nature and cause of the accusation; to be confronted with the witnesses against him; to have compulsory process for obtaining witnesses in his favor, and to have the Assistance of Counsel for his defence.

Amendment VII

In Suits at common law, where the value in controversy shall exceed twenty dollars, the right of trial by jury shall be preserved, and no fact tried by a jury, shall be otherwise re-examined in any Court of the United States, than according to the rules of the common law.

Amendment VIII

Excessive bail shall not be required, nor excessive fines imposed, nor cruel and unusual punishments inflicted.

Amendment IX

The enumeration in the Constitution, of certain rights, shall not be construed to deny or disparage others retained by the people.

Amendment X

The powers not delegated to the United States by the Constitution, nor prohibited by it to the States, are reserved to the States respectively, or to the people.

Amendment XI

The Judicial power of the United States shall not be construed to extend to any suit in law or equity, commenced or prosecuted against one of the United States by Citizens of another State, or by Citizens or Subjects of any Foreign State.

Amendment XII

The Electors shall meet in their respective states and vote by ballot for President and Vice-President, one of whom, at least, shall not be an inhabitant of the same state with themselves; they shall name in their ballots the person voted for as President, and in distinct ballots the person voted for as Vice-President, and they shall make distinct lists of all persons voted for as President, and of all persons voted for as Vice-President, and of the number of votes for each, which lists they shall sign and certify, and transmit sealed to the seat of the government of the United States, directed to the President of the Senate; — the President of the Senate shall, in the presence of the Senate and House of Representatives, open all the certificates and the votes shall then be counted; — The person having the greatest number of votes for President, shall be the President, if such number be a majority of the whole number of Electors appointed; and if no person have such majority, then from the persons having the highest numbers not exceeding three on the list of those voted for as President, the House of Representatives shall choose immediately, by ballot, the President. But in choosing the President, the votes shall be taken by states, the representation from each state having one vote; a quorum for this purpose shall consist of a member or members from two-thirds of the states, and a majority of all the states shall be necessary to a choice. [And if the House of Representatives shall not choose a President whenever the right of choice shall devolve upon them, before the fourth day of March next following, then the Vice-President shall act as President, as in case of the death or other constitutional disability of the President. —]* The person having the greatest number of votes as Vice-President, shall be the Vice-President, if such number be a majority of the whole number of Electors appointed, and if no person have a majority, then from the two highest numbers on the list, the Senate shall choose the Vice-President; a quorum for the purpose shall consist of two-thirds of the whole number of Senators, and a majority of the whole number shall be necessary to a choice. But no person constitutionally ineligible to the office of President shall be eligible to that of Vice-President of the United States.

*Superseded by Section 3 of the 20th amendment.

Amendment XIII

Section 1.
Neither slavery nor involuntary servitude, except as a punishment for crime whereof the party shall have been duly convicted, shall exist within the United States, or any place subject to their jurisdiction.

Section 2.
Congress shall have power to enforce this article by appropriate legislation.

Amendment XIV

Section 1.
All persons born or naturalized in the United States, and subject to the jurisdiction thereof, are citizens of the United States and of the State wherein they reside. No State shall make or enforce any law which shall abridge the privileges or immunities of citizens of the United States; nor shall any State deprive any person of life, liberty, or property, without due process of law; nor deny to any person within its jurisdiction the equal protection of the laws.

Section 2.
Representatives shall be apportioned among the several States according to their respective numbers, counting the whole number of persons in each State, excluding Indians not taxed. But when the right to vote at any election for the choice of electors for President and Vice-President of the United States, Representatives in Congress, the Executive and Judicial officers of a State, or the members of the Legislature thereof, is denied to any of the male inhabitants of such State, being twenty-one years of age,* and citizens of the United States, or in any way abridged, except for participation in rebellion, or other crime, the basis of representation therein shall be reduced in the proportion which the number of such male citizens shall bear to the whole number of male citizens twenty-one years of age in such State.

Section 3.
No person shall be a Senator or Representative in Congress, or elector of President and Vice-President, or hold any office, civil or military, under the United States, or under any State, who, having previously taken an oath, as a member of Congress, or as an officer of the United States, or as a member of any State legislature, or as an executive or judicial officer of any State, to support the Constitution of the United States, shall have engaged in insurrection or rebellion against the same, or given aid or comfort to

the enemies thereof. But Congress may by a vote of two-thirds of each House, remove such disability.

Section 4.

The validity of the public debt of the United States, authorized by law, including debts incurred for payment of pensions and bounties for services in suppressing insurrection or rebellion, shall not be questioned. But neither the United States nor any State shall assume or pay any debt or obligation incurred in aid of insurrection or rebellion against the United States, or any claim for the loss or emancipation of any slave; but all such debts, obligations and claims shall be held illegal and void.

Section 5.

The Congress shall have the power to enforce, by appropriate legislation, the provisions of this article.

Changed by Section 1 of the 26th amendment.

Amendment XV

Section 1.

The right of citizens of the United States to vote shall not be denied or abridged by the United States or by any State on account of race, color, or previous condition of servitude—

Section 2.

The Congress shall have the power to enforce this article by appropriate legislation.

Amendment XVI

The Congress shall have power to lay and collect taxes on incomes, from whatever source derived, without apportionment among the several States, and without regard to any census or enumeration.

Amendment XVII

The Senate of the United States shall be composed of two Senators from each State, elected by the people thereof, for six years; and each Senator shall have one vote. The electors in each State shall have the qualifications requisite for electors of the most numerous branch of the State legislatures.

When vacancies happen in the representation of any State in the Senate, the executive authority of such State shall issue writs of election to fill such vacancies: *Provided,*

That the legislature of any State may empower the executive thereof to make temporary appointments until the people fill the vacancies by election as the legislature may direct.

This amendment shall not be so construed as to affect the election or term of any Senator chosen before it becomes valid as part of the Constitution.

Amendment XVIII

Section 1.
After one year from the ratification of this article the manufacture, sale, or transportation of intoxicating liquors within, the importation thereof into, or the exportation thereof from the United States and all territory subject to the jurisdiction thereof for beverage purposes is hereby prohibited.

Section 2.
The Congress and the several States shall have concurrent power to enforce this article by appropriate legislation.

Section 3.
This article shall be inoperative unless it shall have been ratified as an amendment to the Constitution by the legislatures of the several States, as provided in the Constitution, within seven years from the date of the submission hereof to the States by the Congress.

Amendment XIX

The right of citizens of the United States to vote shall not be denied or abridged by the United States or by any State on account of sex.

Congress shall have power to enforce this article by appropriate legislation.

Amendment XX

Section 1.
The terms of the President and the Vice President shall end at noon on the 20th day of January, and the terms of Senators and Representatives at noon on the 3d day of January, of the years in which such terms would have ended if this article had not been ratified; and the terms of their successors shall then begin.

Section 2.
The Congress shall assemble at least once in every year, and such meeting shall begin at noon on the 3d day of January, unless they shall by law appoint a different day.

Section 3.

If, at the time fixed for the beginning of the term of the President, the President elect shall have died, the Vice President elect shall become President. If a President shall not have been chosen before the time fixed for the beginning of his term, or if the President elect shall have failed to qualify, then the Vice President elect shall act as President until a President shall have qualified; and the Congress may by law provide for the case wherein neither a President elect nor a Vice President elect shall have qualified, declaring who shall then act as President, or the manner in which one who is to act shall be selected, and such person shall act accordingly until a President or Vice President shall have qualified.

Section 4.

The Congress may by law provide for the case of the death of any of the persons from whom the House of Representatives may choose a President whenever the right of choice shall have devolved upon them, and for the case of the death of any of the persons from whom the Senate may choose a Vice President whenever the right of choice shall have devolved upon them.

Section 5.

Sections 1 and 2 shall take effect on the 15th day of October following the ratification of this article.

Section 6.

This article shall be inoperative unless it shall have been ratified as an amendment to the Constitution by the legislatures of three-fourths of the several States within seven years from the date of its submission.

Amendment XXI

Section 1.

The eighteenth article of amendment to the Constitution of the United States is hereby repealed.

Section 2.

The transportation or importation into any State, Territory, or possession of the United States for delivery or use therein of intoxicating liquors, in violation of the laws thereof, is hereby prohibited.

Section 3.

This article shall be inoperative unless it shall have been ratified as an amendment to the Constitution by conventions in the several States, as provided in the Constitution, within seven years from the date of the submission hereof to the States by the Congress.

Amendment XXII

Section 1.

No person shall be elected to the office of the President more than twice, and no person who has held the office of President, or acted as President, for more than two years of a term to which some other person was elected President shall be elected to the office of the President more than once. But this Article shall not apply to any person holding the office of President when this Article was proposed by the Congress, and shall not prevent any person who may be holding the office of President, or acting as President, during the term within which this Article becomes operative from holding the office of President or acting as President during the remainder of such term.

Section 2.

This article shall be inoperative unless it shall have been ratified as an amendment to the Constitution by the legislatures of three-fourths of the several States within seven years from the date of its submission to the States by the Congress.

Amendment XXIII

Section 1.

The District constituting the seat of Government of the United States shall appoint in such manner as the Congress may direct:

A number of electors of President and Vice President equal to the whole number of Senators and Representatives in Congress to which the District would be entitled if it were a State, but in no event more than the least populous State; they shall be in addition to those appointed by the States, but they shall be considered, for the purposes of the election of President and Vice President, to be electors appointed by a State; and they shall meet in the District and perform such duties as provided by the twelfth article of amendment.

Section 2.

The Congress shall have power to enforce this article by appropriate legislation.

Amendment XXIV

Section 1.

The right of citizens of the United States to vote in any primary or other election for President or Vice President, for electors for President or Vice President, or for Senator or Representative in Congress, shall not be denied or abridged by the United States or any State by reason of failure to pay any poll tax or other tax.

Section 2.

The Congress shall have power to enforce this article by appropriate legislation.

Amendment XXV

Section 1.

In case of the removal of the President from office or of his death or resignation, the Vice President shall become President.

Section 2.

Whenever there is a vacancy in the office of the Vice President, the President shall nominate a Vice President who shall take office upon confirmation by a majority vote of both Houses of Congress.

Section 3.

Whenever the President transmits to the President pro tempore of the Senate and the Speaker of the House of Representatives his written declaration that he is unable to discharge the powers and duties of his office, and until he transmits to them a written declaration to the contrary, such powers and duties shall be discharged by the Vice President as Acting President.

Section 4.

Whenever the Vice President and a majority of either the principal officers of the executive departments or of such other body as Congress may by law provide, transmit to the President pro tempore of the Senate and the Speaker of the House of Representatives their written declaration that the President is unable to discharge the powers and duties of his office, the Vice President shall immediately assume the powers and duties of the office as Acting President.

Thereafter, when the President transmits to the President pro tempore of the Senate and the Speaker of the House of Representatives his written declaration that no inability exists, he shall resume the powers and duties of his office unless the Vice President and a majority of either the principal officers of the executive department or of such other body as Congress may by law provide, transmit within four days to the President pro tempore of the Senate and the Speaker of the House of Representatives their written declaration that the President is unable to discharge the powers and duties of his office. Thereupon Congress shall decide the issue, assembling within forty-eight hours for that purpose if not in session. If the Congress, within twenty-one days after receipt of the latter written declaration, or, if Congress is not in session, within twenty-one days after Congress is required to assemble, determines by two-thirds vote of both

Houses that the President is unable to discharge the powers and duties of his office, the Vice President shall continue to discharge the same as Acting President; otherwise, the President shall resume the powers and duties of his office.

Amendment XXVI

Section 1.
The right of citizens of the United States, who are eighteen years of age or older, to vote shall not be denied or abridged by the United States or by any State on account of age.

Section 2.
The Congress shall have power to enforce this article by appropriate legislation.

Amendment XXVII

No law, varying the compensation for the services of the Senators and Representatives, shall take effect, until an election of Representatives shall have intervened.

APPENDIX C

FEDERALIST PAPERS #10 AND #51

Federalist Paper #10: The Union as a Safeguard Against Domestic Faction and Insurrection

From the New York Packet.
Friday, November 23, 1787.

Author: James Madison

To the People of the State of New York:

AMONG the numerous advantages promised by a well-constructed Union, none deserves to be more accurately developed than its tendency to break and control the violence of faction. The friend of popular governments never finds himself so much alarmed for their character and fate, as when he contemplates their propensity to this dangerous vice. He will not fail, therefore, to set a due value on any plan which, without violating the principles to which he is attached, provides a proper cure for it. The instability, injustice, and confusion introduced into the public councils, have, in truth, been the mortal diseases under which popular governments have everywhere perished; as they continue to be the favorite and fruitful topics from which the adversaries to liberty derive their most specious declamations. The valuable improvements made by the American constitutions on the popular models, both ancient and modern, cannot certainly be too much admired; but it would be an unwarrantable partiality, to contend that they have as effectually obviated the danger on this side, as was wished and expected. Complaints are everywhere heard from our most considerate and virtuous citizens, equally the friends of public and private faith, and of public and personal liberty, that our governments are too unstable, that the public good is disregarded in the conflicts of rival parties, and that measures are too often decided, not according to the rules of justice and the rights of the minor party, but by the superior force of an interested and overbearing majority. However anxiously we may wish that these complaints had no foundation, the evidence, of known facts will not permit us to deny that they are in some degree true. It will be found, indeed, on a candid review of our situation, that some of the distresses under which we labor have been erroneously charged on the operation of our governments; but it will be found, at the same time, that other causes will not alone account for many of our heaviest misfortunes; and, particularly, for that prevailing and increasing distrust of public engagements, and alarm for private rights, which are echoed from one end of the continent to the other. These must be chiefly, if not wholly, effects of the unsteadiness and injustice with which a factious spirit has tainted our public administrations.

By a faction, I understand a number of citizens, whether amounting to a majority or a minority of the whole, who are united and actuated by some common impulse of passion, or of interest, adversed to the rights of other citizens, or to the permanent and aggregate interests of the community.

There are two methods of curing the mischiefs of faction: the one, by removing its causes; the other, by controlling its effects.

There are again two methods of removing the causes of faction: the one, by destroying the liberty which is essential to its existence; the other, by giving to every citizen the same opinions, the same passions, and the same interests.

It could never be more truly said than of the first remedy, that it was worse than the disease. Liberty is to faction what air is to fire, an aliment without which it instantly expires. But it could not be less folly to abolish liberty, which is essential to political life, because it nourishes faction, than it would be to wish the annihilation of air, which is essential to animal life, because it imparts to fire its destructive agency.

The second expedient is as impracticable as the first would be unwise. As long as the reason of man continues fallible, and he is at liberty to exercise it, different opinions will be formed. As long as the connection subsists between his reason and his self-love, his opinions and his passions will have a reciprocal influence on each other; and the former will be objects to which the latter will attach themselves. The diversity in the faculties of men, from which the rights of property originate, is not less an insuperable obstacle to a uniformity of interests. The protection of these faculties is the first object of government. From the protection of different and unequal faculties of acquiring property, the possession of different degrees and kinds of property immediately results; and from the influence of these on the sentiments and views of the respective proprietors, ensues a division of the society into different interests and parties.

The latent causes of faction are thus sown in the nature of man; and we see them everywhere brought into different degrees of activity, according to the different circumstances of civil society. A zeal for different opinions concerning religion, concerning government, and many other points, as well of speculation as of practice; an attachment to different leaders ambitiously contending for pre-eminence and power; or to persons of other descriptions whose fortunes have been interesting to the human passions, have, in turn, divided mankind into parties, inflamed them with mutual animosity, and rendered them much more disposed to vex and oppress each other than to co-operate for their common good. So strong is this propensity of mankind to fall into mutual animosities, that where no substantial occasion presents itself, the most frivolous and fanciful distinctions have been sufficient to kindle their unfriendly passions and excite their most violent conflicts. But the most common and durable source of factions has been the various and unequal distribution of property. Those who hold and those who are without property have ever formed distinct interests in society. Those who are creditors, and those who are debtors, fall under a like discrimination. A landed interest, a manufacturing interest, a mercantile interest, a moneyed interest, with many lesser interests, grow up of necessity in civilized nations, and divide them into different classes, actuated by different sentiments and views. The regulation of these various and interfering interests forms the principal task of modern legislation, and involves the spirit of party and faction in the necessary and ordinary operations of the government.

No man is allowed to be a judge in his own cause, because his interest would certainly bias his judgment, and, not improbably, corrupt his integrity. With equal, nay with greater reason, a body of men are unfit to be both judges and parties at the same time; yet what are many of the most important acts of legislation, but so many judicial determinations, not indeed concerning the rights of single persons, but concerning the rights of large bodies of citizens? And what are the different classes of legislators but advocates and parties to the causes which they determine? Is a law proposed concerning private debts? It is a question to which the creditors are parties on one side and the debtors on the other. Justice ought to hold the balance between them. Yet the parties are, and must be, themselves the judges; and the most numerous party, or, in other words, the most powerful faction must be expected to prevail. Shall domestic manufactures be encouraged, and in what degree, by restrictions on foreign manufactures? are questions which would be differently decided by the landed and the manufacturing classes, and probably by neither with a sole regard to justice and the public good. The apportionment of taxes on the various descriptions of property is an act which seems to require the most exact impartiality; yet there is, perhaps, no legislative act in which greater opportunity and temptation are given to a predominant party to trample on the rules of justice. Every shilling with which they overburden the inferior number, is a shilling saved to their own pockets.

It is in vain to say that enlightened statesmen will be able to adjust these clashing interests, and render them all subservient to the public good. Enlightened statesmen will not always be at the helm. Nor, in many cases, can such an adjustment be made at all without taking into view indirect and remote considerations, which will rarely prevail over the immediate interest which one party may find in disregarding the rights of another or the good of the whole.

The inference to which we are brought is, that the CAUSES of faction cannot be removed, and that relief is only to be sought in the means of controlling its EFFECTS.

If a faction consists of less than a majority, relief is supplied by the republican principle, which enables the majority to defeat its sinister views by regular vote. It may clog the administration, it may convulse the society; but it will be unable to execute and mask its violence under the forms of the Constitution. When a majority is included in a faction, the form of popular government, on the other hand, enables it to sacrifice to its ruling passion or interest both the public good and the rights of other citizens. To secure the public good and private rights against the danger of such a faction, and at the same time to preserve the spirit and the form of popular government, is then the great object to which our inquiries are directed. Let me add that it is the great desideratum by which this form of government can be rescued from the opprobrium under which it has so long labored, and be recommended to the esteem and adoption of mankind.

By what means is this object attainable? Evidently by one of two only. Either the existence of the same passion or interest in a majority at the same time must be prevented, or the majority, having such coexistent passion or interest, must be rendered, by their number and local situation, unable to concert and carry into effect schemes of oppression. If the impulse and the opportunity be suffered to coincide, we well know that neither moral nor religious motives can be relied on as an adequate control. They are not found to be such on the injustice and violence of individuals, and lose their efficacy in proportion to the number combined together, that is, in proportion as their efficacy becomes needful.

From this view of the subject it may be concluded that a pure democracy, by which I mean a society consisting of a small number of citizens, who assemble and administer the government in person, can admit of no cure for the mischiefs of faction. A common passion or interest will, in almost every case, be felt by a majority of the whole; a communication and concert result from the form of government itself; and there is nothing to check the inducements to sacrifice the weaker party or an obnoxious individual. Hence it is that such democracies have ever been spectacles of turbulence and contention; have ever been found incompatible with personal security or the rights of property; and have in general been as short in their lives as they have been violent in their deaths. Theoretic politicians, who have patronized this species of government, have erroneously supposed that by reducing mankind to a perfect equality in their political rights, they would, at the same time, be perfectly equalized and assimilated in their possessions, their opinions, and their passions.

A republic, by which I mean a government in which the scheme of representation takes place, opens a different prospect, and promises the cure for which we are seeking. Let us examine the points in which it varies from pure democracy, and we shall comprehend both the nature of the cure and the efficacy which it must derive from the Union.

The two great points of difference between a democracy and a republic are: first, the delegation of the government, in the latter, to a small number of citizens elected by the rest; secondly, the greater number of citizens, and greater sphere of country, over which the latter may be extended.

The effect of the first difference is, on the one hand, to refine and enlarge the public views, by passing them through the medium of a chosen body of citizens, whose wisdom may best discern the true interest of their country, and whose patriotism and love of justice will be least likely to sacrifice it to temporary or partial considerations. Under such a regulation, it may well happen that the public voice, pronounced by the representatives of the people, will be more consonant to the public good than if pronounced by the people themselves, convened for the purpose. On the other hand, the effect may be inverted. Men of factious tempers, of local prejudices, or of sinister designs, may, by intrigue, by corruption, or by other means, first obtain the suffrages, and then betray the interests, of the people. The question resulting is, whether small or extensive republics are more favorable to the election of proper guardians of the public weal; and it is clearly decided in favor of the latter by two obvious considerations:

In the first place, it is to be remarked that, however small the republic may be, the representatives must be raised to a certain number, in order to guard against the cabals of a few; and that, however large it may be, they must be limited to a certain number, in order to guard against the confusion of a multitude. Hence, the number of representatives in the two cases not being in proportion to that of the two constituents, and being proportionally greater in the small republic, it follows that, if the proportion of fit characters be not less in the large than in the small republic, the former will present a greater option, and consequently a greater probability of a fit choice.

In the next place, as each representative will be chosen by a greater number of citizens in the large than in the small republic, it will be more difficult for unworthy candidates to practice with success the vicious arts by which elections are too often carried; and the suffrages of the people being more free, will be more likely to centre in men who possess the most attractive merit and the most diffusive and established characters.

It must be confessed that in this, as in most other cases, there is a mean, on both sides of which inconveniences will be found to lie. By enlarging too much the number of electors, you render the representatives too little acquainted with all their local circumstances and lesser interests; as by reducing it too much, you render him unduly attached to these, and too little fit to comprehend and pursue great and national objects. The federal Constitution forms a happy combination in this respect; the great and aggregate interests being referred to the national, the local and particular to the State legislatures.

The other point of difference is, the greater number of citizens and extent of territory which may be brought within the compass of republican than of democratic government; and it is this circumstance principally which renders factious combinations less to be dreaded in the former than in the latter. The smaller the society, the fewer probably will be the distinct parties and interests composing it; the fewer the distinct parties and interests, the more frequently will a majority be found of the same party; and the smaller the number of individuals composing a majority, and the smaller the compass within which they are placed, the more easily will they concert and execute their plans of oppression. Extend the sphere, and you take in a greater variety of parties and interests; you make it less probable that a majority of the whole will have a common motive to invade the rights of other citizens; or if such a common motive exists, it will be more difficult for all who feel it to discover their own strength, and to act in unison with each other. Besides other impediments, it may be remarked that, where there is a consciousness of unjust or dishonorable purposes, communication is always checked by distrust in proportion to the number whose concurrence is necessary.

Hence, it clearly appears, that the same advantage which a republic has over a democracy, in controlling the effects of faction, is enjoyed by a large over a small republic,--is enjoyed by the Union over the States composing it. Does the advantage consist in the substitution of representatives whose enlightened views and virtuous sentiments render them superior to local prejudices and schemes of injustice? It will not be denied that the representation of the Union will be most likely to possess these requisite endowments. Does it consist in the greater security afforded by a greater variety of parties, against the event of any one party being able to outnumber and oppress the rest? In an equal degree does the increased variety of parties comprised within the

Union, increase this security. Does it, in fine, consist in the greater obstacles opposed to the concert and accomplishment of the secret wishes of an unjust and interested majority? Here, again, the extent of the Union gives it the most palpable advantage.

The influence of factious leaders may kindle a flame within their particular States, but will be unable to spread a general conflagration through the other States. A religious sect may degenerate into a political faction in a part of the Confederacy; but the variety of sects dispersed over the entire face of it must secure the national councils against any danger from that source. A rage for paper money, for an abolition of debts, for an equal division of property, or for any other improper or wicked project, will be less apt to pervade the whole body of the Union than a particular member of it; in the same proportion as such a malady is more likely to taint a particular county or district, than an entire State.

In the extent and proper structure of the Union, therefore, we behold a republican remedy for the diseases most incident to republican government. And according to the degree of pleasure and pride we feel in being republicans, ought to be our zeal in cherishing the spirit and supporting the character of Federalists.

Federalist Paper #51: The Structure of the Government Must Furnish the Proper Checks and Balances Between the Different Departments

From the New York Packet.
Friday, February 8, 1788.

Author: Alexander Hamilton or James Madison

To the People of the State of New York:

TO WHAT expedient, then, shall we finally resort, for maintaining in practice the necessary partition of power among the several departments, as laid down in the Constitution? The only answer that can be given is, that as all these exterior provisions are found to be inadequate, the defect must be supplied, by so contriving the interior structure of the government as that its several constituent parts may, by their mutual relations, be the means of keeping each other in their proper places. Without presuming to undertake a full development of this important idea, I will hazard a few general observations, which may perhaps place it in a clearer light, and enable us to form a more correct judgment of the principles and structure of the government planned by the convention. In order to lay a due foundation for that separate and distinct exercise of the different powers of government, which to a certain extent is admitted on all hands to be essential to the preservation of liberty, it is evident that each department should have a will of its own; and consequently should be so constituted that the members of each should have as little agency as possible in the appointment of the members of the others. Were this principle rigorously adhered to, it would require that all the appointments for the supreme executive, legislative, and judiciary magistracies should be drawn from the same fountain of authority, the people, through channels having no communication whatever with one another. Perhaps such a plan of constructing the several departments would be less difficult in practice than it may in contemplation appear. Some difficulties, however, and some additional expense would attend the execution of it. Some deviations, therefore, from the principle must be admitted. In the constitution of the judiciary department in particular, it might be inexpedient to insist rigorously on the principle: first, because peculiar qualifications being essential in the members, the primary consideration ought to be to select that mode of choice which best secures these qualifications; secondly, because the permanent tenure by which the appointments are held in that department, must soon destroy all sense of dependence on the authority conferring them. It is equally evident, that the members of each department should be as little dependent as possible on those of the others, for the emoluments annexed to their offices. Were the executive magistrate, or the judges, not independent of the legislature in this particular, their independence in every other would be merely nominal. But the great security against a gradual concentration of the several powers in the same department, consists in giving to those who administer each department the necessary constitutional means and personal motives to resist encroachments of the others. The provision for defense must in this, as in all other cases, be made commensurate to the danger of attack. Ambition must be made to counteract ambition. The interest of the man must be connected with the constitutional rights of the place. It may be a reflection on human nature, that such devices should be necessary to control the abuses of government. But what is government itself, but the greatest of all reflections on human nature? If men were angels, no government would be necessary. If angels were to govern men, neither external nor internal controls on government would be necessary. In framing a government which is to be administered by men over men, the great difficulty lies in this: you must first enable the government to control the governed; and in the next place oblige it to control itself. A dependence on the people is, no doubt, the primary control on the government; but experience has taught mankind the necessity of auxiliary precautions. This policy of supplying, by opposite and rival interests, the defect of better motives, might be traced through the whole system of human affairs, private as well as public. We see it particularly displayed in all the subordinate distributions of power, where the constant aim is to divide and arrange the several offices in such a manner as that each may be a check on the other that the private interest of every individual may be a sentinel over the public rights. These inventions of prudence cannot be less requisite in the distribution of the supreme powers of the State. But it is not possible to give to each department an equal power of self-defense. In republican government, the legislative authority necessarily predominates. The remedy for this inconveniency is to divide the legislature into different branches; and to render them, by different modes of election and different principles of action, as little connected with each other as the nature of their common functions and their common dependence on the society will admit. It may even be necessary to guard against dangerous encroachments by still further precautions. As the weight of the legislative authority requires that it should be thus divided, the weakness of the executive may require, on the other hand, that it should be fortified. An absolute negative on the legislature appears, at first view, to be the natural defense with which the executive magistrate should be armed. But perhaps it would be neither altogether safe nor alone sufficient. On ordinary occasions it might not be exerted with the requisite firmness, and on extraordinary occasions it might be perfidiously abused. May not this defect of an absolute negative be supplied by some qualified connection between this weaker department and the weaker branch of the stronger department, by which the latter may be led to support the constitutional rights of the former, without being too much detached from the rights of its own department? If the principles on which these observations are founded be just, as I persuade myself they are, and they be applied as a criterion to the several State constitutions, and to the federal Constitution it will be found that if the latter does not perfectly correspond with them, the former are infinitely less able to bear such a test. There are, moreover, two considerations particularly applicable to the federal system of America, which place that system in a very interesting point of view. First. In a single republic, all the power surrendered by the people is submitted to the administration of a single government; and the usurpations are guarded against by a division of the government into distinct and separate departments. In the compound republic of America, the power surrendered by the people is first divided between two distinct governments, and then the portion allotted to each subdivided among distinct and separate departments. Hence a double security arises to the rights of the people. The different governments will control each other, at the same time that each will be controlled by itself. Second. It is of great importance in a republic not only to guard the society against the oppression of its rulers, but to guard one part of the society against the injustice of the other part. Different interests necessarily exist in different classes of citizens. If a majority be united by a common interest, the rights of the minority will be insecure. There are but two methods of providing against this evil: the one by creating a will in the community independent of the majority that is, of the society itself; the other, by comprehending in the society so many separate descriptions of citizens as will render an unjust combination of a majority of the whole very improbable, if not impracticable. The first method prevails in all governments possessing an hereditary or self-appointed authority. This, at best, is but a precarious security; because a power independent of the society may as well espouse the unjust views of the major, as the rightful interests of the minor party, and may possibly be turned against both parties. The second method will be exemplified in the federal republic of the United States. Whilst all authority in it will be derived from and dependent on the society, the society itself will be broken into so many parts, interests, and classes of citizens, that the rights of individuals, or of the minority, will be in little danger from interested combinations of the majority. In a free government the security for civil rights must be the same as that for religious rights. It consists in the one case in the multiplicity of interests, and in the other in the multiplicity of sects. The degree of security in both cases will depend on the number of interests and sects; and this may be presumed to depend on the extent of country and number of people comprehended under the same government. This view of the subject must particularly recommend a proper federal system to all the sincere and considerate friends of republican government, since it shows that in exact proportion as the territory of the Union may be formed into more circumscribed Confederacies, or States oppressive combinations of a majority will be facilitated: the best security, under the republican forms, for the rights of every class of citizens, will be diminished: and consequently the stability and independence of some member of the government, the only other security, must be proportionately increased. Justice is the end of government. It is the end of civil society. It ever has been and ever will be pursued until it be obtained, or until liberty be lost in the pursuit. In a society under the forms of which the stronger faction can readily unite and oppress the weaker, anarchy may as truly be said to reign as in a state of nature, where the weaker individual is not secured against the violence of the stronger; and as, in the latter state, even the stronger individuals are prompted, by the uncertainty of their condition, to submit to a government which may protect the weak as well as themselves; so, in the former state, will the more powerful factions or parties be gradually induced, by a like motive, to wish for a government which will protect all parties, the weaker as well as the more powerful. It can be little doubted that if the State of Rhode Island was separated from the Confederacy and left to itself, the insecurity of rights under the popular form of government within such narrow limits would be displayed by such reiterated oppressions of factious majorities that some power altogether independent of the people would soon be called for by the voice of the very factions whose misrule had proved the necessity of it. In the extended republic of the United

States, and among the great variety of interests, parties, and sects which it embraces, a coalition of a majority of the whole society could seldom take place on any other principles than those of justice and the general good; whilst there being thus less danger to a minor from the will of a major party, there must be less pretext, also, to provide for the security of the former, by introducing into the government a will not dependent on the latter, or, in other words, a will independent of the society itself. It is no less certain than it is important, notwithstanding the contrary opinions which have been entertained, that the larger the society, provided it lie within a practical sphere, the more duly capable it will be of self-government. And happily for the REPUBLICAN CAUSE, the practicable sphere may be carried to a very great extent, by a judicious modification and mixture of the FEDERAL PRINCIPLE.

PUBLIUS.

APPENDIX D

SELECTED SUPREME COURT CASES

A. *L. A. Schechter Poultry Corp. v. United States, 295 U.S. 495 (1935).* This case represented a challenge to the constitutionality of a law called the National Industrial Recovery Act. This law was a major part of President Franklin D. Roosevelt's attempt to rebuild the nation's economy during the Great Depression. Major industries in the United States, however, objected to the way the law empowered the president to regulate aspects of American industry, such as labor conditions and even pay. In the unanimous decision, the court determined that the act was unconstitutional because it shifted the power to regulate commerce from the legislative branch to the executive branch.

Arizona v. United States, 567 U.S. ___ (2012). This case involved federal attempts to prevent an Arizona state immigration law (S.B. 1070) from being enforced. The United States brought suit, arguing that immigration law is exclusively in the federal domain. Agreeing with the federal government, a federal district court enjoined specific provisions in the law. Arizona appealed to the Supreme Court to overturn the decision. In a 5–3 decision, the court found that specific provisions in the law did conflict with federal law, while others were constitutional.

Brown v. Board of Education of Topeka, 347 U.S. 483 (1954). This case represented a challenge to the principle of "separate but equal" established by *Plessy v. Ferguson* in 1896. The case was brought by students who were denied admittance to certain public schools based exclusively on race. The unanimous decision in *Brown v. Board* determined that the existence of racially segregated public schools violated the equal protection clause of the Fourteenth Amendment. The court decided that schools segregated by race perpetrated harm by giving legal sanction to the idea that African Americans were inherently inferior. The ruling effectively overturned *Plessy v. Ferguson* and removed the legal supports for segregated schools nationwide.

Buckley v. Valeo, 424 U.S. 1 (1976). This case concerned the power of the then recently created Federal Election Commission to regulate the financing of political campaigns. These restrictions limited the amount of contributions that could be made to candidates and required political contributions to be disclosed, among other things. In 1975, Senator James Buckley filed suit, arguing that these limits amounted to a violation of First Amendment protections on free speech and free association. In a series of decisions in this complex case, the court determined that these restrictions did not violate the First Amendment.

Burwell v. Hobby Lobby Stores, Inc., 573 U.S. ___ (2014). This case involved a challenge to the mandate in the Patient Protection and Affordable Care Act that required that all employment-based group health care plans provide coverage for certain types of contraceptives. The law, however, allowed exemptions for religious employers such as churches that held a religious-based opposition to contraception. The plaintiffs in the case argued that Hobby Lobby, a large family-owned chain of arts and crafts stores, was run based on Christian principles and therefore should be exempt as well because of the Religious Freedom Restoration Act of 1993 (RFRA). The 5–4 decision in *Burwell v. Hobby Lobby* agreed with the plaintiffs and declared that RFRA permits for-profit companies like Hobby Lobby to deny coverage for contraception in their health plans when that coverage violates a religious belief.

Bush v. Gore, 531 U.S. 98 (2000). Following voting in the November 2000 presidential election, observers recognized that the outcome of the very close national election hinged on the outcome of the election in Florida. Because the Florida election was so close, manual recounts were called for by the state's supreme court. Then-governor George W. Bush, who was ahead in the initial count, appealed to the U.S. Supreme Court to halt the manual recount and to declare that the method of manual recount being used violated his rights to equal protection and due process. The court issued a two-part *per curiam* opinion on the case. (In a *per curiam* opinion, the court makes it clear that the decision in the case is not intended to set a legal precedent.) In the first part, the court ruled in a 7–2 decision that the manual recount did violate the plaintiff's right to equal protection. In the second part, decided by a smaller 5–4 margin, the court ruled that there was not sufficient time to adjust the recount procedure and conduct a full recount. The effect of this ruling gave the Florida electoral votes, and thus the presidency, to George W. Bush.

Citizens United v. Federal Election Commission, 558 U.S. 310 (2010). In 2007, the nonprofit corporation Citizens United was prevented by the Federal Election Commission (FEC) from showing a movie about then-presidential candidate Hillary Clinton. The FEC noted that showing the movie violated the Bipartisan Campaign Reform Act (BCRA). BCRA prohibited campaign communications one month before a primary election and two months before a general election, required donors to be disclosed, and prohibited corporations from using their general funds for campaign communications. The plaintiffs argued that these restrictions constituted a violation of the First Amendment. The 5–4 decision in *Citizens United v. FEC* agreed with the plaintiffs and concluded that the restrictions imposed by BCRA and enforced by the FEC violated the corporation's First Amendment right to free expression.

Dred Scott v. Sandford, 60 U.S. 393 (1856). This case concerned the constitutionality of the Missouri Compromise, which declared that certain states would be entirely free of slavery. Dred Scott, a slave, was brought by his owner into free territories. When the owner brought him back to Missouri, a slave state, Dred Scott sued claiming that his time living in free territory made him free. After failing in his attempts in Missouri, Scott appealed to the Supreme Court. In a 7–2 decision, the court declared that the relevant parts of the Missouri Compromise were unconstitutional, and that Scott remained a slave as a result.

Gideon v. Wainwright, 372 U.S. 335 (1963). In 1961, Clarence E. Gideon was arrested and accused of breaking into a poolroom and stealing money from a cigarette machine. Not being able to afford a lawyer, and being denied a public defender by the judge, Gideon defended himself and was subsequently found guilty. Gideon appealed to the Supreme Court declaring that the denial by the trial judge constituted a violation of his constitutional right to representation. The unanimous decision by the court in *Gideon v. Wainwright* agreed that the Sixth Amendment required that those facing felony criminal charges be supplied with legal representation.

King v. Burwell, 576 U.S. ___ (2015). When Congress wrote and passed the Patient Protection and Affordable Care Act in 2010, lawmakers intended for states to create exchanges through which residents in those states could purchase health care insurance plans. For those residents who could not afford the premiums, the law also allowed for tax credits to help reduce the cost. If states didn't create an exchange, the federal government created the exchange for the state. While the intention of the lawmakers was for the tax credits to apply to the federally created exchanges as well, the language of the law was somewhat unclear on this point. Residents in Virginia brought suit against the law arguing that the law should be interpreted in a way that withholds tax credits from those participating in the federally created exchange. In the 6–3 decision, the court disagreed, stating that viewing the law in its entirety made it clear that the intent of the law was to provide the tax credits to those participating in either exchange.

Lawrence v. Texas, 539 U.S. 558 (2003). This case concerned two men in Houston who in 1998 were prosecuted and convicted under a Texas law that forbade certain types of intimate sexual relations between two persons of the same sex. The men appealed to the Supreme Court arguing that their Fourteenth Amendment rights to equal protection and privacy were violated when they were prosecuted for consensual sexual intimacy in their own home. In the 6–3 decision in *Lawrence v. Texas*, the court concluded that while so-called anti-sodomy statutes like the law in Texas did not violate one's right to equal protection, they did violate the due process clause of the Fourteenth Amendment. The court stated that the government had no right to infringe on the liberty of persons engaging in such private and personal acts.

Marbury v. Madison, 5 U.S. 137 (1803). This case involved the nomination of justices of the peace in Washington, DC, by President John Adams at the end of his term. Despite the Senate confirming the nominations, some of the commissions were not delivered before Adams left office. The new president, Thomas Jefferson, decided not to deliver the commissions. William Marbury, one of the offended justices, sued, saying that the Judiciary Act of 1789 empowered the court to force Secretary of State James Madison to deliver the commissions. In the unanimous decision in *Marbury v. Madison*, the court declared that while Marbury's rights were violated when Madison refused to deliver the commission, the court did not have the power to force the secretary to do so despite what the Judiciary Act says. In declaring that the law conflicted with the U.S. Constitution, the case established the principle of judicial review wherein the Supreme Court has the power to declare laws passed by Congress and signed by the president to be unconstitutional.

McDonald v. Chicago, 561 U.S. 742 (2010). This case developed as a consequence of the decision in *District of Columbia v. Heller*, 554 U.S. 570 (2008), which dismissed a Washington, DC, handgun ban as a violation of the Second Amendment. In *McDonald v. Chicago*, the plaintiffs argued that the Fourteenth Amendment had the effect of applying the Second Amendment to the states, not just to the federal government. In a 5–4 decision, the court agreed with the plaintiffs and concluded that rights like the right to keep and bear arms are important enough for maintaining liberty that the Fourteenth Amendment rightly applies them to the states.

Miranda v. Arizona, 384 U.S. 436 (1966). When Ernesto Miranda was arrested, interrogated, and confessed to kidnapping in 1963, the arresting officers neglected to inform him of his Fifth Amendment right not to self-incriminate. After being found guilty at trial, Miranda appealed to the Supreme Court, insisting that the officers violated his Fifth Amendment rights. The 5–4 decision in *Miranda v. Arizona* found that the right to not incriminate oneself relies heavily on the suspect's right to be informed of these rights at the time of arrest. The opinion indicated that suspects must be told that they have the right to an attorney and the right to remain silent in order to ensure that any statements they provide are issued voluntarily.

National Federation of Independent Business v. Sebelius, 567 U.S. ___ (2012). This case represented a challenge to the constitutionality of the Patient Protection and Affordable Care Act. The suing states argued that the Medicare expansion and the individual mandate that required citizens to purchase health insurance or pay a fine were both unconstitutional. The 5–4 decision found that the Medicare expansion was permissible, but that the federal government could not withhold all Medicare funding for states that refused to accept the expansion. More importantly, it found that Congress had the power to apply the mandate to purchase health insurance under its enumerated power to tax.

New York Times Co. v. Sullivan, 376 U.S. 254 (1964). This case began when the *New York Times* published a full-page advertisement claiming that the arrest of Martin Luther King, Jr. in Alabama was part of a concerted effort to ruin him. Insulted, an Alabama official filed a libel suit against the newspaper. Under Alabama law, which did not require that persons claiming libel have to show harm, the official won a judgment. The *New York Times* appealed to the Supreme Court, arguing that the ruling violated its First Amendment right to free speech. In a unanimous decision, the court declared that the First Amendment protects even false statements by the press, as long as those statements are not made with actual malice.

Obergefell v. Hodges, 576 U.S. ___ (2015). This case concerned groups of same-sex couples who brought suits against a number of states and relevant agencies that refused to recognize same-sex marriages created in states where such marriages were legal. In the 5–4 decision, the court found that not only did the Fourteenth Amendment provision for equal protection under the law require that states recognize same-sex marriages formed in other states, but that no state could deny marriage licenses to same-sex couples if they also issued them to other types of couples.

Plessy v. Ferguson, 163 U.S. 537 (1896). When Homer Plessy, a man of mixed racial heritage, sat in a Whites-only railroad car in an attempt to challenge a Louisiana law that required railroad cars be segregated, he was arrested and convicted. Appealing his conviction to the Supreme Court, he argued that the segregation law was a violation of the principle of equal protection under the law in the Fourteenth Amendment. In a 7–1 decision, the court disagreed, indicating that the law was not a violation of the equal protection principle because the different train cars were separate but equal. Plessy v. Ferguson's "separate but equal" remained a guiding principle of segregation until *Brown v. Board of Education* (1954).

Roe v. Wade, 410 U.S. 113 (1973). This case involved a pregnant woman from Texas who desired to terminate her pregnancy. At the time, Texas only allowed abortions in cases where the woman's life was in danger. Using the pseudonym "Jane Roe," the woman appealed to the Supreme Court, arguing that the Constitution provides women the right to terminate an abortion. The 7–2 decision in *Roe v. Wade* sided with the plaintiff and declared that the right to privacy upheld in the decision in *Griswold v. Connecticut* (1965) included a woman's right to an abortion. In balancing the rights of the woman with the interests of the states to protect human life, the court created a trimester framework. In the first trimester, a pregnant woman could seek an abortion without restriction. In the second and third trimesters, however, the court asserted that states had an interest in regulating abortions, provided that those regulations were based on health needs.

Schechter Poultry Corp. v. United States. See ***A. L. A. Schechter Poultry Corp. v. United States***.

Shelby County v. Holder, 570 U.S. ___ (2013). After decades in which African Americans encountered obstacles to voting, particularly in southern states, Congress passed the Voting Rights Act of 1965. Among other things, the law prohibited certain congressional districts from changing election laws without federal authorization. In 2010, Shelby County in Alabama brought a suit against the U.S. attorney general, claiming that both section five of the act, which required districts to seek preapproval, and section four, which determined which districts had to seek preapproval, were unconstitutional. In a 5–4 decision, the court found that both sections violated the Tenth Amendment.

United States v. Windsor, 570 U.S. ___ (2013). When Thea Clara Spyer died in 2009, she left her estate to her wife, Edith Windsor, with whom she had been legally married in Canada years before. Because of a 1996 U.S. law called the Defense of Marriage Act (DOMA), this marriage was not recognized by the federal government. As a result, Windsor was compelled to pay an enormous tax on the inheritance, which she would not have had to pay had the federal government recognized the marriage. Appealing to the Supreme Court, Windsor argued that DOMA was unconstitutional because it deprives same-sex couples of their Fifth Amendment right to equal protection. In the 5–4 decision, the court agreed with Windsor, stating that DOMA was intended to treat certain married couples differently in blatant violation of their Fifth Amendment rights.

ANSWER KEY

Chapter 1

Question 1: A
Question 2: B
Question 3: B
Question 4: D
Question 5: B
Question 6: C
Question 7: A
Question 8: A
Question 9: D
Question 10: A
Question 11: C
Question 12: C
Question 13: B
Question 14: B
Question 15: C
Question 16: C
Question 17: C
Question 18: A
Question 19: C
Question 20: B
Question 21: T
Question 22: A
Question 23: D
Question 24: F
Question 25: T

Chapter 2

Question 1: T
Question 2: D
Question 3: B
Question 4: A
Question 5: A
Question 6: B
Question 7: B
Question 8: T
Question 9: T
Question 10: F
Question 11: A
Question 12: F
Question 13: C
Question 14: C
Question 15: B
Question 16: A
Question 17: D
Question 18: B
Question 19: T
Question 20: F
Question 21: B
Question 22: T
Question 23: D
Question 24: F
Question 25: C

Chapter 3

Question 1: D
Question 2: B
Question 3: D
Question 4: B
Question 5: D
Question 6: A
Question 7: B
Question 8: B
Question 9: A
Question 10: D
Question 11: B
Question 12: D
Question 13: C
Question 14: D
Question 15: T
Question 16: D
Question 17: T
Question 18: F
Question 19: F
Question 20: T
Question 21: F
Question 22: T
Question 23: F
Question 24: T
Question 25: T

Chapter 4

Question 1: B
Question 2: A
Question 3: A
Question 4: D
Question 5: B
Question 6: A
Question 7: B
Question 8: A
Question 9: B
Question 10: A
Question 11: A
Question 12: A
Question 13: B
Question 14: C
Question 15: A
Question 16: B
Question 17: B
Question 18: B
Question 19: D
Question 20: A
Question 21: A
Question 22: C
Question 23: D
Question 24: C
Question 25: B
Question 26: B
Question 27: A
Question 28: A
Question 29: B
Question 30: D
Question 31: D
Question 32: A
Question 33: A

Question 34: B

Question 35: A

Question 36: C

Question 37: A

Question 38: C

Question 39: A

Question 40: A

Question 41: B

Question 42: A

Chapter 5:

Question 1: C

Question 2: D

Question 3: A

Question 4: D

Question 5: D

Question 6: B

Question 7: C

Question 8: C

Question 9: C

Question 10: D

Question 11: C

Question 12: C

Question 13: B

Question 14: D

Question 15: C

Question 16: A

Question 17: C

Question 18: C

Question 19: C

Question 20: C

Question 21: D

Question 22: A

Question 23: D

Question 24: B

Question 25: C

Question 26: B

Question 27: D

Question 28: C

Question 29: B

Question 30: A

Question 31: C

Question 32: A

Question 33: C

Question 34: B

Question 35: C

Question 36: D

Question 37: B

Question 38: D

Question 39: A

Question 40: C

Question 41: D

Question 42: A

Question 43: B

Question 44: B

Question 45: C

Question 46: B

Question 47: C

Question 48: D

Question 49: D

Question 50: A

Question 51: C

Chapter 6

Question 1: A

Question 2: A

Question 3: B

Question 4: B

Question 5: A

Question 6: C

Question 7: D

Question 8: A

Question 9: C

Question 10: C

Question 11: C

Question 12: A

Question 13: B

Question 14: B

Question 15: A

Question 16: B

Question 17: A

Question 18: B

Question 19: A

Question 20: A

Question 21: A

Question 22: B

Question 23: C

Question 24: A

Question 25: B

Question 26: B

Question 27: A

Question 28: A

Question 29: C

Question 30: B

Question 31: A

Question 32: D

Question 33: D

Question 34: D

Question 35: B

Question 36: C

Question 37: B

Question 38: B

Question 39: D

Question 40: A

Question 41: A

Question 42: C

Question 43: A

Question 44: D

Question 45: B

Question 46: A

Question 47: A

Question 48: B

Question 49: B

Question 50: B

Question 51: B

Question 52: A

Question 53: C

Question 54: A

Question 55: C

Question 56: A

Question 57: D

Question 58: A

Question 59: C

Question 60: A

Question 61: D

Question 62: C

Question 63: B

Question 64: B

Question 65: A

Question 66: A

Question 67: C

Question 68: C

Question 69: B

Question 70: A

Question 71: C

Question 72: C

Chapter 7:

Question 1: A

Question 2: B

Question 3: A

Question 4: B

Question 5: B

Question 6: A

Question 7: D

Question 8: B

Question 9: A

Question 10: A

Question 11: C

Question 12: C

Question 13: C

Question 14: C

Question 15: B

Question 16: C

Question 17: C

Question 18: B

Question 19: D

Question 20: A

Question 21: C

Question 22: A

Question 23: C

Question 24: B

Question 25: D

Question 26: A

Question 27: D

Question 28: B

Question 29: B

Question 30: D

Question 31: B

Question 32: C

Question 33: A

Question 34: B

Question 35: C

Question 36: D

Question 37: A

Question 38: C

Question 39: D

Question 40: C

Chapter 8:

Question 1: C

Question 2: C

Question 3: A

Question 4: B

Question 5: C

Question 6: A

Question 7: B

Question 8: B

Question 9: C

Question 10: B

Question 11: B

Question 12: B

Question 13: C

Question 14: C

Question 15: A

Question 16: B

Question 17: B

Question 18: A

Question 19: T

Question 20: F

Question 21: T

Question 22: T

Question 23: F

Question 24: F

Question 25: T

Question 26: T

Question 27: F

Question 28: T

Chapter 9:

Question 1: A

Question 2: B

Question 3: A

Question 4: C

Question 5: A

Question 6: B

Question 7: C

Question 8: A

Question 9: C

Question 10: B

Question 11: B

Question 12: B

Question 13: B

Question 14: C

Question 15: C

Question 16: B

Question 17: A

Question 18: D

Question 19: A

Question 20: B

Question 21: A

Question 22: A

Question 23: B

Question 24: A

Question 25: A

Question 26: B

Question 27: B

Question 28: A

Question 29: C

Question 30: A

Question 31: B

Question 32: B

Question 33: B

Question 34: B

Question 35: C

Chapter 10:

Question 1: B

Question 2: C

Question 3: B

Question 4: B

Question 5: C

Question 6: C

Question 7: C

Question 8: C

Question 9: D

Question 10: B

Question 11: C

Question 12: B

Question 13: C

Question 14: A

Question 15: C

Question 16: C

Question 17: B

Question 18: B

Question 19: B

Question 20: B

Question 21: C

Question 22: C

Question 23: B

Question 24: C

Question 25: B

Question 26: A

Question 27: A

Question 28: B

Question 29: C

Question 30: B

Question 31: A

Question 32: A

Question 33: D

Question 34: C

Question 35: D

Question 36: B

Question 37: A

Question 38: B

Question 39: D

Question 40: B

Question 41: B

Question 42: B

Question 43: A

Question 44: B

Question 45: D

Question 46: B

Question 47: C

Question 48: B

Question 49: C

Question 50: A

Question 51: B

Question 52: B

Question 53: C

Question 54: B

Question 55: C

Question 56: B

Question 57: A

Question 58: A

Question 59: D

Question 60: A

Question 61: B

Question 62: C

Question 63: A

Question 64: B

Question 65: C

Question 66: B

Question 67: C

Chapter 11:

Question 1: C

Question 2: A

Question 3: D

Question 4: A

Question 5: A

Question 6: A

Question 7: A

Question 8: A

Question 9: C

Question 10: B

Question 11: D

Question 12: A

Question 13: A

Question 14: D

Question 15: C

Question 16: D

Question 17: C

Question 18: A

Question 19: B

Question 20: A

Question 21: C

Question 22: A

Question 23: A

Question 24: A

Question 25: C

Question 26: A

Question 27: C

Question 28: C

Question 29: C

Question 30: C

Question 31: D

Question 32: B

Question 33: B

Question 34: B

Question 35: C

Chapter 12:

Question 1: C

Question 2: A

Question 3: D

Question 4: A

Question 5: B

Question 6: D

Question 7: A

Question 8: D

Question 9: D

Question 10: A

Question 11: D

Question 12: A

Question 13: D

Question 14: A

Question 15: D

Question 16: A

Question 17: B

Question 18: C

Question 19: C

Question 20: F

Question 21: F

Question 22: C

Question 23: T

Question 24: B

Question 25: T

Chapter 13:

Question 1: C

Question 2: B

Question 3: A

Question 4: D

Question 5: B

Question 6: A

Question 7: D

Question 8: B

Question 9: A

Question 10: D

Question 11: D

Question 12: B

Question 13: A

Question 14: A

Question 15: B

Question 16: A

Question 17: A

Question 18: D

Question 19: D

Question 20: D

Question 21: A

Question 22: B

Question 23: A

Question 24: A

Question 25: C

Question 26: A

Chapter 14:

Question 1: C

Question 2: B

Question 3: D

Question 4: A

Question 5: B

Question 6: D

Question 7: D

Question 8: B

Question 9: C

Question 10: A

Question 11: D

Question 12: A

Question 13: C

Question 14: D

Question 15: A

Question 16: B

Question 17: D

Question 18: A

Question 19: A

Question 20: B

Question 21: B

Question 22: C

Question 23: A

Question 24: B

Question 25: D

Chapter 15:

Question 1: A

Question 2: C

Question 3: D

Question 4: B

Question 5: A

Question 6: A

Question 7: D

Question 8: C

Question 9: A

Question 10: B

Question 11: C

Question 12: D

Question 13: B

Question 14: B

Question 15: A

Question 16: C

Question 17: D

Question 18: B

Question 19: D

Question 20: B

Question 21: C

Question 22: A

Question 23: B

Question 24: C

Question 25: A

Question 26: C

Question 27: D

Question 28: B

Question 29: B

Question 30: A

Question 31: B

Question 32: C

Question 33: A

Question 34: D

Question 35: A

Question 36: D

Question 37: C

Question 38: B

Question 39: B

Question 40: A

Question 41: T

Question 42: F

Question 43: T

Question 44: T

Question 45: F

Question 46: F

Question 47: T

Question 48: T

Question 49: F

Question 50: T

Chapter 16:

Question 1: C

Question 2: A

Question 3: C

Question 4: A

Question 5: D

Question 6: A

Question 7: B

Question 8: T

Question 9: T

Question 10: D

Question 11: A

Question 12: A

Question 13: C

Question 14: T

Question 15: B

Question 16: D

Question 17: T

Question 18: T

Question 19: B

Question 20: T

Question 21: T

Question 22: D

Question 23: F

Question 24: A

Question 25: T

Question 26: D

ABOUT THE AUTHOR

R. L. Cohen is a university professor residing in Redlands, California. His current research focus is on political science, ethics, and religious studies. R. L. Cohen has a passion for social justice in order to create a better world for his children. When he is not lecturing, he often can be found at the beach, at a unique coffee bar, or traveling back to his home in New Zealand.